This WAR NEVER ENDS

Michael McKernan has written extensively in the area of Australian social history, charting in particular the effects of war on Australian society. He was a senior lecturer in History at the University of New South Wales, before accepting the position of Deputy Director at the Australian War Memorial. Now working as a consultant historian, Michael McKernan is an experienced writer, reviewer, public speaker and broadcaster. His regular history programs on ABC Radio reach a wide audience. His publications include *Australian Churches at War*, *The Australian People and the Great War*, *The Makers of Australia's Sporting Traditions* (ed.), *Here Is Their Spirit: A History of the Australian War Memorial* and *Beryl Beaurepaire*. Michael McKernan is co-leader of the *Australian* Battlefield Tours, journeys which give him the opportunity of sharing his extensive knowledge of the Australian story.

This WAR NEVER ENDS

THE PAIN of SEPARATION and RETURN

MICHAEL McKERNAN

University of Queensland Press

First published 2001 by University of Queensland Press
Box 6042, St Lucia, Queensland 4067 Australia

www.uqp.uq.edu.au

Typeset by University of Queensland Press
Printed in Australia by McPherson's Printing Group

Distributed in the USA and Canada by
International Specialized Book Services, Inc.,
5824 N.E. Hassalo Street, Portland, Oregon 97213–3640

Cataloguing in Publication Data
National Library of Australia

McKernan, Michael, 1945–   .
   This war never ends : Australian prisoners of war come home.

   1. Prisoners of war — Australia. 2. Veterans — Australia.
   3. World War, 1939–1945 — Prisoners and prisons, Japanese.
   I. Title.

   Includes index

940.547252

ISBN 0 7022 3274 2 (Paperback Edition)

ISBN 0 7022 3285 2 (Cased Edition)

*For Jaraslaw (Joe) Stawyskyj, national serviceman, grievously
wounded in Vietnam, and for his parents, sister and brother,
whose love for him and generous care have been inspiring.
For these people, too, their war never ends.*

Contents

Acknowledgments   *ix*
Introduction   *xi*

1. 'Tragedy after tragedy'   *1*
2. 'If only I knew what has become of him'   *19*
3. 'That's the Eighth Division colour patch, isn't it?'   *45*
4. 'Twilight liberation'   *61*
5. 'I will turn up like the proverbial penny'   *84*
6. 'It wasn't as I had expected'   *109*
7. 'You are not going home as prisoners'   *132*
8. 'Stirring up trouble by segregating POWs from their fellow
   servicemen'   *153*
Conclusion   *173*

Notes   *177*

Acknowledgments

In 1999 I was appointed inaugural Frederick Watson Fellow at the National Archives of Australia. The Fellowship gave me the facilities and the time to conduct, in Canberra and in Melbourne, much of the research on which this book is based. I particularly appreciated special access to the collections of the National Archives of Australia and the professional and courteous support of staff who were assigned to assist me. I deem it a very great honour to have been the inaugural Fellow.

I cherish the memory of the late Hugh Clarke, former prisoner of war, historian and author, and, I am proud to say, friend. The influence of Hugh Clarke's books is evident in this book as is his story-telling and wise counsel. I am grateful, too, for the interest and encouragement of Hugh's widow, Patricia Clarke, herself a fine historian.

The following people helped in a variety of ways, generously sharing aspects of their lives with me, as members of libraries or archives, assisting in the provision of information, or as friends, encouraging and enquiring: Nola Ashcroft, Noel Blundell, Les Bolger, Joyce Braithwaite, Jim Busine, John Buxton, Owen Campbell, John Carmody, Shane Carmody, Ros Casey, Caroline Connor, Denis Connor, Lloyd Ellerman, Muriel Ellerman, Russ Ewin, JOhn Fenton, Stephen Foster, Morag Fraser, Mary Gibson, Thomas Giles, Brenda Heagney, Rosalind Hearder, Allan Herd, Ian Hibberson, Tony Hill, Gabrielle Hyslop, the late Max Jagger, Kerry Jeffrey, Enid Johnson, Brendon Kelson, Margaret Kenna, Paul Macpherson, Max McGee, John McQuilton, Lil Mangoni, Harry Medlin, the late Roy Mills, Merilyn Minell, Ann Moyal, Beverley Mutch, George Nichols, Geoffrey Pryor, Les Read, Rosemary Reynolds, John Ringwood, Sandra Riordan, Nan Rivett, Gerard Sampson, Anne-Marie Schwirtlich, Judith Shaw, Peter Stanley, Lembit Suur, Kemble Thompson, Joanne Tier, Alison Todd, David Todd, Don Tweedie, Chris Uhlmann, James Valentine, Philip Wallbridge, Isabel Watson, Ray Wheeler, Ashley White, Gerard Windsor, Stephen Yorke, Tom Young.

I rejoice in the support and love of my wife, Michalina Stawyskyj, and my daughters, Katherine and Jane McKernan.

Introduction

Australians go away for war and they are expected to come home to a clean slate and a new beginning. The legacy of war might mean supporting the widows and children, or helping men in hospital wards or those temporarily down on their luck. For the rest, those who fought must simply get on with being civilians again. I have written this book to suggest that the reality is probably not like that for any soldiers and their families, and certainly not for former prisoners of war and their families.

It was at Sandakan, the site of an appalling Australian tragedy, that the force of the problem faced by the returning prisoners hit me most powerfully. I was with a group of people making an 'Australia Remembers' pilgrimage to Sandakan and also in the group was Owen Campbell. Owen was one of the six Australians to have survived Sandakan and the death march to Ranau during the Second World War. More than two thousand men in the prison camp at Sandakan had been deliberately and cruelly killed. How, I wondered, had Owen Campbell ever had the guts to go back home and try to take up his life again.

We had a brief but powerfully moving ceremony at Sandakan. Later, walking in the camp site, now a picturesque garden, as peaceful a place as you will find in that hectic region, I came across a journalist, Peter Harvey, whose job it was to tell the people at home what this pilgrimage was all about.

'Why has this story been kept from us?' he asked me insistently. 'I grew up in Australia immediately after the Second World War and yet until now I knew nothing about what went on here. Why has this not become one of the defining stories of the nation?'

I had no answer for Peter Harvey, and here was another question to which I wished to find an answer. How could we have forgotten or have pushed away that terrible story? Why did it take so long for the account of the prisoners in the hands of the Japanese to find its place in our history books? Are we such an impoverished nation that we take no account of the sufferings and traumas of our own people? Why had the stories of the prisoners at Changi, on the Railway, and most disastrously at Sandakan, not become a core element of our understanding of ourselves and our past?

Working at the Australian War Memorial for many years had given me access to some of the stories that would help me to respond to Peter Harvey's question. I had met men and women who had shown me how hard it was to return too readily to the past. They had also shown me that the impact and tragedy of war extends beyond the front-line soldiers right into the homes from which these men and women had enlisted. All those who served Australia in war would have some problems in resuming the lives they had once lived. But the former prisoners of the Japanese would have far greater problems. This book explores the story of the prisoners and their families and attempts to find out how they coped. It tells the stories and examines the silences.

Two men, both from Gippsland in Victoria (unknown to each other I presume), in their own life stories gave me elements for the enquiry on which this book is based.

John Gow, a straight-backed, lean dairy farmer had migrated to Australia from Scotland as a boy, without family. He learnt farming the hard way, as an underpaid rural worker while still a lad, paying his way on the farm for the privilege of being an immigrant. John Gow might never have expected to have owned a property of his own, but the war had made that possible. He had fought overseas, and then he took up a soldier settlement, raised a family, and prospered. Now he was in the Labuan War Cemetery, one of the veterans on an 'Australia Remembers' pilgrimage. He had left his dairy herd in the care of a son and a neighbour to make this pilgrimage, but it worried him to be away, you could see that, as he scanned the sky for clouds that might bring rain. He knew, of course, that conditions in Gippsland would be different from the oppressive weather of Labuan, but old farmers are constantly thinking of the weather and home.

After a brief ceremony of remembrance at the Labuan Cemetery I walked with John Gow past the rows of headstones. He was looking for names that he might remember, but he seemed to want some company too. After a while he stopped walking; he wanted a rest from the burden of memory. 'I'll never understand,' he said, 'why these men, much better men than me, with families to live for, why they died and I survived. I'll never understand.' And we walked on. The burden, of course, could not be shifted.

'Survivor guilt', the glib psychiatrist might call it, but naming the condition does not defeat it. Fifty years after the end of his war this good man was still grieving. He remained uncomfortable with the fact of his own survival. And I, who could do nothing for him, was saddened by that.

Another Gippsland dairy farmer had earlier shown me that it was not only the people who fought the wars who remained troubled and scarred for the rest of their lives. This man had served in the Second World War too and his son had asked me to show the old man around the War Memorial on one of his rare visits to Canberra. The son had told me that his father had a gammy leg and foolishly, given the strong independence of the man, I had offered him the use of a wheelchair as we started to make our way through the Memorial's galleries.

The look of contempt at that offer made me feel the fool I had been, but when we reached the Mont St Quentin diorama, less than halfway through the upper floor galleries, I thought perhaps I might have been vindicated. The old man asked if he could sit down for a bit. It was the leg, I thought. Gazing for a few minutes at the model of Australians fighting at Mont St Quentin — the greatest feat of arms of the AIF, General Monash had called it — this man suddenly said to me: 'That was the whole damn trouble.' What? I wondered. Thinking I had not heard, he repeated himself: 'That was the whole damn trouble.' Or was he even speaking to me? 'What?' I asked him. 'What was the trouble?'

'My dad fought there,' he replied. 'They told us he was a good man, a kind man, before he went off to war. He enjoyed life; he had married well and happily; he was a man for a few beers and a laugh. But the war changed him; Mont St Quentin changed him. He came back morose; he had moods of black depression that rarely seemed to lift; he had few good words for my mother and even fewer for me. We lived in some fear of him, and God how he made us work. Only in the last couple of years of his life, around 1939 before I enlisted, when he came under the spell of my own new wife, did the depression ever seem to ease. His war had scarred us all.'

It was 1994 when this man was telling me this; Mont St Quentin was a battle of 1918. The tentacles of war stretched far into the Australian story. It was 1995 when I was at the war cemetery at Labuan. But two world wars, so remote from so many of us, except through books and ceremonies and perhaps even cemeteries, lived on in the lives of these two men, and surely, too, in the lives of their families. Wars, for some at least, do not ever end.

So much of Australia's writing about war concentrates on the fighting soldier and the immediate moment of battle. That is as natural as it is necessary. Charles Bean's history of the First World War, the model of Australian military historical scholarship, places the reader as if in the trenches alongside the men, men whom Bean seems to know personally. There are, it is true, some after-the-battle moments in Bean's personal diary, but the focus of his history is what is happening at this moment in battle.

One after-battle moment occurs when he calls on 'Pompey' Elliott whose 15th Brigade had just been destroyed in the battle of Fromelles: 'I felt almost as if I were in the presence of a man who had just lost his wife. He looked down and could hardly speak. He was clearly terribly depressed and overwrought.' Perhaps Bean held that moment in his mind, because, years later, when he wrote of Fromelles in the history, his anger at the debacle of planning and execution was apparent. But he did not tell us in the history if Brigadier Elliott ever recovered from that dreadful moment at Fromelles or how he managed to keep on going at war. In fact, 'Pompey' Elliott died by his own hand in 1931.

When Charles Bean came to write the last words of his monumental history of the AIF, the force had been repatriated for more than twenty years. Its officers and men had long since thrown away their drab khaki uniforms and had embraced other uniforms of office and factory, farm and shop. When Bean was thinking about how he might write the final pages and reflecting, possibly, on what it had all meant, he had already attended the funerals of dozens of the survivors of the war, his friends. He had cared for and helped to finance the future of the children of dozens of men with whom he had served: men who had died before they could provide for their families, or men who, although alive, were temporarily or permanently incapable of so providing. Bean could trace the consequences of war in the lives of men he knew and also in the lives of their families.

But when he came to write those last few paragraphs, he steered clear of life after the war as a theme, as if it were too bitter or too contested. In moving and simple prose he worked around, but of course did not use, the cliché that 'old soldiers never die, they simply fade away'. 'The Australian Imperial Force is not dead', he wrote; 'that famous army of generous men marches still down the long lane of its country's history, with bands playing and rifles slung.' This was a hopeful and positive statement.

But those words were written when Australia was at war again: in North Africa and Greece, in the air over Europe, and soon in the jungles of the Pacific. He could not possibly say that war had damaged its survivors so badly that some, at least, would gladly have swapped places with those in the war cemeteries. He could not say that 'Pompey' Elliott had greeted the few survivors of the slaughter at Fromelles with tears streaming down his face as he shook hands with them and that in that moment Elliott's own fate was sealed. Australians go away for war and they are expected to come home to a clean slate and a new beginning. But Bean knew that it was not like that.

Searching for an answer to Peter Harvey's perplexing question I looked at as many of the books written by former prisoners of war as I could find. There are dozens of them; some are well known, like Rohan Rivett's *Behind Bamboo* or Russell Braddon's *The Naked Island*, some have found only a small number of readers, and some have been self-published 'for the family', often by men in their retirement years.

The story these books tell is remarkably consistent in describing the brutality and terror of captivity and in the nobility of spirit that allowed men to rise above their confinement, although the individuality of the writer and the variety of experiences is evident. But there is another common feature of this literature: the story ends with the end of the war. They may briefly tell their readers how it was that they got home; they will not say, in any detail, what it was like to come home.

Take, for example, the final paragraphs of Jessie Simons' *In Japanese Hands*:

> So it was that Margaret Anderson [another nursing sister, prisoner of the Japanese] and I took off over Bass Strait on Saturday, October 27th, 1945, on the last leg of the long journey home. I had acquired so much gear that Margaret took some over temporarily to keep down my excess baggage charges! … at last we touched down.
>
> It seemed to take an age to get the gangway down, and even then my way was blocked by the matron of the Campbelltown Military Hospital and a few military officials before I could get through to my parents and family. By special arrangement only my family was there to meet me, a much increased family — three new sisters-in-law, a new brother-in-law, and numerous lovely nieces and nephews to get to know …
>
> Dr Thompson gave me twenty-four hour's leave, starting immediately. What an ordeal my return must have been to him; his only son had been drowned while a P.O.W. up in the Islands.
>
> Still chattering, asking questions and half answering others, we came in slowly to Launceston in the car … We had a family party at my sister's home in Trevallyn that night and gossiped. *I was home.*

In those simple paragraphs Jessie Simons opens up many of the themes that this book explores but she does not comment on any of them herself. The war had ended on 15 August 1945 and yet it was more than two months after this that she was returning home. Why had it taken so long for her to return to her beloved Tasmania? She was greeted by a vastly expanded family, and significant aspects of Australian life had also changed while she and the other prisoners were away. How easily would she settle back into this new family and into this new Australia? For how long would she feel an outsider, a stranger even in familiar circumstances?

Nurse Simons had survived her ordeal, but several of her most intimate friends had died in captivity. Almost the first official that she had to deal with in Tasmania, Dr Thompson, had lost his only son to a prison camp. How would she cope with his grief in her happiness, and how would she deal with the questions from those who needed to know the fate of their own loved ones? And what could she say to her own family about the story of her captivity?

The reader will not find the answers to these questions in Jessie Simons' book. Like almost every other account written by an Australian who had been a prisoner of war of the Japanese the end point of the story is the simple fact of the return home. '*I was home.*'

In Jessie Simons' account all is happiness and joy at home, as we, the readers would sincerely wish it to be after the horrors that she had lived through as a prisoner. But this was not the case with another informant whose story will be told more fully later in the book. This father had never seen his son, the boy having been conceived on leave and born after the father had sailed off for war. Brought up by his mother and grandparents the boy was four when it was known that his father was coming home. A woman in the country town where he lived suggested to the boy that he must be very excited at the prospect of his father's return. 'My father?' the boy replied, puzzled. 'He's not my father; this is my father.' And he pointed to his grandfather. There was conflict and confusion in the making there, but 'a few weeks loaf at the beaches, that will put them all right', someone had said. Would it really be like that?

Many Australians now know the outlines of the story of the captivity of the Eighth Division and the treatment of the Australian prisoners of the Japanese. I would have preferred not to repeat the details of that sad tale, but I felt I had to give glimpses of what it had been like, through the words of the prisoners themselves, in order to remind us of the trauma that these Australians would have to overcome before they could take up their civilian lives again.

It is a central argument of this book that families and officials were expecting the worst in the return of the prisoners. The military had made a careful study of the possible medical and psychological problems that the returning prisoners were likely to present. For their part the prisoners were somewhat reluctant to come home. Aware that they stank, that they were diseased and terribly malnourished, and that their minds were just not right, the prisoners feared that they would be a burden and a worry to their loved ones. 'I don't want Mum to see me like this' was a constant refrain in the camps in the first days of peace. But the human body is remarkably resilient. Within weeks the bodies filled out, not to their pre-war condition, to be sure, but enough to allow people the fiction that 'they weren't too bad really'.

There is an ambivalence in the moment of the first meeting, whether of recovery teams and prisoners in Japan or Singapore, or of former prisoners and family and friends in the depots and camps of Australia. Had the prisoners presented as had the victims of Belsen to the liberating Allied troops, there would have been outrage and anger directed towards the Japanese that would have taken more than a generation to surmount, and there would have been medical and all kinds of other assistance for the prisoners returning home. Perhaps they would have been held in military hospitals for months and months, and the folks at home would have understood the need for this and would have accepted it. But the men pretended that they were a lot better than they were and their loved ones played along with them. Discharged to the care of their families within hours of making Australian landfall, and despite all the medical preparations, on paper, for recovery and rehabilitation, the prisoners were largely on their own.

The loneliness of this and the burden of it saw former prisoners abandoning those at home, who themselves had suffered so much during the years of their loved one's captivity. The families at home had had virtually no news about the prisoners and about conditions in the camps. Neither the Australian government officially nor the families through private correspondence had received much news at all with which to console themselves while this long war dragged on. And when the prisoners were finally at home and all the terror and anxiety for wives and parents was at an end, then, most cruelly to the families who had been expecting so much, the former prisoners seemed to turn away from them, clearly missing their prisoner mates and obviously dissatisfied with their resumed lives. The heartbreak of observing this and not being able to speak of it was near enough to the hardest thing of all for those who had waited at home.

Men 'shot through', or they could find pleasure only in the company of former prisoners. They found it hard to take up again the job kept open for them in factory or office, and they feared, deep to the core of their being, that they would never be able to truly provide for their families again. Men whose most treasured possession had been a family picture of wife and children, of parents, now discovered that they had been nurturing a fantasy. 'When I get home everything will be wonderful', wrote many of them to daughters or wives, mothers or lovers in the first heady days of peace. Both sides expected so much and the reality was so very different. Some, a small minority certainly, found cherished relationships at an end; the wife or girlfriend was with someone else, convinced, perhaps, that their beloved had died years before. For the majority though the news from home was far less traumatic and few expected that they would have to work so hard in renewing the ties.

'I've changed so much', one man said to his fiancee. 'Take a good look at me and if you don't like what you see well I'll understand if you want to call it quits.' In his case, happily, the relationship was picked up from where it had been before the man went away. But even in this happy story both husband and wife would suffer dreadfully from disturbed sleep, nightmares and vomiting in the first years of the peace, and the nightmares even now sometimes return.

This is a book about suffering and about trauma but it is not a book about blame. Occasionally in my research and writing I have become incensed by the insensitivity of a senior military officer or a medical man who should have known better. The government's response could have been more imaginative, but recrimination will not make the story any more palatable. In any case, in view of the numbers involved, in the determination of all to see the men in their own homes as soon as possible, and in the popular belief that 'she'll be right', there was little real prospect that the government could order long periods of care and rehabilitation, except in cases of obvious illness and wounds.

There was justification for all the positions adopted and decisions taken. Staggered though we may be by the army officer who counsels his minister about making too much of a fuss of the returning prisoners, nevertheless we have to agree with him that those who had borne the 'heat and burden of the battle' on Kokoda, at Tobruk, in bomber command over Europe, had no less right to assistance and to the community's deep-seated gratitude and admiration. The best we could have said to him was that surely it did not have to be either/or.

Nor would I suggest that the parents of a son killed in war would not have swapped places instantly with the parents of those who had to nurse their prisoner son, over many years perhaps, through the terrors and traumas of his terrible memories. At least, they might have said, you have your son back, whereas we are left with a cold emptiness of the heart.

In this tale of anguish and suffering, of hopes unfulfilled, of misunderstandings, of fear and torture and death, there are very few — prisoners or their loved ones at home, politicians, military leaders, community workers, doctors and public servants — whom we have the right to condemn, whose motives we can contest. It is war that we should learn to hate through the telling of this story; war is the dreadful evil that makes these things happen. For most of the people in this book, war was an atrocity from which they could be liberated only slowly, if at all. For this war, like all wars for those captured by it, never ends.

CHAPTER 1

'Tragedy after tragedy'

Australians were quite unprepared for defeat at Singapore; defeat was, literally, unthinkable. For too long deluded by concepts of British grandeur and might, despite the ineptitude and bungling at Gallipoli and more recently in Greece and Crete, Australians clung to a notion that they were secure from Japanese aggression so long as Singapore stood. And Singapore, they had been told repeatedly, was impregnable.

Although the troops would actually be fighting for only another three weeks at Singapore and the situation there was desperate, Melbourne's *Age*, for example, calmed readers by asserting that 'despite all the disadvantages we may continue to suffer as a result of Japanese surprise and treachery, there would seem to be reasons for recalling, not boastfully, but reassuringly, how powerful a stronghold Singapore is. For there is becoming current among some groups in Australia facile talk to the effect that Singapore is likely to fall … this is the spirit of defeatism in subtle guise'.[1]

The editorial writer may, indeed, have believed what he wrote. If so, he had little contact with senior military or political leaders in Australia who had recognised the vulnerability of Singapore even as Britain's leader, Winston Churchill, began sounding out opinion for a staged withdrawal of troops from the island fortress. Withdrawal, John Curtin told Churchill, 'would be regarded here and elsewhere as inexcusable betrayal', and even in the dying days, reinforcements continued to arrive at Singapore instead of the governments taking the sensible option of evacuation.[2]

Before the Japanese had begun the Pacific war in December 1941 Australia had committed one of its five AIF divisions — the Eighth

— to the defence of Malaya and Singapore. The Eighth Division, formed in 1940 after the fall of France and commanded by Lieutenant-General Gordon Bennett, consisted, in the words of Lieutenant Colonel C. G. W. Anderson VC, one of the Division's most inspirational leaders, of men 'who had to make a special sacrifice to join up'.[3]

Despite what Anderson believed, it would be foolish to try to characterise as numerous a body of men as those in an Army division (about 15 000). Some will believe that a division acquires a distinguishing ethos or characteristic, often because of the purposes to which it is put or the training it has been given. Or its history might indelibly determine how it is remembered. It would be the fate of the Eighth Division, in perpetuity, to be known as the captured division, a unique situation in Australian military history. Members of the Division, those few remaining today, bridle at such a characterisation and want to insist, with good reason, on the fighting qualities of the division. Against impossible odds, the Eighth held up for as long as it could the unstoppable Japanese advance down the Malaya peninsula. This was a fighting division, they still insist, with battle honours and real heroes. They are right, of course, but nevertheless captivity dominates their story.

It has not been possible to test the notion that different Australian divisions took on different 'personalities' or identities, because there has not been as yet any divisional history for any of the Australian divisions of either the First or the Second World War. Military historians have traditionally preferred to work at the battalion level, and more recently at the company or smaller-group level. But to make sense of the story that will unfold in this book, we do need to have some picture of the 'family' that comprised the Eighth Division of the Second Australian Imperial Force.

Military history often describes only what occurs at the frontline or within the military formation, as if those who are fighting have no remaining connection with the world from which they have been recruited, with the family, friends and experiences of their pre-military life. Of course this simply cannot be the case. Men at war carry with them the same personal histories that mould and shape the lives of all of us regardless of the work we do or the circumstances in which we find ourselves. Our family shapes, influences and pervades all of what we are and how we live; education and friendships settle other aspects of our personalities and determine some of our major choices in life, including work, values and partners; experiences contribute to the way we look at the world. The soldier at war brought all these influences and experiences to his new situation, as the best of Australian military history has constantly shown. It was Charles Bean who asserted so strongly in his history of Australia in the Great War that the individual really mattered. Bean introduced us, with succinct footnotes, to the individuality and personal life story of every soldier and officer who played a part in his narrative.

The hunger that the Australian soldier, in all conflicts and in all situations across time, has shown for letters from home, for news and for glimpses of the past is well known to historians. And the deter-mination of soldiers at the front to write it all down for family and friends at home has shown the continuing nature of the links between those at war and those at home. When writing of action at Lone Pine or Pozieres, for example, Charles Bean or Bill Gammage instinctively reached for the personal letters or the diaries of the men in that action to find the individual response and the mood of the soldiers in the thick of things. They could rely on such writings because Australians, yearning for home and fighting for home, had been so diligent in describing what they had been living through. The extent of the Australian personal archive on war in homes and libraries across the nation indicates the strength of the engagement between the home-front and the battlefront.

The hunger for home news and for the feeling of home that has been so strong among Australian soldiers is evidence of the connect-edness of life for soldiers. In seeking to write about these links, for this book is essentially about the disruption of these connections in the story of captivity, it is important to bear in mind that family in its broadest sense (friends, neighbours and former workmates are included) did not simply represent the past. Family was a part of the important reality of the present. When an Australian prisoner was huddled in his hut at the end of a shift on the Burma–Thailand railway his thoughts were more likely to be of home than of his present whereabouts. Home sustained him but it also drained him in his concern for those he loved. Family, then, is more complex than a simple distinction between what was 'then' and what is 'now', because family profoundly influenced 'now' and was a part of 'now'. With such reliance on family in captivity, the return of the soldier to his family was an extremely important part of his and their rehabilitation.

We need to keep this image of family before us as we attempt some understanding of those who comprise this book. Any military grouping can be analysed statistically to help us understand the individuals whose lives we are trying to understand. The statistics can be supported by a few stories and portraits of individuals to add humanity to the bare facts. But in its generality this statistical picture can evade the issue. Each soldier in Australia's Eighth Division had a personal story that nourished and supported him. For the vast majority, that personal story embraced parents, possibly wives or sweethearts, certainly brothers and sisters, close homefront mates, workmates, and a myriad mix of sporting, cultural and religious associations. It is possible to give some statistics for a portrait of, for example, a battalion. It is not possible to hint at the personal stories of more than a few members of that battalion. But in knowing the few we may know something of the many.

For the 2/19th Battalion, for example, one of those groupings of about 750 men that made up the Eighth Division, we do have a good and somewhat personalised statistical picture. The 'Battalion Postman', invited by a historian to recall those with whom he served, used his special position within the Battalion and a 'retentive memory' to give a feel for who they were — as he put it, 'to write down all sorts of details about the battalion'. Largely recruited from the Riverina district of New South Wales, the 2/19th Battalion comprised 714 'general rural workers', 12 bank clerks, 5 railway workers, 20 shop assistants and 130 labourers. There were two doctors and one dentist. And so on. Seven hundred of the men were single, 50 of them were aged 16–18 years, 150 were 19–20 years, 550 were 21–30 years and the remaining 250 men were over 30 years. With just less than one-third of them under 21 years they were younger than we might have thought, perhaps, and in less 'educated' jobs probably, but do these simple statistics bring us any closer to knowing who these men were?[4]

On his return to Australia in mid-October 1945 Lance Corporal Barney Porter, formerly of the staff of the Melbourne *Argus*, reported that 'there was one kid, back today, 14 when he enlisted … Junior we called him. The boys all fathered him. He had his 15th, 16th, 17th and 18th birthdays at Ambon. He's a kid still'. A dramatic demonstration of difference, but eloquent in telling us how varied were the stories of each prisoner. We treat them merely as 'soldiers' at our peril.[5]

What does the information about the old battalion, remembered so strikingly by its postman, actually tell us about these individuals? It would be absurd to suggest that the life experiences of all 'general rural workers' or even all bank clerks were similar, although there would have been more points of similarity than between rural workers and city doctors. But those soldiers who were caught up in the story that this book tells were more than rural workers or doctors; they were connected, vitally, to people and places in Australia, and we will explore that connection.

Take Rohan Rivett. Knowing him as a writer, a journalist and an educated man, fellow prisoners, even in the despair of their suffering, would say to him: 'You've got to write a book about this; we're counting on you.' Or: 'You'll have to put this in your book. The folks at home will never believe it.' And so he did, with long newspaper articles almost instantaneous with his release. And then came a book, *Behind Bamboo*, first published in April 1946, a book that sold 100 000 copies. People queued in the streets of Sydney waiting patiently for their turn in Angus & Robertson's store where they obtained their prized copy. Rivett wanted to tell the story of captivity, the jailers, the work and deprivations, the railway, the heroism. He wanted to celebrate what the human spirit had achieved, to tell the story of the men he knew. And so he kept himself out of it and we learn nothing directly of his background and home life. But his personal story, the remembrance of the past, and the story of many of the men he describes is at the core of his explanation of survival: 'Few officers did a better job all along the line than Lieutenant Harry Farmer … we discovered a common devotion to cricket and, in recalling the glories of past afternoons at the Sydney Cricket Ground and the MCG, we forgot the sweltering heat, the choking dust and even the sentry squatting grimly behind us.' Home, in this example, was sustaining and diverting; it was an ideal; it kept men going.[6]

The defeat at Singapore profoundly shocked Australians and was regarded as the national calamity that indeed it was. Surrender was on 15 February 1942 and perhaps Australia has never awoken to worse national news. As if fulfilling the theory that while Singapore stood Australia was secure, hard on the heels of the surrender, four days after in fact, came the bombing of Darwin and the first attack on Australian soil since the white occupation of this continent. Death in Darwin and the almost complete destruction of the town alarmed an already jittery homefront, which wondered where the heavy blow would fall next. These were Australia's darkest days. Is it any wonder that, except for the immediate families of the men who became prisoners, the fate of the Australians of the Eighth Division occupied less attention in the national imagination than it otherwise might have?

In any case, there was not much for the politicians, the service chiefs and the newspapers to say. For suddenly the news shut down from Singapore and Malaya. There was a silence now where for the past months there had been busy reporting and glowing, optimistic expectations of hard fighting and victory. An entire Australian division had been swallowed up by an enemy despised and belittled, and, with Rabaul lost in January, the humiliations continued in Java, on Ambon, and all through Asia. Within a matter of weeks some 22 000 Australians had become prisoners. Terrible though this was for the nation, it was the fact that no one had any certain knowledge of the fate of these Australians that was the first, greatest and most enduring anxiety. No one could say who was alive and who had died in the fighting or the retreat. No one knew the fate of those who had become prisoners, where they were being held or how they were being treated. Many months would drag by, in some cases years, before Australian families could be certain that their son had survived the fighting to live out the war as a prisoner. Some families would never know, until the peace, that their loved one had not died, as years without contact might have led them to expect. It was the responsibility of the government to care for the men and women of Australia's armed forces and to keep the next of kin informed about their circumstances.

But the government was as much in the dark as everyone else, despite frantically cabling to London to try to find out what was going on.

There was no immediate news, to be sure, and that was terrible, but Australians had also to absorb the fact of captivity on this mass scale; they had to try to integrate that news with their previous understandings of Australian soldiers and what it meant to be Australian. There was not much to be said for being a prisoner of war; not much nobility; not much glory. In the Air Force, for example, long-existing regulations required officers to conduct an enquiry to ensure that each captured member had not willingly or cravenly gone over to the enemy. These regulations, admittedly borrowed from Britain, indicate a way of thinking about being a prisoner of war. It could be seen to be, not to mince words, dishonourable. Indeed, all Australians, at the front or at home, had enjoyed the jokes from North Africa's desert campaign, the first engagement of the Australians in the Second World War, as an ill-equipped and dispirited Italian opponent poured into prisoner of war camps in numbers that were hitherto unimaginable. People amused each other with reports of Italian tanks with one forward gear and four for reverse. They looked upon those Italian prisoners as men who would not, or could not, fight. The Australian experience of war, in history and the popular imagination, was something quite different.

Few of the Anzacs had ever become prisoners of war; it was not part of the Australian story. In the First World War there had been a couple of hundred prisoners of the Turks, and a couple of thousand prisoners from the Western Front, the majority of them taken at Bullecourt in April 1917 when British incompetence had hung the Australians out on the wire. In Greece in 1941 there was disaster on a grand scale as the British again led the Australians to a campaign that was doomed before it began. But by fighting a rearguard action down the length of the Greek peninsula, before hopping over to Crete and then leading the Germans a dance there too, many Australians evaded or fought their way out of capture and those who were in the bag had at least shown what they could do. At Singapore there had not been much chance of that. Cooped up on a small island, and obeying when ordered to lay down their arms, Australian troops had capitulated before an enemy that was despised and mocked. Pre-war, 'made in Japan' was a label for all that was shoddy, second-rate and slightly laughable. Now 'these little men with glasses', as Australians then characterised them, had taken off one-fifth of Australia's overseas fighting strength. The empire was humiliated; Australia was embarrassed.

And for the families of those who knew their sons to be in this theatre of war there was nothing. Silence. The agony of waiting and not knowing. Take the parents and other family of Aircraftman Class I Donald Wilfred Bruce, formerly of Brighton, South Australia. Donald Bruce had enlisted in the Air Force, aged 20, in September 1940. He was captured in Java in a campaign where the Australians did not even see their enemy. Their commander, a South Australian like Don Bruce, Brigadier Arthur Seaforth Blackburn VC, was incensed when ordered by the Dutch to surrender. The consequences would be felt in faraway Adelaide. At 9.15 in the morning of 14 March 1942, just a month after the defeat at Singapore, Donald Bruce's father, his next-of-kin, took delivery of a telegram from the Air Board in Melbourne. As this was the first communication since the general news of the defeat, the telegram would have been grasped eagerly, for mother and father had long agonised over the fate of their son. A month and no news at all. The telegram contained a spare message for these anxious people: 'Regret to inform you that your son ... is missing and believed to be a prisoner of war as result of enemy occupation of Java. If further information is received it will be immediately conveyed to you.' They would hold on to that hope for months — 'believed to be a prisoner of war' — but it was little enough. Exactly a month later, in April 1942, a letter came from M. C. Langslow, Secretary of the Department of the Air, but it merely confirmed the telegram. The letter gave no further clues about Aircraftman Bruce, his whereabouts, condition or fate:

> Although your son has been reported missing he is not necessarily killed or wounded, and in view of this it may be of assistance to you in your anxiety to know what action is being taken to trace missing members of the Air Force. I am, therefore, forwarding herewith a leaflet which gives full information concerning this matter ... I desire to extend to you the sincere sympathy of the Department in the anxiety you are suffering.

It would be September, a full six months later, before the family would hear again from the Department. In the meantime all that they could say to anxious questioners was that their son Donald was 'believed to be a prisoner of war'.[7]

What everyone wanted to know, beyond that the son, daughter, husband or brother was alive and safe, was just how the Japanese would handle all these prisoners for whom they had suddenly become responsible. Japan was not a signatory to the 1929 Geneva Convention on Prisoners of War, but the Australian government believed or hoped that the Japanese would hold fast to the spirit of the convention. First among the responsibilities imposed upon the 'detaining power' was a requirement to provide accurate information about who had been captured and where each prisoner was held. Then the 'detaining power' should allow representatives of the International Red Cross, or representatives of the 'protecting power', to inspect the camps and the condition of the prisoners and to provide the prisoners with some of the necessities of life — food, clothing, books and other leisure materials to help them to endure their captivity.[8]

If they could have seen what was happening to the prisoners of war through the global television on which we have come to rely, or if their sons or daughters had been allowed to send their stories home, the first news would not have been all that bad. There were possibly more than 100 000 Allied prisoners on Singapore Island, nearly 15 000 of them Australians. The Japanese were at first quite friendly. Within two days the prisoners were moved by route march to Changi on the north-eastern tip of the island, formerly a British garrison, with large and airy barrack buildings and a large number of bungalows. And with parade grounds and well cared for lawns and gardens there was 'a pleasant suburban atmosphere to the area'. Forever after in the Australian mind 'Changi' would become shorthand for the worst excesses of Japanese brutality, but it was never as terrible a place, in fact, as others were to become. The prisoners were at first permitted to roam freely through the entire camp and outside it to the straits of Jahore or to the beach on the east. By mid-March, however, prisoners were confined to their own divisional areas. The provision of food was adequate, although hardly generous, the real difficulty being that the Australian cooks had little experience in cooking with rice. Their first efforts were terrible: '[Rice] appeared on the plate as a tight ball of greyish, gelatinous substance, nauseous in its lack of flavour and utterly repulsive.' Australian officers took responsibility for the discipline and employment of their troops and soon effected change in all matters of common interest; they ordered the creation of gardens to provide vegetables, set up an AIF poultry farm, insisted on urgent improvements to the latrines, and established educational and entertainment activities. There was organised sport, too, until the weakness of the prisoners from a defective diet, and the need to conserve medical supplies, meant that football and other games had to be forbidden.[9]

The story 'Football Behind Bamboo' tells us much about the prisoners in these early days.[10] They wanted their lives to bear some of the marks of normality and they wanted, passionately, to remember the lives they had left behind. Noting that the football season was under way in Australia in April 1942, several prisoners, among them Wilfred 'Chicken' Smallhorn, a Fitzroy player, and winner of the Brownlow Medal, the Victorian Football League's highest accolade for a player, established an Australian Rules competition. Chicken's nickname had preceded him to Changi; it is said that his mother, looking on her newborn and pondering his small and scraggy appearance, instantly bestowed upon him the name that he would be stuck with for life. But it would also eerily prefigure his Changi story. Modelled on the dominant VFL, the football competition at Changi had six teams named after VFL clubs and boasted clearances, a system for trading players, tribunals and even its own Brownlow Medal. A player wanted by one team was offered a 'clearance fee' of three bowls of rice; 'if you think that was pretty paltry you're wrong', one of those involved later reported. Among the sportsmen assisting with the organisation of the teams was Ben Barnett, a Victorian and Australian test cricket wicket-keeper. There were three matches each week, played on Saturdays and Wednesdays, and, to a participant, 'believe me, they weren't picnic matches. It was very serious football ... occasionally there were fights on the field'. Chicken Smallhorn was born in 1911 and had won his Brownlow Medal in 1933, so he was perhaps too old to play at Changi, and certainly not well enough. Some have suggested, although it hardly seems credible, that he weighed not much more than four or five stone on his release from captivity. But he wrote up many of the games in the manner of Melbourne's *Sporting Globe*, making a special feature of the final match, Victoria v. The Rest, which Victoria won by 10 points. Football, its accoutrements, and all the other sports and entertainments, tell us that at first captivity was not what it would become. The activities also tell us that these men of spirit would attempt to live the lives they had once lived.

Shortly after the arrival of the prisoners at Changi the Japanese began to understand the potential of the resource they represented. Forbidden, under the Geneva Convention, to require their prisoners to assist the enemy's war effort through their own labour, nevertheless the Japanese soon had the Australians and all the other Allied prisoners working. Work parties were popular with the troops, as they relieved the boredom of captivity and gave them more in terms of rations and canteen goods. On the wharves unloading ships, in godowns (warehouses) piling goods up, or in repairing the roads and other facilities damaged in the fighting, the prisoners were soon a massive source of labour for their captors.

Work would become the centrepiece of the prisoner's experience, and the brutal, savage and inhumane treatment of the prisoners centred to a large extent on the work that was expected of them. Football, the garden and the poultry farm soon gave way for the overwhelming majority to the brutality of the Railway or, later, of coal mines in Japan. By March 1943 the number of Australians at Changi had fallen to less than 2500, with the bulk of the prisoners at work elsewhere. The first parties to leave Changi, in May 1942, were put to work on airfield construction along the coast of Burma. Conditions at first were not severe, although the trip by boat to their places of work was terrible. The equipment given to the prisoners for the type of work expected of them was primitive in the extreme, anticipating problems that would come later. With the airfield work completed, and with more labour battalions on their way from Singapore, the workers were taken either further into Burma or to Thailand to begin work on a railway that was intended to supply the large Japanese army in Burma. It had been decided that the sea route for supply to Rangoon was too hazardous for Japanese shipping and that a railway must be urgently completed if the army was to survive. This was, therefore, vital war work for the Japanese.[11]

The men were forced to build a railway deep in the jungle, with virtually no mechanical assistance, relying instead solely on their own muscle power. They were situated in such remote sites that the provision of their own food supply would be difficult in good weather and near impossible in bad. And it was impressed on their guards that the railway would be completed on time regardless of the human cost, thus consigning these prisoners to a misery that is, for those of us merely reading about it, impossible to comprehend.

Described as one of the most extraordinary engineering feats of the Second World War, the Burma–Thailand Railway was almost primitive in its simplicity when compared with the sophisticated military engineering being employed in the European and other theatres of war. Soil, for example, was moved by hand, with men in chain gangs of buckets or carting bags stretched on poles. There were no excavators or dump trucks, no pile drivers for bridges, no cranes for heavy rails. The Railway was constructed by manpower and willpower in near equal parts. With a labour force of 51 000 British, Dutch and American prisoners of war, 9500 Australians, and 270 000 conscripted Asian civilians, the Railway would wind 415 kilometres through the jungle and would include 15 kilometres of bridging. 'Hell Fire Pass', forever synonymous with the Railway, was a cutting about 500 yards long and about 80 feet deep. Men had to take off the surface soil and then cut into solid rock to find a level path for the line. Shifts in Hell Fire Pass blew out to 18 hours a day and work continued around the clock, with primitive lamps providing light through the night, so determined were the Japanese not the allow the Pass to delay progress. One officer estimated that 68 men were beaten to death while working in the cutting.[12]

The Railway owed its existence to the Battle of Midway, the first significant Allied victory in the first year of the Pacific war. That victory, in June 1942, permanently removed Japanese naval superiority in the Pacific and placed in some jeopardy Japanese supply by sea to its army formations in Burma. Approved by the Japanese Cabinet as a direct response to Midway, the Railway was originally intended to be completed by August 1943 to enable the Japanese

Army to begin an assault on British forces in India. This was an impossible timetable, but in fact the work was finished on 16 October 1943, a completion date that was achieved only by terrible conditions of work and by hideous demands imposed on the labourers. Those in control appeared to have no interest at all in the survival of their labourers; their sole concern was the early completion of the line. Thus sick men were rarely excused work, and with disease and starvation their constant companions the labourers were pushed beyond all reasonable human limits. The death toll was terrible; 2646 Australians died on the Railway, as did 10 000 other Allied prisoners and probably around 70 000 Asian workers.[13]

The location of the railway camps and the type and amount of work expected of the prisoners was bad enough. Worse, by far, was the attitude of the Japanese commanders and their force of Japanese and Korean guards. To some extent the Japanese would have denied any humane treatment to their workers in their determination to have the railway built on time. This can be seen in their brutal treatment of the native labour force, in whose name, ironically, this conquest of the West's Asian colonies was taking place. But there was a further problem for the prisoners: a significant cultural difference. Australians were somewhat embarrassed about being prisoners of war, because captivity seemed to clash with the dominant Anzac legend. But to the Japanese the circumstance of being a prisoner went far beyond mere embarrassment; a soldier who had been defeated in battle and had not died for his Emperor had brought generations of deep shame on his family. Effectively he was dead to decent society already. Therefore the prisoners over whom the Japanese now had control were as nothing to their guards; disgraced by their captivity they were now men without value. In Japanese eyes, in surrendering, no matter that it was in strict compliance with orders and may have represented a triumph of discipline, the prisoners had thrown away whatever claim they may have had as human beings to decent treatment.

There were ominous indications of this attitude even in the early days of captivity. Brutality seemed so excessive and so little remarked upon by the Japanese that it could have been seen as a sign of the insignificance of the prisoners in their captors' eyes. At the Bicycle

Camp at Batavia, to take but one chilling example, there was an initial period of relative calm for the thousands of prisoners there, but by May 1942 a regime was being imposed that was becoming more rigid and incomprehensible by the day. Towards the end of May the Australian officers were detached from their men and were subjected to an intense, month-long examination that was remarkable for its brutality. It seems that the Japanese had made a huge miscalculation and had confused the brigade of Australians put on Java (Black Force) for a division, the Seventh Division, returning from the Middle East. This confusion meant that the Japanese had mistakenly deployed forces to Java that might have been used more effectively elsewhere.

Not unexpectedly, therefore, the Japanese, anticipating the capture of a division, wanted to know where the rest of the Australian troops were and they looked to their interrogation of the Australian officers to provide the answers. Colonel J. M. Williams, commanding the 2/2nd Australian Pioneeer Battalion, was one of those questioned for a month. The brutality was staggering: '[He] had been tied to a chair and his whole body bashed so badly, even his tormentors believed he was dying. When he did regain consciousness, dry rice was forced down his throat and a hose thrust into his mouth, allowing water to surge into his body. When the rice began to swell, his stomach was so swollen [it caused] intense agony.' When Colonel Williams and his fellow officers returned to their units in June, 'the Japanese were none the wiser militarily'.[14]

On the Railway, far from being isolated to a few instances, Japanese brutality and inhumanity extended to the entire labour force. The working conditions were bad enough, as in this account of the laying of rails and sleepers:

> Eighteen or twenty sweating men would grasp the rail and holding it up the leading end, quickly run it clear of the bogie and jump clear as it fell on the sleepers … following the laying gangs at a slower pace came the back spiking gang. Their job was to spike the rails to each sleeper … It was all hard work, performed at high pressure. By the time the sun began to drop towards the west the auger-man was certain that his arms would drop off as he drilled his next hole … and as fatigue began to tell, the blows of the hammer men were not always accurate and the spike was sometimes bent. If the Jap engineer saw the work stop for a minute for

a bent spike to be straightened or pulled out, he bound along muttering or screaming abuse, and laid about him with his heavy metre stick.[15]

Punishment was almost random, consisting of beatings, brutal kicks to ulcerated leg wounds or private parts, or punches of such force as to knock a man down. And it all seemed so senseless, because it could hardly be said to be advancing the building of the Railway which was the only priority. Equally senseless were the hours of work, with 16-hour days being not uncommon. Exhausted men would drag themselves from their camps for another day of excruciating labour, day after day after day. Life revolved around work and rest. At some camps, at some stages, the rations were adequate, but in the wet, at almost every camp, rations were totally inadequate, so these hard-working men were also being starved. Beyond the brutality lay the danger of the work itself. Bridges were built without the least regard to the danger to the men working high above the ground, moving very heavy weights; accidents were common. Men died at a terrible rate. Literally there was a life lost for every sleeper laid, and yet somehow the work proceeded and was finished in remarkably good time.[16]

The Railway has captured most of our attention as the central example of Japanese brutality and inhumanity; it was most certainly an extraordinary and shameful project. But the contempt for the prisoners and the callous disregard for their lives was not restricted to the Railway. Those moving from south-east Asia to Japan endured appalling conditions of overcrowding and lack of food and sanitation on the boats. Those working in the coal mines of Japan likewise suffered long hours of labour, appalling working conditions with primitive equipment, lack of food, and as a constant accompaniment to it all the terrible, mindless brutality. It is hard to understand how anyone survived these atrocious conditions, and yet two-thirds of the Australian prisoners of war in the hands of the Japanese would return to Australia at the end of the war. That statistic alone speaks for the spirit of these men.

Lloyd Ellerman enlisted in the AIF in February 1941. He had worked for the Bank of New South Wales before enlistment, and, posted to Grenfell, he had formed a special friendship with Muriel, one of the daughters of the local postmaster. Lloyd was a keen, skilled and highly competitive tennis player who enjoyed his work, his sport, the town he worked in, his friends and the family of the girl he would marry. His was a good Australian life but he knew that he had to do his duty to his country. Lloyd Ellerman became a prisoner on Singapore when the Allied cause collapsed and he admits that he 'felt a bit ashamed'. In November 1942 he was sent to Japan to work at the Kawasaki ship yards at Kobe as a member of a rivetting gang. It was dangerous work, he remembers, carrying heavy metal plates to the ships being built; balancing across thin planks of wood with a drop many metres to the ground below. Always pushed and often brutalised, Lloyd constantly feared serious injury or death more from the conditions at work than from the guards whose brutality was random and haphazard. He received only one Red Cross parcel in all the years he was a prisoner, and Muriel received only one letter from him, and that in 1945. It was by then twelve months out of date. In May 1945, after the Americans had blown the shipyards 'skyhigh', Lloyd was transferred to Yoshii, a mining village, where he became a coal miner. He detested the work. The mine had been out of use, but was brought back into production in the desperation of Japan's position in 1945. The coalface was a kilometre below the surface and it took the miners an hour to walk underground to their jobs. Lloyd Ellerman lost half of his bodyweight while he was a prisoner, and his experiences in Japan demonstrate how universal was the brutality, the suffering and the unremitting hard and dangerous work.[17]

No one at home could have believed what the prisoners were enduring. Had they known, they would have been driven almost to madness in their grief and in their frustration at their inability to put a stop to it. Instead people at home had to assume that their sons and husbands were not being treated too badly. They had to assume the best for their loved ones. They worked diligently to provide for them, raising money for the Red Cross or packing Red Cross parcels, writing regularly, perhaps each week, long letters of love and news, into a void, to be sure, but in the hope that the letters were being read. And in the refinement of cruelty, the captors were carefully storing up these Red Cross parcels as they were received, or piling up the letters that continued to arrive at their destinations, not distributing them simply out of perversity. When peace came, the prisoners were astonished to discover the quantities of now rotting food that might have been made available to men dying of starvation, or of tins of good, unspoiled food that might have supplemented hopeless diets. They saw with amazement the quantities of medicines that had been so carefully and lovingly packed in Australia, medicines that would have saved hundreds, probably thousands, of lives. And medical equipment that could have substituted for the improvised tools that the doctors crafted themselves from whatever was to hand. They found clothing in these stores that might have been distributed to men who had no new clothing for the period of their captivity and who were reduced to loincloths, making many of them seem, as they became in Japanese eyes, degraded and wretched beggars. The failure to distribute what was freely available and what might have made a tremendous difference shows an attitude of mind that says that to the Japanese these men were already dead in the shame of their surrender. They were non-persons to their captors, but deeply loved by those still spending a part of every day thinking of them, speaking of them with affection, and often praying for them.

One-third of the Australians who became prisoners of war of the Japanese died in captivity: 7700 men. And yet from what we know of the conditions under which they were held, it seems miraculous that any, in fact, survived. Part of the key to survival lies in the work of the doctors, on the Railway and elsewhere. Deprived of medicines and forced to operate in makeshift theatres, with few instruments and improvised conditions, the doctors did the best they could. They stood up to the Japanese, seeking to keep from work those they judged most incapable of it. Sometimes they succeeded and this saved lives. The doctors also insisted on high standards of hygiene and sanitation and this certainly helped to save lives too, and they encouraged the allocation of better rations to the sick, wherever this was possible. 'Weary' Dunlop is rightly remembered as a magnificent Australian in his work for the prisoners, but there were dozens like him, less well-known now, but nevertheless of the greatest importance to the men whose lives they saved.

If part of the answer to the question of survival lies in the strength and determination of the medical staff, another part lies in the spirit

of the men themselves. Lloyd Ellerman claims that he 'always remained optimistic' and Colonel Williams, so brutally treated in
interrogation, would, on his release, attribute Australian survival rates
to a 'sense of humour'. That sounds trite yet it is impossible to find
the words to describe the reality of what Williams and Ellerman, and
thousands of others, discovered. 'Mateship' is now a discredited word
in some quarters perhaps, but it was then an extremely important
aspect of survival. No man need be alone, mateship asserted, no
thought or fear need be unspoken, no anxiety need be hidden. A man
would scrounge food for his sick mate; he would listen and counsel
in depression; he would bind wounds when needed. And his mate
would do the same for him when his time came.

Much of the talk between mates was of the old days at home, and
of the days to be again. In his love for cricket, and in shared memories
of two great Australian cricket grounds, Rohan Rivett entered
another world with his mate, the existence of which gave him a reason
for living. Mates were not limited in their intimacy as between lovers;
they shared entire worlds from the past and the future. It was in those
shared worlds that they escaped the present horrible reality. And in
this sense, the family of the prisoners was a key to survival. A
remembered world, for Lloyd Ellerman, of the bank, of Grenfell, of
tennis and its parties, of a warm family, of the postmaster who was a
good churchman, an honest worker and a fine father, was a joy to
recall and recapture. It was also a joy to share its meaning with a mate
and in speaking of it to make it real. And the anticipation of regaining
that world gave some sense to the Railway, the shipyard or the coal
mine. Home was not merely an aspiration; it was present as a reality
to be enjoyed between mates; it was a reality that forced a man to
keep going. Family was present in the life of the prisoner in the person
of his mate and in each man's shared memories and anticipations.

CHAPTER 2

'If only I knew what has become of him'

No one at home could have known how vital home was to the men who were trying to survive the most brutal captivity imaginable. Indeed, families knew almost nothing at all about the fate of their men and women in the hands of the Japanese and their most urgent need was to find out. As a War Office official in London reported to Australia House in August 1942, 'so far the silence of the East reigns unbroken'.

Yet there was optimism on the homefront despite the silence from Singapore. The Australian commander of the Eighth Division, Major-General Gordon Bennett, had escaped Singapore in controversial circumstances just as the men were being assembled to surrender. Bennett was quoted in Australian newspapers in early March 1942 as saying that there was every reason to believe that the Australian prisoners would not be badly treated by the Japanese. 'Evidence so far is', he said, 'that Australians in Japanese hands have been treated quite well, and there does not seem to be any need for undue worry by relatives.' Bennett excused his desertion of his troops on the grounds that he needed to get back to Australia to tell the government what this new enemy was really like. Reassuring relatives in this way was a kindness; perhaps Bennett's private advice to the government was more accurate. He would have known, at least, of the massacre at Hong Kong and possibly of other atrocities.[1]

Cables travelled furiously between Canberra and London about proposals for the Red Cross to organise sending a couple of ships, packed with food, to relieve the prisoners. A London official solemnly advised H. V. Evatt, the Australian foreign minister, that it was 'obvious that the Japanese scale of diet will be hopelessly insufficient for Australian soldiery' and so supplementary foods should be shipped from Australia. The cabling officials believed, or hoped, that the Japanese would provide an adequate diet to their own standards, but these officials spent much time throughout 1942 trying to arrange extra supplies, down to the minutest detail of how the ships were to be loaded. As they believed that even the Indian prisoners (41 000 in Singapore) would be caught short by the type of fare the Japanese would consider reasonable, one of the ships should contain 'rice, flour, golden syrup, figs, dates, nuts, chillies, curry powder'. It was essential, the officials believed, to time the arrival of the European and Asiatic supplies so that they coincided, thus preventing the Japanese from unsettling the Indians by alleging that the Empire did not care for them. It was cloud-cuckoo-land in London.[2]

On the same day that the Melbourne *Argus* published Gordon Bennett's encouraging bromide to relatives, the *Daily Telegraph* in Sydney was at last reporting 'shocking stories of atrocities by the Japanese in Hong Kong'. That was in March, but the Australian government had already received the bad news in a cable from London dated 18 February, three days after the defeat at Singapore. 'Atrocities at Hong Kong were considered by [the British] Cabinet on 16 February and conclusion reached that it was inadvisable to give immediate publicity to the matter … publicity at present would have a bad effect on morale in the Far East and would cause great distress to the relatives of those concerned.'[3]

But the British had changed their minds by early March, hoping perhaps that publicity would influence the 'detaining power' to play the game. Anthony Eden, the Foreign Secretary, in the House of Commons on 7 March 1942 gave members a gruesome picture of Japanese atrocities against prisoners of war and civilian internees. He concluded: 'The Japanese claim that their forces are animated by a lofty code of chivalry is a nauseating hypocrisy … we can best express our sympathy with the victims of these appalling outrages by redoubling our efforts to ensure [Japan's] utter and overwhelming defeat.' Eden's statement, cleared with the Australian government beforehand, was given widespread publicity in the Australian newspapers, as the government would have expected. But it was cruel for relatives to know of these atrocities before they even knew if their own folk were alive and safe in some camp. For Eden's statement preceded by a few days the despatch of the first and most cursory telegrams to Australian next-of-kin of the kind received by the Bruce family in South Australia. The tension at home was already extreme.[4]

The Australian government had expected that the Japanese would compile full lists of prisoners in their hands soon after the defeat at Singapore and would forward these lists to a neutral source. This was what the Geneva Convention stipulated. It was normal behaviour. But given the extraordinary numbers of prisoners (a cable in July suggested there were some 300 000 of them), the governments were prepared to tolerate some delay in the transmittal of names. Only slowly did it dawn on Canberra and London that the enemy had no intention of following their civilised expectations. In April, John Curtin wondered whether an element of pay-back, 'reciprocity' in the polite talk of the cables, might bring the Japanese to their senses. The High Commissioner, S. M. Bruce, in London, sympathised with what Curtin was trying to achieve and explained that there was also 'considerable feeling here re lack of information'. But, he continued, 'our representative is doubtful whether method suggested will have desired effect, particularly as so few Japanese are in British hands'.[5] That was only part of the problem. It soon became obvious that the Japanese despised those who had become prisoners, from either side, and there was no element of leverage with the enemy by threatening rough treatment for their soldiers in captivity. But at least John Curtin was trying to find some sort of solution.

Curtin's own natural sympathy and humane concern would have propelled this great Australian war leader to try to do something for the men and their families in this new and intensely worrying difficulty, but Curtin was also being importuned from all sides to act. Organisations, unions, at least one Labor Party branch, and individuals all reinforced the widespread community concern for the prisoners, still by mid-year largely unknown in name or location. The Randwick North Branch of the Labor Party in florid terms called on Archbishop Gilroy to ask the Pope to ensure that 'the superabundant bounties of God of Australia's surplus reserves of wheat and meat and wool for clothing ... should be given unmolested transport to provide sustenance for the sick and wounded and all Allied Prisoners of War'.[6]

Two individuals capture the tone of the correspondence that Curtin was receiving. F.J. MacKenzie of Sydney reminded his prime minister that 'the relatives and friends of our men feel that the position is desperate and calls for some immediate action, even though such action does not follow the set methods of approach'. 'Let us do something', he pleaded, and then suggested an expedition to Rabaul with food and medical supplies. And Mrs Grace Harrison of South Melbourne, who conceded that her prime minister was 'very busy' and had 'a great worrie', nevertheless had to tell him how she felt:

> I have a great worrie too my son is missing in Malaya and I am a very sad mother. If only I knew what has become of him. I am going to make a surjestion to you and that is to alow a mother to make a broadcast to Japan to appeal to the mothers of Japan to appeal to their menfolk to send in the names of the men they have prisoners. Look at all the sad wives and mothers in Australia … again please forgive me taking the liberty and may Our Lady of Good Council [her spelling] help you in a task that is very great.

This last letter was written in November 1942; nearly a year had passed and still no real news. John Curtin probably did not need to be reminded of 'all the sad wives and mothers in Australia'.[7]

There was some exchange of diplomats, foodstuffs and information at Lourenco Marques, Mozambique, in mid-1942 but still no names from Singapore. As London plaintively cabled in September: 'Have you received any lists by wireless.' The reply from Australia was even more depressing. Only eight names had been officially communicated: five prisoners of war airmen and three others who had been killed in action. Eight names officially communicated in seven months since this captivity began — this was, without doubt, an appalling situation. The Australian government was in a terrible position, with a real duty of care to the families of prisoners, yet unable to do anything to alleviate their suffering. There had been one bizarre and unique occurence when, at the end of April 1942, Japanese planes, flying low over Port Moresby, dropped bags containing letters from

Australian prisoners. There were 395 letters in the cache, but the meaning of this event has never been adequately explained.[8]

The Japanese seemed set to take advantage of the Australian anxiety about the prisoners and to exploit the near total silence from the camps. By mid-year they had begun to use the lack of names as a propaganda ploy, broadcasting some names and news from prisoners on Radio Batavia, which could be picked up on shortwave in Australia. The promise of information was a means of hooking listeners into the broadcasts which also contained morale-sapping information of Allied defeats and disasters. From these broadcasts the names of 1685 Australians had been gained — a small enough titbit indeed, but names nevertheless and of enormous comfort to those who had won in this distressing lottery. Radio Tokyo was even more generous, broadcasting the prisoners' own voices as well as their names. In July 1942, in a carefully written and lengthy memo, the Short Wave Department of the Australian Broadcasting Commission analysed the news from the camps that Radio Batavia was sending out. The analysis showed how carefully listeners needed to interpret what the men were saying and how sketchy was any true picture of conditions in the camps. Listeners not searching for the nuances could easily have believed that the Japanese were caring for the prisoners pretty well.[9]

Alison Todd had just turned nine years of age when war broke out in 1939; her brother David was five. Their father, William Angus Todd, was an officer in the Merchant Navy, working for the Union Steam Ship Company. Late in 1941 Bill Todd was transferred as first officer to MV *Hauraki*, a ship his father had brought out from England twenty years before on its maiden voyage. Sailing first to the Middle East on this newest posting, Bill Todd returned in May 1942, to leave again in convoy from Melbourne on 9 June 1942. After repairs due to storm damage the *Hauraki* finally left Fremantle for Colombo on 7 July 1942. Within days there were rumours flying about the ship's offices and wharves in Sydney, but it was not until 18 August that Alison's mother was officially informed that the *Hauraki* had been captured in the Indian Ocean by a Japanese raider. It was probable, the telegram concluded, that the crew were prisoners of war. Nearly a year later, in June 1943, the International Red Cross confirmed that Bill Todd was indeed a prisoner in Japan. The strain on her mother of waiting for this morsel of news, Alison remembers, was terrible.[10]

Alison cannot now remember how, but at some stage this worried family learnt that Radio Tokyo broadcast messages from prisoners for fifteen minutes every weekday evening from 7.15 pm. The family listened in every night on the first-class shortwave radio that Bill Todd had brought back from America around 1935. 'There was a rush to get the evening meal over,' Alison recalls. 'We listened to the 7 o'clock news in Australia and went straight over at 7.15 to Radio Tokyo.' They did this for many months: 'It was routine.' Then on 10 August 1943, the day after Alison's 13th birthday, 'we heard that Dad and several others from the *Hauraki* would speak the next evening. We were ecstatic'. The telephone started to ring immediately, with some friends but predominately total strangers calling to make sure that the family had heard the good news. Alison went to school in a state of high excitement, telling everyone that she was to hear her father's voice that evening. Returning home she found that her mother had been swamped with telegrams and phone calls, one from as far away as Western Australia, from people anxious to alert the family to the coming broadcast. All of these callers were strangers, Alison remembers, just good people keen for the family not to miss the chance of hearing their loved one's voice once more.

They were in the lounge room that evening, around the fire, Alison, her mother, and David now nine years of age. With them were 'Dad's sister and one of Mum's', intent on copying down every word. 'Could you recognise your father's voice?' I asked these two, brother and sister, who were telling me their story. 'Oh yes,' they replied, instantly and without hesitation, transported back to that evening long ago when they heard their father speak to them for the last time. 'Hello Natalie, Alison and David,' he started, 'hope you are listening.' Bill Todd then told them that he was in a camp with Australian, British and American soldiers, that they worked each day and received rations from the Japanese and Red Cross food parcels. Although he had been a prisoner for twelve months, he said, 'I have not been fortunate enough to receive letters; am hopeful each mail delivered.' He hoped, he said, that 'Alison and David are doing well at school. Both must help mother all they can in my absence'. 'You are always in my thoughts,' he concluded, 'and fortunately I still have your photograph … Hope to be home soon, so will close with fondest love to you all.' And then he was gone. It had been a fleeting embrace with the person around whom that whole house revolved, who was never out of their thoughts and for whom there was so much concern. There were two letters and two cards to the family beyond this radio broadcast, the last delivered in April 1944. It was on 3 October 1945, seven weeks after the war had ended, that the family learnt that Bill Todd would not be coming home; he had died on 19 April 1944. The official notification from Canberra, addressed to David Todd, Alison's young brother, clearly the only male in the family that the department could find, was received on 17 December 1945. David told me, in a quiet sort of way, that it was hard to remember anything of his father.[11]

Radio Batavia and other Japanese broadcasts provoked a dilemma for a government that was keen to discourage people from listening-in to enemy propaganda. The government might have ignored the broadcasts and might actively have discouraged people from tuning in; but that would have involved asking families to surrender the only available source of news and might well have portrayed the government as indifferent to the fate of the prisoners and the anxieties of their families. Or the government might have openly acknowledged the importance of the broadcasts, but this would have run the real risk of promoting Japanese propaganda in Australia. The broadcasts were widely available and, it would seem, widely listened to, as the experience of the Todds and many letters in government files testify. What was the government to do?

A public servant, Frank Davidson, a press officer in the Department of Information, wrote to a more senior officer, L. G. Wigmore, of the same department to explain just how great an audience Radio Batavia had:

> A cousin of mine has been missing since he went into Java just ahead of the Japs. One night last week Batavia radio read a letter from him to his mother etc. Of course they didn't hear it although they have often tinkered hopefully with a short wave set. But in a very short time half a dozen people — all strangers — had arrived at the house to tell them of the broadcast and one woman even shut up her shop in a nearby suburb to come down and tell his mother. On the following days a number of

other people called and his mother had about 40 letters from different parts of the State, some of them giving extracts from his message. This week the correspondence continued.[12]

Alison Todd's story, it would seem, was far from unusual.

Radio Batavia was, therefore, a serious problem and it merited deep consideration within government, including a full airing of the issues at War Cabinet. The 'Australian Home News Service' of Radio Batavia, as notes to the prime minister on the War Cabinet Agendum explained, consisted of a daily reading of the names of some prisoners of war, a letter from a prisoner to his family and 'propaganda directed towards creating an Australian opinion in favour of surrender or appeasement'. The Defence Committee wanted to ban all references to Radio Batavia in the press, and to severely limit access, if possible, to the broadcasts, while providing a summary to the relatives concerned. The Prime Minister's Committee on National Morale, presided over by the shadowy Alf Conlon, recognised that a refusal to pass on information of such vital personal interest 'would produce widespread resentment ... it would give the impression ... [of] a bureaucratic indifference to the deep feelings of those suffering anxiety and loss'. The government decided that it would monitor the broadcasts, transcribe them faithfully for relatives, and pass the news on promptly to relatives to assure them that they would not miss out on any news. The government would also explain through the press and other channels that official action, relying on the best wireless equipment available, would be likely to more efficient than local 'hams'. The text of any messages would be communicated, officially, to the next of kin by Service channels. The Prime Minister's statement made all these points and concluded that 'since any such letters or messages are received through enemy sources, the Government feels it should warn people against a too ready acceptance of them as completely authentic'.[13]

And so it was. The next telegram to be received in the Bruce household in South Australia arrived in September 1942:

Information just received states that your son Aircraftman Donald Wilfred Bruce was mentioned in a broadcast from Batavia as being a prisoner of war. This information should be treated with reserve pending official confirmation. In the event of further information being received same will be immediately conveyed to you.[14]

At least, now, Donald's father and family knew that he was alive. It had taken more than six months to reach that stage. And the Bruce family was one of the lucky ones in a random selection from Radio Batavia.

In an age of near instant communication, when a travelling daughter or son can provide the family with a regular e-mail from even the most remote places or a can send a quick greeting via mobile phone, it is difficult to comprehend the total silence that existed between the prisoner and his loved ones. It is easy, however, to understand the anguish. Some prisoners would come home in October 1945 having heard nothing at all of home since late January 1942; some parents would never have any personal news of a son or daughter again; many would have only the most rudimentary news during the years of captivity, and that many months or years after the initial imprisonment.

The prime minister wanted to know the true dimensions of the agony relatives were experiencing and in May 1943 Australia's postal authority, the Postmaster General's Department, briefed him. This was then the picture: at the end of April 1942, 395 letters and 'three other bundles' had been dropped over Port Moresby; in October 1942 a packet of postcards and one letter had been brought to Australia by a returning member of the Australian legation, Tokyo; in February 1943 seven letters had been mailed from Zentsuji camp, Japan; in February 1943, 49 message forms had arrived from camps in Thailand, and one other letter on 24 May 1943. Apart from a few letters from civilians at the Stanley internment camp, Hong Kong, that was it. The total communication from 22 000 Australian prisoners of war in 15 months captivity amounted to not much more than 500 individual letters, postcards or forms.[15] In addition, several thousand names had been broadcast from unreliable enemy sources, but no exact listing of all prisoners had ever been received. Was a son or daughter alive or dead, enduring terrible privations or torture, or relatively well cared for? No one knew — neither parents nor governments. This was cruelty most refined, driving some at home over the brink from misery to madness.

It is not my intention to highlight the sufferings of the families of prisoners in the hands of the Japanese by contrasting their circumstances with those of families of prisoners in the hands of the Germans, but a letter of complaint to John Curtin from a mother whose son was in Germany does underline the difference. This woman, Mrs Burton from Enfield, New South Wales, was worried about the irregularity of mails to and from Australia and Germany, because, although she had written some time ago that her other son (his brother) had died in battle, the prisoner son had not yet commented on this. The mother wrote weekly but was alarmed that some of her letters apparently had not got through. And Mrs Burton enclosed a letter from her son in Germany so that the Prime Minister could better understand the nature of their correspondence. In view of his concerns for Australians in the hands of the Japanese, the issue Mrs Burton raised was probably a second-order problem for Curtin:

> I received two letters from you last week. I was very glad to know everyone is alright and especially glad for news of Jean since it is ages since I heard from her … Everyone seems to be getting married according to your letters. I'm sure missing a lot, but I guess I'll make up for it when I get home.[16]

Mothers and wives writing weekly and blindly to their sons in Singapore and Thailand would have dreamed of this regular interchange, and the Burton letter serves to remind us of what might and should have been the norm for them too.

It is hardly surprising that some of the relatives of the prisoners thought of forming a self-help group, for there were so many now in the same boat and it has been a notable characteristic of Australians in time of war to band together for all sorts of purposes. But the establishment of the Australian Prisoners of War Relatives Association (APOWRA) seemed to depend on the organising ability, habits of life and drive of one particular individual, Sydney Smith, more than on the impetus of the many. Smith's son was a prisoner of war in Germany and, as President of the New South Wales Cricket Association, Smith had access to an office and facilities in Cricket House,

George Street, Sydney. He had played first-grade cricket for Petersham and then Gordon in the Sydney competition and joined the
Australian Board of Control for International Cricket in 1911. He
was one of those people, it seems, who just liked to do good, and as
honorary secretary of APOWRA Smith was indefatigable in the
interests of members, as hundreds of letters in government files testify.
A public servant until he retired in 1944, Smith was tireless in
numerous honorary jobs of which 'about twenty concerned cricket
and tennis'. He was also honorary secretary of the Sailors', Soldiers'
and Airmen's Fathers Association. Although he was involved in cricket
administration for three-quarters of a century Smith 'tended to see
players as cogs in the administrative machine, whose duty was to do
as they were told'. His correspondence with ministers sometimes
adopted a similar tone.[17]

Syd Smith could claim, by April 1943, that APOWRA had 9000
members thoughout Australia. He saw the association as a group to
lobby government in the interests of prisoners and their families and
hoped that families would feel less isolated knowing that there were
many others in the same boat. In his work with government Smith
watched closely all the issues and was constantly urging the government to take action. He was also the editor and principal writer for
P.O.W., a journal first published in January 1942.[18]

The aim of the journal was 'to spread news of prisoners and prison
camps and, through the publication of letters and news, to carry
mental comfort to those who have relatives in the Enemy's camps'.
Smith sincerely wanted to keep the relatives 'in good heart', a worthy
objective, but one that increasingly gave a pollyanna tinge to the
journal. In March 1942 Smith asserted that 'although Japan has never
agreed to the Geneva Convention under which Red Cross works,
she is probably the most Red Cross-minded country in the world'.
This was an audacious assessment that Smith based on the reported
number and size of Japanese Red Cross branches. By May 1942,
although worrying about the lack of news that was already so
disturbing to relatives, Smith remained optimistic, merely asking
whether the 'delay is due to the deliberate withholding of the names
by the Japanese, or the speed of their advance having disorganised
their Prisoner of War and Red Cross Departments'. In October Smith

had some real news to impart from the few members of the AIF who
had escaped from the prison camp on the island of Amboina: 'They
report that our prisoners there were healthy and fit. Our men had
been allowed to keep their personal belongings. They had ample
medical supplies and lived in a large compound in which was a
hospital.'[19]

Good news indeed and followed up the next month with the first
letters from Japan. Just three of them, to be sure, and short, but
headlined 'Comforting News for Prisoners Families'. For the life of
the journal Smith had been printing large quantities of news from
Germany, and a mother with a son in the hands of the Japanese, and
no news, would have been tough-minded to keep on reading *P.O.W.*
In relaying the news from Germany, Smith delighted to put the best
gloss on captivity: 'Saturday I'm Playing Football; Work, Sport, Good
Food and Warmth are the Lot of Our Men in Stalag VIII B.' A steady
diet of this, and no news at all from Singapore or Thailand, must have
been a saddening mix.[20]

It was the Victorian RSL which first questioned what Smith was
up to. 'The influence of the pacifists appears in many guises', warned
Mufti, that branch's journal: 'In the periodical circulated by the P.O.W.
movement, there is gratuitous propaganda for the enemy worth
countless thousands of pounds … it is the type of propaganda that
was responsible for the fall of France.' The RSL wanted something
altogether tougher and more resolute: 'If, in depriving relatives of the
comfort of news of their loved ones, one should be accused of
callousness towards the sufferings of wives and mothers, we appeal to
them to see the need of the nation and the danger confronting us.'
Smith countered: 'We do not gain strength by heaping anguish on
the relatives'. He passionately believed that, in writing that things
were reasonable, the prisoners were either doing no more than
telling the truth or were showing the 'courage and cheefulness' that,
he believed, had always characterised the Australian soldier. So what
if they were cracking hardy, he seemed to be saying, they were doing
it for the best of reasons. 'There is not a grizzle in a hundred of
them', he wrote, and there would not be either, because they were
Australian.[21]

Sydney Smith was putting into print what thousands of parents and wives must have been doing every day anyway: hoping for the best. He was prepared to hear good news from any source. A parent told him of men who had returned from Malaya and Singapore during the war but before the defeat and surrender. They reported: 'The Japs are not as cruel as we are given to believe. I saw them move wounded men to the side of the road [in the Malayan campaign] so that they should not be run-over.' Smith used this 'analysis' as his counter to the government's ill-considered 'Hate Campaign', launched and quickly abandoned in mid-1942, which had as its theme: 'We've always despised them, now we must smash them.' Even after Anthony Eden had again painted the most appalling picture of life in a Japanese prison camp, in January 1944, Smith was capable of running a report of a lecture from a 'Mr Mack' who spoke to relatives somewhere in England of his experiences of living in Japan for many years. The incidents used by Eden in his statement, Mr Mack complained, were all taken from the early weeks of captivity and this was at a time when the Japanese war policy was of brutal conquest: 'but there seems to be sufficient evidence that later things improved a great deal', he said. Mr Mack also claimed to have known, before the war, several missionaries who had adopted Japanese ways to such an extent that they had trained themselves to live on native food: 'when they were accustomed to it, it had no ill effects'. The prisoners ought to be able to adapt to Japanese food just as readily, was Mack's unspoken assumption.[22]

In the absence of news and reliable testimony it is easy to understand Sydney Smith's motivation, if not necessarily to agree with what he was doing. How much anxiety and worry could people bear? If there was nothing provable to be said, was it not better to assume that the enemy would do the right thing? And, in any case, would any prisoner of the Japanese suffer one extra agony, beating or deprivation on account of the 'she'll be right' hopefulness of the prisoners' advocate in Australia. As will emerge, the prisoners themselves, on release, minimised their sufferings in deference to the feelings of relatives of the men and women who did not return. Was Sydney Smith doing any more than they would have wanted him to do? If the needs of the relatives were the only consideration, Sydney

Smith's pleasant gloss could be justified, but there were other issues for the government to consider.

The optimism and hopefulness of these reports soon came to the attention of the Australian censor, who had to juggle the interests of the relatives against the wider national interest, and who, with no great certainty or confidence in his own judgment, tried to find a way for all viewpoints. The Australian Red Cross Society publicity material along with *P.O.W.* came to the censor's attention in October 1942. Both publications purported to summarise what was known of Japanese prisoner of war camps. The Red Cross material told of one camp, 'location unknown', that had two doctors and one dentist present, a 'fair supply' of medical goods, plenty of facilities for washing and laundering, a 'fair supply' of games, books and cards, two cricket pitches and a gymnasium. At another 'location unknown', 'prisoners [were] treated with consideration. Food mostly rice, which seems to suit the men. The prisoners are healthy and the mortality very low'.[23]

In *P.O.W.*, and to some extent in the Red Cross material, the information came from the prisoners themselves in the few letters that had been received. The censors suspected, quite rightly, that the prisoners were putting a gloss on their circumstances to allay fears and worry at home. It was gallant of the prisoners to do this, and quite understandable, but should the censor intervene in this playing out of humane impulses on the part of individuals and organisations? It was a matter 'which I find difficult to decide', the chief censor, E. G. Bonney, wrote. 'There is no doubt that cheer-up letters from a prisoner allay fears not only in the minds of his relatives but in the minds of readers whose sons and brothers are in captivity. Whether peace of mind is established at the cost of determination to wipe out our enemies is the problem to be solved.' An internal adviser in the Censor's office had already suggested to Bonney that 'if our prisoners are being ill-treated it is highly important that we should know this so that we may get a proper appreciation of the sort of people we are fighting'. The censor reported that he had discussed the matter with the military where he found a view hardly complimentary to Australian troops. It was an attitude that re-emerged after the war when governments were dealing with the question of compensation to former prisoners. It was a mean assessment, which Bonney reported to his fellow censors: 'G.H.Q.'s view, with which I concur, is that the constant repetition of stories indicating favourable treatment ... is definitely detrimental to the fighting qualities of our armed forces. The only way to combat a possible tendency to surrender is to convince our soldiers that a prisoner's lot is not a happy one.' Bonney made the sensible point that *P.O.W.* could not be printed if the prisoners' letters were cut out. Therefore censorship would lead to the collapse of the magazine and might be seen as callous. Bonney 'hoped to have this difficult question finally clarified further by a decision of War Cabinet at an early date'.[24]

The matter was referred to War Cabinet in late December 1942 and that body produced a ruling that was truly delphic in its wording: 'that the publication of letters or extracts of letters from prisoners of war be permitted subject to censorship'. The evidence thereafter would indicate that the censors gave free rein to Sydney Smith and the like, hoping, probably correctly, that few beyond the immediate families of prisoners would ever come across the material anyway. Whether any Australian troops thereafter succumbed to 'a possible tendency to surrender' can never be known with any certainty, although surveys of soldiers and their ideas about the Japanese makes the notion of voluntary surrender quite implausible.[25]

It is doubtful that Sydney Smith and the Relatives' Association ever knew how closely they had been scrutinised by the Censor and by War Cabinet. But Smith certainly understood the importance of censorship, and as much more was coming to light in the later years of the war, though still in general terms, about conditions in Japanese camps, he sought to encourage the government to clamp down on reports of brutality and barbarism. Such reports, he believed, caused 'unnecessary worry to the relatives of [prisoners]'. Hope, and a naive respect for Japan as the 'most Red Cross-minded country in the world' encouraged Smith to dismiss without question suggestions of brutality or a high death toll in the camps. Perhaps many relatives were of a similar mindset, but the worry and anxiety caused by the newspapers was only too obvious to those working with the relatives. Sydney Smith had read an account in Australian newspapers that '20 000 prisoners of war had died in the building of a railway in Burma'. This was just press talk, he believed, which caused great worry to relatives of Australian prisoners of war. 'In such a case there should have been a footnote from the Government to the effect that there was no verification of such statement and, furthermore, there was nothing to indicate that any Australian Prisoners of War were involved, other than those whose next-of-kin had already been notified.' The prime minister's reply informed Smith that censorship would not be imposed 'merely for the maintenance of morale or the prevention of despondency and alarm', and the censor reported to the prime minister that the railway story had originated from the Press Association in Chungking and reached the world news services before being printed in Australia. It would be futile to try to keep such stories out, the censors believed. There seemed, however, to be a degree of scepticism all round about the claimed death toll on the railway. It looked high and therefore unrealistic even to the censors.[26]

But increasingly the government was learning some of the truth of the treatment of prisoners of war in the hands of the Japanese and increasingly the news was dreadful. The agonising question for the prime minister and his ministers was how much of this information should be made publicly available. It was an issue that was hotly debated in Canberra and, through constant reference to London, more widely. Much of the information about conditions in the camps came by way of cable from London. A Chinese missionary, able to move about more freely than most, was reported as having been in Thailand where '[he] saw many prisoners clearly. They were merely skin and bone, unshaven and with long matted hair. They were half naked and looked longingly at the train'. The weekly intelligence summary from the South East Asia Command (SEAC) confirmed such reports. For example, in June 1944 SEAC reported on the camps along the Burma–Siam Railway: '[The railway] can be described without exaggeration as slave labour in its vilest form' with a death rate of 450 men per month. The report concluded: 'Few of the original 60 000 P.O.W. are likely to survive to tell the tale of the most inhuman treatment of P.O.W. the world has seen in modern times.'[27]

This news was terrible and it was now becoming constant. No Australian government minister could be left in any doubt as to the fate of Australian prisoners as the veil of secrecy began to be lifted from mid-1943 onwards. The relevant ministers, parliamentarians, and the prime minister especially, were under siege from the public, prisoners' relatives particularly, demanding that the government tell what they knew and that they do something to alleviate the suffering and brutality. It was an appalling dilemma for government, because the voices of the parents were clearly so honest and so agonised.

Mrs D. H. Wallace of Glenbrook, New South Wales, wrote to John Curtin in February 1944: 'All my living progeny, four sons, are in the combatant forces, one being a prisoner in Thailand.' This patriotic mother had had a couple of cards from her prisoner son, but they had been hopelessly delayed and were quite out-of-date by the time she received them. 'If this delay of prisoners mail is systematic it is refined cruelty', she wrote. 'I have written to him many times it seems he has received none of my letters'. She concluded: 'I am alone and greatly worried about my son in Japanese hands, who is my best boy.' A reply carelessly addressed to Mr D. H. Wallace was detailed in its explanation of the circumstances facing the government, but it could give no joy as nothing could be done, beyond pressing on to win the war. To have told Mrs Wallace the truth would have been further 'refined cruelty'.[28]

Another mother, Mrs Evans from Heathcote, Victoria, reported in March 1944 that her youngest son was with the 2/22nd Battalion in Rabaul when the Japanese invaded: 'I received one letter from him the letter was in a mail bag that was dropped from an airplane over Pt Moresby. It was written in my son's handwriting and said he was in the best of health, that he was well treated and that I was not on any account to worry about him. I have not heard of him since.' She had endured just on two years of total silence. Mrs Evans wanted to let her prime minister know that she was suffering. She would learn, when the war was over, that her son had died on 1 July 1942, nearly two years before she had written to John Curtin.[29]

Some letter-writers were angry. P. Timmens of Glenelg, South Australia, had a son lost on HMAS *Perth*. 'At that time our boys went into battle without any chance', he wrote. 'No plane protection etc so anything the Commonwealth can do for us to get in touch with them would be greatly appreciated.' One mother discovered that although the International Red Cross was prepared to send money to prisoners in Japanese camps on behalf of Australian relatives, who would pay in Swiss francs, the Australian government prevented sending such foreign exchange. 'It is now over two years since the Fall of Singapore and Malaya', Mrs Murison of Moonee Ponds, Victoria, wrote to John Curtin in April 1944, 'and not a finger raised to help those brave boys that were let down like sheep ... [then] when we can get the opportunity ... to get help to them you are the one that is making it impossible ... [yet they are] the Flower of our Country in men that saved Australia and kept the war from our own doors'.[30]

And sometimes fear did creep into the letters too, because many relatives had begun to believe some of the things that the newspapers were printing. And some of the letters that did get through from the prisoners did in fact describe at least part of the reality. Thus in December 1943 Mrs Quinn from Darlinghurst, Sydney, wrote to her local member, E. J. Ward, about her brother. 'Is it possible', she pleaded, 'that our Government could do something or try to do something for our prisoners of war.' She had received a card from her brother who was in a camp in Korea and he wrote that the winter was very severe and that they still had only the clothes they had been wearing when captured. As well as the inadequacy of tropical clothes in the Korean winter, Mrs Quinn added that 'they must be in a very bad condition [now]'.[31]

The interesting aspect of much of this correspondence with the prime minister was the personal regard and concern for his own welfare that many of the correspondents expressed. They seemed to understand the heavy burdens and the responsibility that the war imposed on John Curtin. But it was more than that. There was something of a personal bond between suffering Australians and their anguished leader. 'Wishing you all the best', Mrs J. A. Lyons of Fullerton, South Australia, concluded: 'I realise what a tremendous burden you have to carry in these strenuous days.' They were all a part of John Curtin's 'all-in' war effort.[32]

There was some flow of mail from the Japanese camps, of course, but nothing that could satisfy those who wanted regular and current news. In August 1943 the Army advised that 14 000 items of prisoner of war mail from those in the hands of the Japanese had been received by the Post Office in Switzerland and would be in Australia soon. It would be scrutinised very carefully, the Army pledged, to help to determine the fate of many soldiers still posted as 'missing, believed to be a prisoner of war'. In fact the mail was greater than the Army had been led to believe, comprising some 18 000 items in all, enabling the Army's Prisoner of War section to reclassify 7500 soldiers whose status until then was indeterminate. All next-of-kin would receive the welcome news within days of the mail being examined. Indeed, the officer-in-charge reported, 'in several cases [the mail] has established the fact that personnel who were reported killed in action prior to the fall of Singapore are in fact alive and held as Prisoners of War'.[33]

Occasionally a prisoner would escape and make his way back to Allied forces and it was difficult for the government to suppress the story that he might tell. Thus the minister for the Army, Frank Forde, made a statement to Parliament in November 1943 that contained an account of the Japanese treatment of prisoners, based on a rescued Australian's information. Forde spared his hearers the details, but even so, the Labor member for Parkes, Leslie Haylen, said that while he listened to Forde's statement 'it struck me what bitter hearing this must make for the parents and friends of prisoners of war'. But Haylen was prepared to weigh their interests against the national interest, declaring that 'the story must be told sometime, and I think it is better that it should be told now'. While Haylen sympathised with the government's dilemma — 'the women of Australia are wracked and anguished over the fate of relatives' — nevertheless, he believed, 'the truth, no matter how stark, should be revealed at the earliest opportunity'. It was hard to know what was best to do. One woman remembers her aunt's agony waiting for news of her husband: 'When the newspapers began to print stories about the mistreatment of POWs the situation at home grew even worse. It was a time of great strain for the family.' In March 1945 John Curtin gave the House of Representatives a comprehensive picture of what the government then knew of the position in the prison camps. He pulled no punches. 'Conditions Appalling', the newspapers trumpeted. 'Brutal Discipline', 'Callous Disregard for Welfare'.[34]

Yet the government had never seemed certain about the correct approach throughout the entire period of captivity. Often taking a lead from London, where there had been considerable discussion about the appropriateness of another statement by Anthony Eden to

the House of Commons, senior ministers were concerned that
publicity about brutality and even atrocities would have a bad effect
on morale and would 'cause great distress to the relatives of those
concerned'. As the war progressed, tighter security over atrocity
stories was imposed, partly in recognition of the agony of waiting
that the relatives of prisoners endured, and partly, or perhaps substan-
tially, for military reasons. In a message to state-based censors, the
Australian Chief Publicity Censor in June 1944 reported that atrocity
stories were 'known to be having a bad effect on the morale of Allied
airmen. The fear of mistreatment by the enemy in case they are forced
to land in enemy territory cannot but have a bad effect upon the
morale of the air forces'. Therefore, as almost an inversion of previous
military thinking, censors should enforce rigid censorship of almost
any atrocity story emanating from the prison camps.[35]

One story to evade the tightening censorship was that which
detailed the fate of an Australian airman beheaded by the Japanese in
1943. Somehow this story was printed in the Australian newspapers
and it caused considerable anxiety among families of aircrew and
prisoners, and severe and apparently genuine grief to the government.
Sydney Smith immediately claimed that the report was worrying to
relatives and lowered rather than raised morale. He believed that
people were already suffering enough and called on the government
to prevent the repetition of such a censorship lapse. In the New South
Wales parliament a government member asked the premier, William
McKell, to find out from the federal authorities 'what public and
national value publication of such gruesome narratives possesses; also
whether the nerve-racking distress, pain and fear suffered by parents
and relatives of Servicemen, particularly mothers of men fighting in
New Guinea, were taken into consideration before publication ...
was authorised'.[36]

Prime Minister Curtin decided to minimise the damage that this
unfortunate incident had caused and stated that the government
would tell the beheaded airman's next-of-kin all that was known
about the death. While this would distress the grieving family, it would
remove the immediate doubt and anxiety from all other relatives of
captured or missing airmen, although the publicity given the incident
had alerted relatives to the certainty that atrocities were being

committed by the Japanese. At the urging of the RSL, Curtin stated that the government would not reveal the name of the Australian who had suffered this atrocity, for 'this was a private and intimate matter associated with the deep grief of the next-of-kin'. He felt, however, that the family could be assured 'that there would be no bounds to the sympathy felt [for the family] which would be nation wide'. In an off-the-record briefing for the press, Curtin explained that these stories must not be released to the public in time of war because of the widespread anxiety caused to relatives and because 'it may provoke or lead to demands for reprisals on our part. Should this lead to counter-proposals, we are incapable of competing with a barbarous foe'.[37]

We have few ways of knowing how the families of Australian prisoners coped with the years of waiting and anxiety, although we may reasonably assume that they suffered more grievously than almost any other class of Australians on the homefront. At great personal risk, some Australian prisoners did keep diaries during their captivity, but if family members also kept diaries they are unlikely to have been collected by the institutions that have pursued the prisoners' records so assiduously. Few of the prisoners' narratives that have been published in considerable numbers over the last twenty years or so make much mention of what was happening at home. It is the letters in the government files that gives us the best indication of the grief and anxiety on the homefront.

But occasionally a prisoner's memoir or personal recall will glimpse part of the story on the homefront. Ray Denney's book, *The Long Way Home*, published in 1993, draws on his then girlfriend's diaries and shows some of the suffering that one who was 'spoken for' could endure. Gwen, whom Ray Denney would marry in 1945 within a month of his return to his native Tasmania, lost contact with her boyfriend early in 1942, and did not hear from him at all during his years as a prisoner. Even so, she wrote to him every Sunday night throughout those years, perhaps 180–200 letters all told, and although she would not have known it, only three or four of these letters ever reached their destination. She was a bridesmaid three times and she watched her younger sister and brother start their families. 'She cared for their babies', he wrote, 'and wondered if she would ever have her own to cherish'. As she read the casualty lists in the newspapers and worried over the accounts of the brutality of the Japanese regarding their prisoners, at the same time she feared that life was passing her by. Several other men, Ray Denney reports, 'who were available, admired her, and showed considerable interest in her, to complicate matters'. Although Gwen threw herself into farm work and church and community activities to cover her anxiety and her isolation, 'she had the constant feeling of wasted years ... the fruitful years were passing in loneliness and dirty farm work'.[38]

It was a terrible business, this writing off into a void, not knowing if your man was still alive. And because there was rarely a response from the prisoners, few of the writers could imagine that their letters were being regularly received. So with little news flowing into Australia, and with great uncertainty about the news flowing out of Australia, the misery was simply compounded. There was another way of communicating, of course, and increasingly relatives and friends appealed to the government to organise radio broadcasts to the prisoners in the hope that they might pick something up. If Radio Batavia could broadcast messages into Australia, why wasn't Australia sending messages out, relatives increasingly asked.

Indeed Radio Batavia had stepped up its propaganda in its broadcasts and had even offered to broadcast messages to Australian prisoners if families would send them in. Still the Defence Committee rejected any cooperation with or official acknowledgement of Radio Batavia, but other views began to surface as a realisation of the sufferings of the relatives developed. Notes on a War Cabinet agendum discussing this issue in October 1943 acknowledged that 'this is a most difficult and delicate subject' and suggested that 'the opinion of the Services has not been found to be very sound on questions of this nature, as they tend to place too great emphasis on military considerations to the detriment of a sound judgement of what public opinion considers should be done'. In the opinion of this anonymous official, 'the earlier suggestion of the Defence Committee that the Australian people should be discouraged from listening in to broadcasts containing letters and messages from Australian prisoners was one which was quite divorced from any real comprehension of the feelings of the next-of-kin or any realisation of public opinion on such a matter'.[39]

The radio, of course, could be such a personal medium and could provide not only news of a prisoner, but on rare occasions his own words and voice, his personality, his reality. Arthur Calwell as Minister for Information was closely involved in these debates and a friend, Eleanor Glencross, provided, coincidentally, just the kind of information he needed to understand the importance of the broadcasts. In May 1945 she wrote:

> Nearly two years ago some broadcasts were given through Japan by Prisoners of War, and one of them was a beautiful message from my nephew ... we were all, naturally, in a rather emotional condition when we listened to this lad's broadcast [and wonder whether we might be able to hear it again] ... My sister is practically a physical wreck, as this is her only child, and I knew that if it could be done, your kindly spirit of which I have evidence would enable us to hear this record.[40]

The family had a card from the boy in December 1943, but had not heard from him since then.

Even though armed with the knowledge of the extraordinary importance placed on the exchange of news, War Cabinet had a great deal of difficulty in developing a policy on radio messages to prisoners of war. Two factors helped to change the government's thinking, both provoked by a service offered by All-India Radio. This government station had begun broadcasting messages to prisoners and civilian internees 'into the air' as one Australian official described it in a note for file. Until hearing of this unilateral broadcasting, the Australian government had been looking for a reciprocal agreement with the government of Japan as some guarantee that the messages meant for prisoners would actually be received by them. Now there was enough evidence that these All-India Radio broadcasts were being picked up by the men for whom they were intended, regardless of the fact that the Japanese were not cooperating in any way at all. The second factor shaping a change of government policy was simply the sheer popularity of the All-India service in Australia. As a courtesy the Indian officials had indicated that they would accept a few Australian messages, perhaps around 15, for broadcast each week. Within a short time the radio station was flooded with messages from Australia. In two days the station received 700 air letters from Australia, showing the intense desire of Australian families for this service. Later a steady pattern developed with All–India Radio receiving some 300 to 400 air letters each week and some 40 cables. Such a 'flood of messages', as the official described it, meant that All–India radio had to withdraw their generous offer to Australian prisoner of war families, but these family members were now asking, 'If India can do it, why cannot Australia?'[41]

The minister for External Affairs, H. V. Evatt, encouraged officials to come up with a scheme that would satisfy both the military insistence on security and the relatives' hunger for some sort of communication. The government was under some pressure on this issue. As John McEwen, Country Party member and a member of the Advisory War Council, wrote to John Curtin, 'it appears to me that the lack, for two and a half years, of any satisfactory plan to deal with this very urgent, human problem should be sufficient justification [for a solution]'. It was, in fact, becoming a scandal. Mrs Mary Bourke, writing from Petersham, Sydney, in September 1943 conservatively estimated that, if each Australian prisoner had six relatives and close friends 'worrying on his behalf', this 'would make a total of approximately 138 000 people interested on the home front'. They might all be voters, she seemed to be implying. But her appeal was to Curtin personally: 'You have done so much for the betterment of conditions for our fighting men, and in the improvement of their financial status, for which we are deeply grateful, but in the course of a life time, there are some things that count even more than financial security and well-being, and one of them is peace of mind.' Mrs Elsie Salter, of Epping, Sydney, wrote to Mrs Curtin, the prime minister's wife, noting that as she too had a son in the forces 'you will be able to help us through your husband'. Mrs Dawn Rickerby, of Bellingen, New South Wales, had a husband and a brother captives of the Japanese: 'I have a baby daughter who was born two months after the fall of Singapore. If I could only just mention her name in a message, it, I am sure, would be very comforting to my husband.'[42]

Mrs Anderson, of Melbourne, was one of the lucky ones to have her message broadcast on All–India Radio in December 1943 and her husband subsequently acknowledged that he had heard the broadcast. This was the first communication between this husband and wife since captivity. 'If all prisoners in Japanese hands are suffering from the same lack of news of dear ones, it seems to me a worse punishment than captivity and separation, and it also seems to me quite an unnecessary punishment.'[43]

Slowly the government appeared to agree. Evatt was advised, in May 1944, that technically a radio service was feasible from the Australian transmitters but that difficulties remained. Officials worried about the volume of messages that 'could be expected to reach alarming proportions' and calculated that 'if we spent twenty minutes daily on broadcasting individual messages it would take something like eight years to broadcast one message to every Australian prisoner in the East'. The solution, again, was to borrow from All-India Radio, where messages were bunched around units of men who might be expected to be in the same area. In this way, many more men could be covered in a shorter time, for no one by 1944 could envisage another eight years of war. The Australian service used the Prisoners of War Relatives Association to solicit the messages from families and to bundle them. Broadcasts, announced in August 1944, actually began in September. Within a couple of weeks of the announcement the Relatives Association had received 10 000 messages for broadcast and by the end of September the Association registered 14 414 messages. Relatives, Sydney Smith assured Curtin, 'are just aching for news of their men'.[44]

By March 1945, the radio message service was in full swing and apparently making some difference to the lives of the prisoners. By early March, 7260 messages had been despatched and 627 replies or acknowledgments had been received by letter, card or return broadcast. It was not a high ratio of success, but showed that the service was worthwhile, nevertheless. While the overwhelming majority of next-of-kin were only too keen to use the service, there were some problems, as Sydney Smith reported:

> We have several cases arising from time to time where wives are not further interested in their husbands, and are not sending any messages, and where we have reliable evidence to this effect, we are sending on

messages from the mothers or near relatives … so that these men will not suffer through not receiving messages.[45]

From a variety of sources and by the most patient work the government had been compiling and cross-referencing news of prisoners since the early months of 1942. It was this work that enabled the Department of the Air to send a further telegram to the family of Donald Bruce, in late August 1943, nearly a year since the last communication: 'Desire to inform you that your son Aircraftman Donald Wilfred Bruce previously classified as missing believed prisoner of war is now reported to be a prisoner of war in Japanese hands stop any further information received will be conveyed to you immediately.' In this case, as the file shows, Donald Bruce's name was to be found in a list of 41 names sent to Australia from the Australian Legation, Washington. In December the family was informed that Donald Bruce was in an unknown camp in Thailand. The file of this one airman shows how hard the government was trying to follow up leads and to compile the fullest information on its prisoners. By September 1944 the government released some statistics which showed that there were 20 045 prisoners in Japanese hands who had been accounted for but that there were still 2877 personnel of whom no news had been received and who were, therefore, still posted as missing. The painstaking work would simply have to go on.[46]

CHAPTER 3

'That's the Eighth Division colour patch, isn't it?'

Some mail was coming through from the prisoners, and a voice, well remembered from the past, would occasionally penetrate the silence, to the intense joy of the family involved. But contact was so terribly random and limited; the prisoners were so remote. Furthermore, families knew that anything the prisoners did send had passed through the hands of their captors and must be studied cautiously for that reason. If only someone could come from that other world to tell the government and the people what it was really like. It seemed a fantasy, this homecoming, a wistful dream, until late in 1944 when a handful of prisoners did mysteriously appear in the Australian community, at first almost as an apparition.

With the completion of the Burma–Thailand railway, groups of the fittest prisoners were being moved to Japan for work in the mines and on the wharves there. Ever vigilant relatives, hearing of these transfers, had fresh reason for anxiety. For example, Mrs J. L. Thompson, of Gunnedah, New South Wales, wrote to John Curtin to ensure that 'the necessary precautions are being taken by the Allies to see that the ships conveying prisoners will not be sunk'. Although the reply from the prime minister's department assured Mrs Thompson that 'your letter has been brought urgently to the notice of the appropriate authorities', there was, in reality, little that the government could do to ensure the safety of the transported prisoners. The Japanese were not marking prisoner transport in any way that would warn off the Allied warships that were increasingly applying a stranglehold to the supply of goods to Japan.[1]

A force of 2300 prisoners was shipped from Singapore on 6

September 1944 on two transports, which were part of a larger convoy, eventually comprising seven transports, two oil tankers and six escorting vessels. The *Rokyu Maru*, one of the prisoner ships, normally held 187 steerage passengers; for this trip it contained 599 British and 649 Australian prisoners. Les Bolger, of Concord, Sydney, was one of those Australian prisoners. Born in October 1920 into a devout Catholic family, Les had never known his father who had died in 1921 from the effects of gas, a legacy of the First World War. This man, who had fought in the Boer war and then had enlisted again, in the 7th Light Horse, to serve in Gallipoli and in Palestine, had five sons and a daughter. Four of the boys enlisted in the Second World War, perhaps spurred on by their father's example. One served in the Middle East, one in the Air Force in New Guinea, and another never got further than Western Australia. Only one son was not in the forces during the war; Ted, a professional golfer, was knocked back for flat feet when he tried to enlist.

Les was the baby of the family and enlisted in 1941. His mother had died in 1939, before the war had started, sparing her the worry of four sons at war. Les was posted to the 2/15th Field Regiment, an artillery unit, reaching Malaya in January 1942. Churchill was advising evacuation, and Curtin was arguing for reinforcements to bolster morale at home. But Les Bolger could not have known that; he was simply a soldier. Les saw some fighting in Malaya and then his regiment had their guns at the ready at the Causeway to batter the Japanese invaders as they made their way to Singapore. Before opening up with a last-ditch battle they were given the word to hold their fire as General Percival had caved in. Les was very downhearted at becoming a prisoner of war; he worried for his future and he wondered what his father, an Anzac, would have thought. It was odd for Australians, he thought, to capitulate meekly.

Les Bolger was one of the first to go from Changi to Burma. He was drafted into 'A' Force, as one of the fittest Australian prisoners and in the younger group. He worked first on airfields at Victoria Point and Tavoy, but inevitably he was assigned to the Railway. All up, he spent eighteen months as a labourer in Burma. The toughest time, he recalls, with a gentle enthusiasm and a joy in telling his story, was during the wet season. Food then was almost non-existent. A mug of rice a couple of times a day; nothing else. The work was onerous, digging, moving earth, breaking up rocks at the 4 Kilo camp, then the 55 Kilo camp and then the 75 Kilo camp. His mate, Bill Scarpello, was a mountain of a man and very strong; he could do the work of two men and they all pleaded with him to slow down in case the Japanese imposed his standard on all of them. Bill was from Melbourne, with Italian parents, and was such a gentle, good man.

How does Les Bolger explain his survival? Youth, he said, and his faith. He served Mass every Sunday night with a chaplain of the Railway, Father Correy, a Dominican priest from South Australia. Didn't the evil he witnessed daily shake his faith in a loving God? No, he replies, it was the way I was brought up. Taken ill with malaria 25 times, with an ugly and painful tropical ulcer on the side of his foot, and on the receiving end of frequent bashings, Les learnt to love the ministrations of his doctor, Dr Bruce Hunt from Western Australia, a big man. On one occasion Les thought his end had come. He was given an order by one of the guards but could not understand it and the guard picked up a monkey wrench to bash him. In the instant before the monkey wrench crashed into his skull an Australian officer intervened, saving Les's life.

The railway finished, Les went to Saigon to work on the docks and things were much better there. A Frenchman, an electrician inevitably called 'Sparks' by the Australians, collected money and hid it around the wharves for the prisoners so that they could buy eggs and bread. Then it was back to Singapore in late 1943, travelling along the railway he had helped to build, in terror for his safety as he knew all the things they had done to sabotage the railway and its many bridges.

Les Bolger went aboard the *Rokyu Maru*, bound for Japan, on 4 September 1944. It was terrible on the ship, he remembered, packed into the hold so tightly that men could hardly move. Only the 'sick blokes' were allowed up on deck and it was they who yelled down, on 12 September, as the convoy was off Hainan, that they were being attacked by American submarines. The attack started at about 2 o'clock in the morning, he recalls, and once the ship was hit, an officer, Captain Sumner, told them to get off the ship as quickly as they could because as it started to sink it would suck them all down with it. The evacuation was orderly, and once in the water the men had to try to find something to hang on to. Les was not a good swimmer, but with luck he found a raft designed for four or five people. There were fifteen men depending on the raft, treading water nearby, hanging on to ropes when they could and occasionally taking a breather on the raft itself. Les had got off the ship with his shorts, a jacket, and his slouch hat that he had kept throughout all the years as a prisoner. He also had his water bottle, but that leaked and was soon full of sea water. The slouch hat drifted off but he would never get rid of his jacket as it contained four holy medals that had been with him since he became a soldier. One was a medal of St Joseph, given to him by a nun in Sydney who had said, 'This medal will bring you back home safely'. It was her own medal, given to her by her mother when she was professed as a nun and it had helped her in low times in the convent, she had told him. But she wanted Les to have it.

The *Rokyu Maru* did not instantly sink as they had all expected and after a couple of hours in the water Bill Scarpello said that he was going to swim back to the ship to see if he could find something to eat. However, he could find nothing left on board. Major Chalmers, a doctor, died of malaria, so 'we just pushed his body off the raft'. Many of the men around the raft were exhausted or sick. One of the Japanese destroyers in the convoy returned to the scene and started dropping depth charges in the hope of despatching the marauding American submarines. The impact of those charges on the men in the water was dreadful, recalls Les: 'It was like as if someone had got a sledge-hammer and had hit you right in the guts … I was violently ill in the water from these depth charges.' The crew on the destroyer started to pick up the Japanese survivors and 'we asked them if they they were going to pick us up. No, they said, you can stay there and die'. And with that, 'I'll never forget it … you could hear it all over. All the boys started to sing "Rule Britannia".'

On the second day Bill Scarpello swam away again — 'I don't know where he went'. On the third day he came back to the raft and he said to Les, 'I've just had a lovely cup of coffee.' He'd been drinking the sea water and that was the last they saw of him. 'If anyone should have come through it, he should have … just bad luck,' says Les. On the fourth day in the water, Les started to hallucinate, imagining that there was a beautiful green island with some native women on it 'and I asked them for a drink and they wouldn't give me any water'. He was screaming abuse at them. So he knew on the fourth day that he would not be there much longer. 'I made my peace with God, I asked Him to forgive me.' For what?

On the fourth day two of the American submarines returned to the scene to survey the damage they had caused. The Americans saw survivors in the water but they were covered in oil from the tankers and were assumed to be Japanese. There was no reason to expect that prisoners of war had been present. One of the men, 'Curly' Martin, was on a raft with his mate Frank Farmer. The Americans circled them and the captain of the *Sealion* said to a sailor, 'That's funny, the Japanese don't have fair, curly hair'. They hauled Curly in and the captain looked at him in astonishment. 'Who are you?' he asked. 'We are prisoners of war, English and Australian, who were torpedoed four days ago. There were 2300 of us,' he stated. 'You could see the blood drain from his face', Martin later told the others. The Americans immediately leapt into action, radioing for assistance and picking up as many of the men as they could find. Hearing the sub coming, but nearly blind from the oil and the dehydration, Les Bolger at first thought it was a plane and started looking to the sky. The *Sealion* just glided to his raft, now holding only four of the original fifteen. The sailors threw a rope to these survivors but they were too weak even to lift it over their heads to tie it on and so a sailor swam out to help them. They would be taken to Saipan, they were told, to an American hospital there. On the way they crossed the path of another Japanese convoy and to avoid detection the *Sealion* sat for a while on the bottom of the ocean. 'Have you ever heard of Frank Sinatra?' the Americans asked, trying to calm and encourage these men whose mates they had killed. Les knew nothing of Sinatra, but there he was, Les Bolger of Concord, sitting at the bottom of the sea listening to an American crooner. How profoundly had his world already changed.

The survivors from the *Rokyu Maru* were able to provide the government and the people with the first authentic news of conditions in Burma, Thailand and Singapore. News of the rescued prisoners' existence was flashed to Canberra and other national

capitals, but it was kept from the people at this stage as the governments considered how to deal with the news of the tragedy that was
the story of the *Rokyu Maru*. Given the hunger of Australians for news
of the prisoners, it is hardly surprising that the release of news of these
survivors needed to be handled with the greatest care by the government. The return of these men to Australia would also provide a small
rehearsal for the return of the main body of prisoners, whenever this
might occur.[2]

The survivors soon discovered that the Americans wanted to do
everything possible for them. Even as they were returning to Saipan
a destroyer was despatched with four doctors, to begin the work of
healing even before the men reached hospital. Les Bolger was
overwhelmed by the kindness and the gentleness of the Americans.
They took his clothes from him but he explained about the medals
and they were carefully returned, cleaned and well wrapped. Every
time he left his bunk he would find on his return a little present,
something from the sailors' own possessions. Les has never smoked,
but he keeps on his mantlepiece still the small corn-cob pipe that was
an anonymous gift from a sailor who wanted to make him feel better.

On Saipan for about three weeks and hospitalised for all that time,
Les and his mates could hear the sounds of fighting as pockets of
Japanese soldiers resisted the Americans even after the main body had
surrendered. It was a grim foretaste of what might be expected as the
the Allies moved closer to Japan. Visitors poured into the wards to talk
to these first few returned prisoners of war. One of them, Admiral
Chester Nimitz, the architect of the victory in the Pacific war, told
the men that he would like them to return to their homes via the
United States, so that people there could show them due honour.
That was vetoed in Canberra by the Army minister, Frank Forde, who
wanted the Australians home as quickly as possible. But he also vetoed
the offer of planes to take the men to Australia, believing that a slow
sea voyage would be better for them.

The 84 rescued Australian prisoners made landfall at Brisbane in
late October 1944 after intensive recuperation with the Americans.
They were met by General Blamey at Hamilton wharf and there was
a military band too to make them feel welcome. But it was wartime
and even this prominent event could be censored out of existence.

No one outside the inner circle, not even next-of-kin, had any idea that they were home. The Americans had recently evacuated a substantial Catholic convent school at One Tree Hill, Toowong, a suburb of Brisbane, and this became the rescued prisoners first convalescent home. They were there for about three weeks. General Blamey visited them again, stressing that they must not talk to anyone. They were not allowed out of the convent grounds and no one was allowed to see them. They were effectively in strict quarantine, but there was a war on, and perhaps no one regarded this segregation as unusual. Les Bolger remembers that General Stantke, commanding the Queensland region, sent in a four-gallon keg of beer every day to make life in the convent more bearable. The Queensland Supreme Court and later High Court judge Sir William Webb, now investigating allegations of atrocities against Australian prisoners, took a statement from each of the men. Les Bolger gave him seventeen pages.

The public was informed of the survivors' rescue and their return, in the most general terms, towards the end of October. The question that exercised officials and ministers was what facts might be released. Clear cases of atrocities against Australian prisoners had already come to the attention of the authorities in early 1944 and there was a strong belief that this news had to be kept from the Australian people: 'It is imperative', wrote one official, 'that [news of] calculated extermination should be prevented by whatever means possible, even if it means distressing several thousands of female relatives.' When a story of cannibalism reached the censors it was decided that publication would 'only arouse morbid interest and create distress … [and] it might lead a lot of anxious relatives to imagine that their husbands, brothers etc had been cooked and eaten'. Although the government had appointed Webb to examine the atrocities thoroughly and judicially, ministers decided that they could not possibly allow his investigations to come to public notice. There would need to be management, too, of the news regarding the returning survivors. They would be the first real links with the story of the Australian prisoners since February 1942.[3]

The Navy, for example, on instructions from the Naval Board, was arranging for 'controlled press interviews' of its members returning to Australia, but no reference was to be made to four topics: how the men were rescued; details of the tragic loss of HMAS *Perth*, from which these survivors came; casualties on *Perth*; and 'internment conditions, atrocities, and experiences at the hands of the Japanese'. It might be wondered what these sailors could possibly find to talk about at their press interview, except, perhaps, their pleasure at returning to Australia.[4]

As might have been expected, the Australian Prisoners of War Relatives Association, was eager for news as soon as the existence of the survivors was made public, especially as it could not be concealed that many lives had been lost in the sinking of the Japanese transport. Relatives would want to be assured immediately that their son or husband had not perished in the South China Sea. Sydney Smith telegramed the prime minister on 26 October 1944 to say that he was 'greatly concerned' that no statement had yet been made about the rescue, as 'thousands of relatives of prisoners of war in Japanese hands are extremely worried as to whether their men were on the torpedoed vessel and we are inundated with inquiries from all over Australia'. It was eight days, he explained, since the most general news had broken in Australia and it was not hard to understand the desperation of relatives for news.[5]

Sydney Smith could not know that the government was under some pressure from the Americans not to release the men's stories as it was feared disclosure of atrocities, brutality and deprivations in the camps would jeopardise an exchange of prisoners between the Americans and the Japanese that had been in prospect for some months. While governments in Canberra and London did not ultimately accede to the American demands, the issues to be worked through did delay matters somewhat.[6]

As late as the end of October the department of the Army was counselling against 'any immediate announcement' which would 'merely arouse the anxiety of all next-of-kin, whereas a later announcement that can include advice that next-of-kin concerned have been notified will allay anxiety in the minds of all other next-of-kin'. It was a fair point. The highly influential secretary of the Department of Defence, Frederick Shedden, also counselled against the early release of news: 'the paramount consideration should be the effect on the relatives of those who did not survive and of those who are still in Japanese hands'. Curtin agreed and the statement was finally released on 19 November 1944 when it could include the crucial disclosure that 'the number of Australian prisoners lost is … 184 … next-of-kin of all personnel identified on the Japanese lists have been appropriately informed'. This meant, of course, that unless next-of-kin had received a casualty telegram, they could continue to believe, with some confidence, that their son was still alive; at least they could have confidence that he had not perished on the *Rokyu Maru*.[7]

That, of course, was not the only issue that the arrival of these men provoked. Once their existence was publicised in Australia they would become the focus of intense interest as the possible bearers of personal news and information about a husband or brother. A survivor might have been in camp with my son; or he might at least know that my husband is alive and fit; he might be able to tell me something of the conditions and work that my brother is enduring; I might be able to learn how my best mate is coping. All the pent-up frustration of the lack of news, of the wall of silence that had existed between Australia and the prisoners since February 1942 would suddenly be thrust on these hapless 84 men. For this reason War Cabinet decided, on 15 November, that a list of the names of the Australian survivors would not be published, 'as to do so would expose the men to unlimited enquiries from next-of-kin of other prisoners of war'. Instead the government decided, in view of the sufferings and privations of the returning prisoners, to grant them 90 days leave immediately, a kindness, it seemed, and generous too. The War Cabinet also decided that 'interrogation of recovered prisoners of war by newspaper representatives is not to be permitted'. Again, it is easy to understand the thinking behind this prohibition, but it was hard on those with a frustrated expectation for news.[8]

Sydney Smith bombarded John Curtin with demands that the recovered prisoners speak openly about their experiences, expecting to calm relatives' concerns and anxieties, but the government well understood the dangers of allowing the survivors to speak freely, even if they had wanted to. And indeed their wishes for peace and privacy must have carried at least equal weight with the hopes of the relatives for news. When news was released from the survivors, it was in line with government instructions. All that would be upsetting and demoralising to those at home was avoided and a bland account emerged. In Parliament, however, the minister for the Army, Frank Forde, was more forthright, sharing with members in some small way some of the information that he had of Japanese brutality and some of his fears for the fate of the Australians. A correspondent, Mr Lindsay Pegler of Quilpie, Queensland, was quick to pick up the discrepancy and naturally he believed the survivors and sided with their version of good news. They explained, he wrote, that 'they were well treated, were paid a small sum of money which they could spend at a canteen, that they did not know of any atrocities, and that some even had wireless sets with which they could hear the outside news'.[9] He continued:

> Imagine the amazement of those concerned when the Minister for the Army gave out the public statement that the Japanese were ill-treating Australian prisoners of war … This statement caused those with sons, husbands, etc extreme distress, but in two cases to my knowledge this distress was overcome by the reports given by the returned men … Obviously someone is not speaking the truth and it is not thought that returned prisoners of war would put out false statements … If the statement made by the Minister was for propaganda purposes, then it is a cruel and disgraceful thing.

How is it, Mr Pegler finally asked, rehearsing a question that would emerge again with much force later, 'that if the men were ill treated and ill fed, that those who have returned look extremely well and show no signs of the supposed ordeal … What is the answer?'

In effect, the answer was a suggestion that Mr Pegler might look at the situation with a little more clarity and human understanding, although, of course, cautious government officials could not write so directly. But the bureaucrats did invite him to reflect on the problem survivors and government faced: 'a point which should not be overlooked is the probable, and natural, desire of the men concerned to alleviate the sufferings of the relatives of their comrades still in enemy hands, as a result of which they would be likely to make light of their harrowing experiences'. There were matters here beyond political point-scoring; there were matters here as profound as any Australian community had ever been called upon to confront. The return of the survivors to Australia from the *Rokyu Maru* opened up questions that would become the major issues in the return of the great body of recovered Australian prisoners of war.

Frank Forde had asked that the relatives of prisoners not seek to contact the recovered survivors of the *Rokyu Maru* because these men simply could not provide the answers that so many relatives were, understandably, seeking. The burden the men would confront would be too great for them to bear, and relatives, the Minister was saying, should continue to try to exercise patience. But his was a counsel of perfection. 'One rescued man', Forde wrote to Sydney Smith, 'has reported that he has received over 500 letters of enquiry for information. This is regarded as probably typical of most cases'. Forde asked for the Association's help in trying to stop this embarrassing harassment of the survivors. In preparing his reply, Forde was relying on a briefing paper from the Army which included the story of Private E. A. Pearson who had reported receiving approximately 500 letters. He had approached his superiors 'for guidance, owing to persistent requests from relatives for information of personnel whom Pte Pearson believes to be dead. This is believed to be typical of what is happening to every other recovered member', the Army reported.[10]

After about three weeks at the convent at One Tree Hill, unaware of the paper war the government was fighting on their behalf, the rescued prisoners were to be allowed to return to their homes to begin their leave. Les Bolger had nominated an unmarried aunt as his next of kin; she lived with his grandmother. It was to her that the news of Les's return first came, and then she was told that he was coming home. Kitted out with new uniforms, and with more than two months of restful living, and the memories of Japanese captivity receding, if only slightly, Les Bolger stepped off the Brisbane express at Strathfield railway station, in suburban Sydney, on his way home. Expecting his aunt, instead he was embraced by his sister and a brother. 'I couldn't look at eggs and bacon, or a baked dinner', Les now admits. 'It used to make me violently ill.' And that persisted for six months. He stomach had shrunk, he believed, 'to the size of a small baby' and he subsisted on jellies and custards. Warm welcomes, yet the homecoming was clouded.

There was more than 1000 pounds in Les Bolger's pay book when he was released from captivity, a small fortune in those days, and with 90 days paid leave the world looked pretty good. Officials preparing for the return of all the former prisoners would later suggest that the leave granted to these few men was excessive and that the men were left with time on their hands, time to think of the recent past. Les will have none of that. He took a month's holiday in Manly, where a cousin lived, but the trip across from Sydney on the ferry 'brought it all back'. Les became ill: 'I couldn't stay up [on the deck] looking at the water.' But the holiday itself was just what he wanted.

Les Bolger received more than 400 letters from people asking for information about a relative and people came to see him as soon as they heard that he might have some news about a loved one. 'It was very distressing to have to tell them, the ones that had died … It was distressing to have to tell them that they wouldn't be coming back.' Another recovered prisoner described the job of telling families what had happened as 'one of the greatest difficulties of my life'. How did people handle whatever these returning men had to tell them? 'Well, some of them broke down', but these were people whom Les had never met before. It was all so random but their pain was real. Some of them came in person to his grandmother's house. A father, mother, brothers and sisters of one prisoner stand out. They were in bad shape and just hoped that Les might know something. The provincial superior of the Dominicans in Australia, Father Crofts, took Les to lunch at Tattersall's Club in Sydney to hear how his prisoner-priest, Father Correy, was surviving, and Les undertook to visit the priest's two sisters in Melbourne. Archbishop Gilroy (later Cardinal) invited Les to afternoon tea 'and of course he was asking me about the priests, did they have to work, how they were treated'. Everyone wanted to know.

The sister of Private Eddie Anderson, a Queenslander, was desperate to hear news of her brother and wrote to one of the recovered prisoners, a Mr Hutchinson. She had got his name, she told him, from the Red Cross. All that she wanted was for him to 'spare a few minutes to drop me a line and tell me if you can help'. Would that it were that simple: 'I am hoping that perhaps you being a Queenslander knew him and that perhaps you may have been the one that gave his name. Did you know him or did you know the soldier that knew him? Am so glad you were lucky and it must be wonderful for you to be back home.' The file does not disclose what answer, if any, the soldier sent back, but the cumulative effect of hundreds of these letters must have been daunting to those who were, indeed, lucky to survive.[11]

The Bruce family had last heard from the Air Force in December 1943, a simple statement that their boy was in an unknown camp in Thailand. In November 1944 there was a further letter to say that 'information has come to hand from a member of the Royal Australian Air Force recovered from the Japanese ... that your son was last seen by him at Tamarkand in Thailand ... in April 1944'. 'Any news, however scanty ... is appreciated beyond words', Don's father wrote back immediately, asking for the home address of the recovered airman 'so that it may be possible to find out any further news of my son'. But the Department would not help. This recovered airman was the 'sole survivor' from among airmen on the *Rokyu Maru* and would be inundated with enquiries if his name was given out, the Secretary explained. The Bruce family would just have to continue to wait. They were not told that the survivor had reported that Donald Bruce's health was 'indifferent'. That would have caused too much anguish.[12]

In Melbourne there was a public welcome at the Town Hall in early December to 22 of the men who had been rescued and 'there were several deeply moving incidents'. As the survivors 'modestly' mounted the steps of the platform and took their seats there was loud applause and the full house sang 'Land of Hope and Glory'. Only two of the survivors, both of them sergeants, spoke, and 'with difficulty'. When one of them touched on the sufferings in Burma 'he broke off abruptly'. The other made a simple appeal: 'Over there we had no doubt that our womenfolk were carrying on bravely. We ask them to keep doing this for the sake of the boys still there.' A former leading general, who had served in the Desert and in New Guinea and was now Chief Justice of Victoria, Sir Edmund Herring, then took over proceedings with a long speech intended to allay relatives' concerns. It was as if Herring had been briefed by the Army or the minister. All the prisoners, he reported, said that they had been better treated this year than in the past, as the approaching victory was knocking much of the cockiness out of the Japanese 'who were extraordinarily anxious that the world should regard them as a highly civilised people'. Relatives, discomfited by the recent revelations of barbarity and brutality, 'could take comfort from the fact that the world-wide publicity would act as a definite deterrent to the enemy'. How people felt as they filed out of the Town Hall into an early summer's night can never be known. For these men who had spoken so bravely at the Town Hall, the process of rehabilitation still had a long way to go.[13]

In Sydney the mood was less imperial and the behaviour certainly less restrained. There were 17 recovered prisoners in attendance at a packed Town Hall, seven of them from the *Rokyu Maru*, the remainder from camps in Europe. So large was the crowd, around 3000, that people blocked aisles and even sat in the organ loft. The audience stood and sang 'For They Are Jolly Good Fellows' as the servicemen walked onto the stage and the men answered about 100 questions from the 400 or so that had been submitted in writing before proceedings began. When it became clear that the men would not answer the majority of the questions, describing them as 'too personal to answer', about 100 women rushed the stage. They climbed over press tables and chairs and were waving letters, photographs and names written on scraps of paper. Several women who asked for information left in tears when they were unable to obtain news, and other women surrounded the repatriated prisoners, asking questions and refusing to leave. One soldier collapsed and was unable to answer questions for several minutes. The servicemen were escorted to a back room but were mobbed again when they tried to leave the Town Hall. The pressure on them, and on the families seeking answers, was intense.[14]

After his leave expired, in February 1945, Les and his mates were back in the Army and off to Melbourne. Housed in officer's quarters at Royal Park and 'fed as officers', the soldiers were taken to Prahran every day to go slowly through the unit books in Army Records and to comment, where they could, on each man listed. Was he dead, was he a prisoner, when had he last been seen? This work was building on the painstakingly slow work of pulling together information from letters, broadcasts, the Red Cross and other sources, and was confirming how little information the government had about the fate of the prisoners. The rescued prisoners worked slowly through this debriefing for a couple of months. On their days off the Red Cross would take them out, to the Dandenongs or elsewhere. 'There was never a dull moment.'

Even so, at a bit of a loose end one day Les and a mate went into the city and found themselves at a soldiers' club run by St Francis church in Lonsdale street. Serving that night were Catholic women, officeworkers, who were giving some of their time to entertain the troops. They were in their uniforms and a girl said to Les, 'That's an Eighth Division colour patch, isn't it?' She then asked Les if he knew her brother who was a prisoner of war. 'Yes I do', he replied. 'Is my brother still alive?' she nervously continued, and when told that he was, and what camp he was in, 'she flew to the phone to ring her mother'. And her mother said, 'Bring them out now'. They had dinner 'at a beautiful home in South Yarra and we were able to tell her that it was OK'.

To the family of Bill Scarpello, Les also believed that he had to tell the truth even though it was much less palatable. He told of how strong Bill had been on the railway, of his hard work, his friendship and his care for others. Of how he had tried to be helpful while they were all struggling for days in the water, covered in oil, and of how he had lost his mind and had died. 'Oh, that was hard, his poor old mother breaking down.' There was a pause as Les remembered things about the past he preferred to forget. Then he broke off the interview. 'I'm getting dry', he said. 'Would you like a cup of tea?' The moment was gone.

After two months in Melbourne all the rescued prisoners were given the option of a convalescent camp in Ballarat or going back to their own states. The New South Wales soldiers all decided to go back home and they were sent to Ingleburn on light duties: 'We could do what we liked.' Les wandered around with a spray on his back, to the water holes, spraying to cut down the mosquitoes. In early May 1945, though, the former prisoners were taken to the Showgrounds in Sydney and discharged. In total their convalescence and recuperation had taken nearly eight months. The pace had been slow, the men had been kept together, and the facilities had been generous and the care thoughtful. By way of contrast, many of the prisoners recovered at the end of the war would be in their homes immediately they returned to Australia and back at work very quickly too.

Counselled that clerical work would suit him, Les Bolger joined the Public Service on discharge, working first for the Repatriation Department. He found it hard to adjust to work and the days were very long. He suffered from nightmares for the first year or so, jumping clear out of his bed and screaming, and was cared for and nursed by his two unmarried aunts. He moved out of his grandmother's home in 1947 — he 'had to get on with his life' — became engaged in 1948 and married in 1949. But there were no children, although he and his wife would dearly have loved a family. They both did tests but there was nothing wrong. Les, like many other former prisoners, puts it down to the malnutrition that he suffered in the camps.

CHAPTER 4

'Twilight liberation'

Rarely in history do we find complete agreement in the records relating to any particular event. Different viewpoints and different perspectives are almost always present, even in records from a single source such as a government department. But there is a striking similarity, almost unanimity, in the various accounts from former prisoners on the first days of their liberation. Whether in camps in Japan, on Singapore, in Thailand or the islands, Australian prisoners seem to have responded to the news that the war was over in near identical fashion. The uniformity of response is not just unusual, it is uncanny.

The Australian government had no real idea of the number of prisoners in the Japanese camps, but ministers did expect to find some 8000 Australian prisoners in Japan, 5000 in South East Asia, 500 in Java, 2000 in Borneo, 2000 in other locations, with 3500 unaccounted for. The government was hoping that some 21 000 prisoners would be liberated. This figure proved to be sadly optimistic and it is a reminder of the almost total ignorance of the government to the true situation that the depressing facts were such a long way off this assessment. In reality there were only some 2700 Australians in Japan, Korea and Manchuria, 150 at Kuching in Borneo, 750 in the islands of what is now Indonesia, 265 in Indo-China, 4830 in Thailand and 5549 on Singapore island. Just over 14 200 prisoners in all. Yet wherever these prisoners were located, they responded to the news of peace with restraint towards their captors and happiness at the thought of going home, but with a real sense of apprehension and impatience. It was an ambiguous response, difficult to classify accurately.[1]

From early 1945 prisoners in Japan understood more clearly than those elsewhere that the war was going well for the Allies, but knowing this, they feared that their own situation was becoming dangerously worrying. So although some of them heard good news on the clandestine radios and every day saw evidence of the Allies' domination of the air, they did not attempt to look too far into the future. Most of them feared that the Japanese would kill them all before surrendering to the Allies, and none of them, increasingly weakened, wanted to think about liberation for fear of yet another false dawn. They doubted that they could go on much longer anyway and stuck fast to the prisoners' method for survival: take one day at a time.

There were some 63 000 Allied prisoners of war in Japan, scattered around individual prison camps. Many of these camps were no longer the large-scale affairs of earlier years with many hundreds, possibly thousands, of men giving mutual support to each other by their sheer weight of numbers. So devastating had been the destruction of the Japanese economy from the loss of workers and the Allied bombing of factories that prisoners had been brought into work-places all around Japan to keep the engines of war going. In various factories, in manufacturing plants, on the wharves, in lumber yards and in stores prisoners now comprised a significant part of the labour force. And they camped close to wherever the factories were found, even if this meant, in some cases, quite small and isolated locations. This dispersal meant that there were more than a hundred prisoner of war camps throughout Japan, largely unregulated, unvisited by the Red Cross, and supplied most haphazardly. Many of the prisoners in these camps were now literally starving to death, and it was becoming increasingly difficult for the Japanese to feed them, even if they had wanted to. Other prisoners in Japan worked in the mines, desperately extracting coal even in disused and abandoned mines, fearing that if the Allied forces came too close to the home islands the prisoners would be herded into the mines to be entombed there.[2]

The Allied mastery of the skies was obvious to the prisoners in Japan, who silently cheered on the huge waves of bombers, while prevented, under pain of severe beatings, from even looking up at them. The prisoners pondered the extraordinary devastation that the bombing was causing and wondered for how long the Japanese could fight on. Yet the fanaticism of which they had been the victims in the long years of captivity convinced them that the Japanese would never surrender without a massive struggle. They had heard rumours of, perhaps even seen preparations for, the intended extermination of all the prisoners. This would be followed, they believed, by the mass suicide of women and children, and finally a fanatical fight to the finish from the men who were left.

In Singapore and Thailand the knowledge the prisoners had of the progress of the war was not quite so well developed. The well-hidden camp radios told of sensational Allied successes throughout 1945, but no one dared to suggest a timetable for the eventual invasion of these Japanese strongholds. Each day the prisoners went out to work, as they had done for so long now, and while they may have prayed privately or shared a shy hope with a close mate that soon it might all be over, they dared not speak freely of that great day for fear of further, devastating disappointment. Terribly weakened by the years of neglect, the brutality, and the demanding physical work to which they had all been subjected, and with even the meagre supplies now dramatically contracting because of the tightening of the Allied stranglehold, some prisoners now began to lose hope, even as victory seemed closer. They asked whether it could come quickly enough to save them, and they watched in terrible sorrow the increasing number of deaths of mates who could hold on no longer.

At Sandakan, in Borneo, the Japanese exterminated an entire prisoner of war camp, an appalling tragedy in itself, but a reminder, too, of what might have been the fate of many thousands more of the prisoners if the war had not ended so abruptly. The rice ration at Sandakan, pitifully little enough, was reduced in the second half of 1944, before being cut out altogether in early 1945. Terribly weakened men then faced relocation by walking to Ranau, some 300 kilometres away, as the Japanese commander at Sandakan feared an Allied invasion. He wanted to keep his prisoners as far away as possible from the prospect of liberation.

The country over which these death marches, as they came to be called, were conducted would have been forbidding to trained and fit young men; to prisoners in the last stages of starvation the terrain must have seemed, quite simply, impossible. And yet such was their spirit, and their determination to hang on and so defy this bestial foe, that large numbers of them made it into Ranau. Those who fell out on the march were shot, yet remarkably only 20 of the 470 prisoners in the first death march died on the track. Those on the first march were the fitter men of those who had suffered so much at Sandakan. The second march lasted four weeks in all; of the 560 men who set off, 142 Australians and 61 British mustered at Ranau.

This attractive hill station then became their killing ground. By 18 July 1945 only 72 of perhaps 650 men were still alive. Ten days later this number had dwindled to 30, the others starved and brutalised to death. These remaining prisoners were executed, most probably on 1 August 1945, cruelly so close to the victory, their deaths ordered for fear that they would reveal the shocking truth of their mates' slaughter. Only six Australians of the 2500 Australian and British prisoners who had been located at Sandakan would survive to tell this tale of horror. Those who had been too sick to begin the march to Ranau at all were either shot or left to starve to death at Sandakan. Then all traces of the camp were destroyed to hide the evidence.[3]

The awesome point of this tragic story is that the fate of the Sandakan victims might also have been the fate of thousands of other Allied prisoners. Certainly Australians in Japan particularly, but elsewhere too, feared that this was the plan the captors had drawn up. Victory to the Allies, or even the likelihood of victory, they feared, might not bring liberation; it might bring, instead, summary execution.

In some of the camps in Japan work began to be scaled back from about 10 August onwards, but none of the prisoners could really know why and certainly their guards would not tell them. Elsewhere in the Asian camps life ground on, despite the encouraging if clandestine war news. Prisoners with access to radios might have heard of the Potsdam declaration, issued by the Grand Alliance on 26 July 1945, which called on the Japanese government to proclaim 'the unconditional surrender of its armed forces' and looked to the elimination of 'the authority and influence of those who have deceived and misled the people of Japan into embarking on world conquest'. The declaration brought about a complete split within the

Japanese government, with the 'no surrender' party at this stage in the ascendancy. Of course there had been appalling destruction and loss of life from the Allied bombing campaign, but when the first atomic bomb was dropped on Hiroshima on 6 August and the second on Nagasaki on 9 August, the balance within the Japanese cabinet altered. The Russian declaration of war and the invasion of Manchuria also intensified pressure on the war party. Although the army bitterly held out against surrender, the majority agreed to refer the matter to the emperor for decision. Emperor Hirohito, on receiving undertakings that the Allies would permit his continuance on the throne, and the maintenance of imperial government, directed his government to surrender. It was not entirely certain that the army everywhere would conform, and indeed on 15 August leading military figures and lesser commanders opened their veins to death rather than subject them-selves to the humiliation of surrender.[4]

None of the prisoners, of course, could have known of these momentous events. Most even refused to believe the rumours of the atomic bombs, so incredible did the destruction of two entire cities seem. But the prisoners could not ignore the local evidence and the strange occurrences that were taking place all around them. Hugh Clarke, working in a lumberyard at Fukuoka, in the far north of Japan, watched the guards gather before a loudspeaker for what appeared to be an important statement. Other prisoners remember seeing guards and officers listening with heads bowed, as if the speaker was a person of exalted significance. The broadcast the prisoners were observing was, in fact, the first time in history that the emperor of Japan had addressed his subjects directly and his words had a profound impact. The listeners, these hardened and brutal guards of yesterday, were stunned, and prisoners recall them drifting away from the broadcast with tears rolling down their faces. No further work was ordered after the broadcast and it seemed to the prisoners that the guards and camp officials had suddenly lost interest in them.[5]

So long had the period of captivity been, and so life denying, that many of the prisoners could not believe that it might all be coming to an end. When, in Ray Denney's camp in Japan, the guards explained in the mid-afternoon of 15 August that there would be no more work, Denney reported that 'there were different reactions according to

whether you were an optimist or a pessimist. The view was expressed
by some that we would now be gunned down … but most of us were
optimistic'. Bombardier Lang Fraser observed that his mates' jubila-
tion 'was restrained by uncertainty and doubt' and some even 'cried
with bewilderment and fear that it might be wrong'. But, he adds,
'we could hardly be classed as rational at that time'. At Private Alan
Chick's camp the commandant paraded his prisoners and explained
to them that the war was over. 'He was heard out in silence to the
end', Chick remembered. 'No shouting, cheering or hilarity of any
sort. In fact we may well have been told we were to be executed.'[6]

Douglas McLaggan was in Changi, in the hospital, fast losing the
battle for survival. On 10 August there was a ripple of excitement
throughout the camp as the radio monitors had picked up the news
that Japan was now considering the Allies' demands. The good news
was enough to make 'even the pessimists wonder'. Then, on 11 August,
prematurely, a cry went through this camp, the centrepiece and
symbol of Australian captivity: 'It's all over.' 'Of course it shook our
nerves up', McLaggan wrote, 'and made the heart palpitate, but there
was no exuberance, cheering or anything like that … it would take
more than words to convince us of our freedom.' That night Douglas
McLaggan sat down and wrote out a new will; 'I was not morbid, just
prepared.' As the days dragged on with no definite news, the waiting
became more difficult to bear than confinement itself; 'we were not
normal people', he wrote. The next day, Sunday, two of the prisoners
died in the hospital, and one more on Monday. 'It was pathetic that
they died at that stage, even if they had really no chance at all [of
survival], either [here] or at home. But there were others who still
had a chance if the relieving force came quickly enough.'[7]

No one had any idea how long it would take for relief to arrive.
McLaggan's mates speculated that Allied ships would be in Singapore
harbour within a couple of days and that the released men would be
taken to 'Columbo or Geraldton' in Western Australia for recuperation and rehabilitation. 'I did not want to go home just then',
McLaggan remembered, 'in the deplorable condition that I was in,
underweight, unable to eat proper food, fever-ridden and God knows
what else.' So now there was tension, too, between the hope of an
early release into the care of Australian troops, and a fear of moving

too quickly to the homes of their dreams, for fear of being seen as they were — wretched, degraded, wasted. Many men feared that they emitted a strong and unpleasant smell, confirmed for them when eventually the liberating troops did arrive. The prisoners certainly did not want to go home looking dreadful and smelling fearfully.

They need not have worried about an early release from their captivity. There were no ships to appear magically in Singapore harbour and in Japan the situation was even more difficult to predict. But certain it was that no troops would move forward until the peace treaty was signed and, ever the showman, General MacArthur would delay this until he had created a grand piece of theatre in Tokyo Bay. It was not until 2 September that MacArthur took the surrender, and nothing could be done for the prisoners before then.

If restraint and a lack of exuberance was universal in the prisoners' response to the news that they were soon to be liberated, universal too was their post-liberation response to the Japanese guards and camp officials. For years the prisoners had suffered dreadfully at the hands of these men. They had watched them brutalise and kill men they had loved, they themselves had been degraded by them and beaten, they had been tormented and humiliated. Some guards in each camp stood out especially in the prisoners' minds as thugs, sadists and worse, and prisoners had survived, many of them, on the notion that one day they would be able to get even with their tormentors. When that day came, remarkably, the desire for revenge and retribution vanished. Whether in Singapore, Thailand or Japan, the Australians turned their backs on these people as if they were beneath their dignity. 'We were so glad after three years to be able to ignore them, that we gave them not a glance, not a word, not a blow.' But the prisoners were realists, too. 'We had all reached the stage of exhaustion', Frank Hole reported, 'where even the effort of revenge was beyond us.' Gunner Kitch Loughnan agreed: 'We were too weak to do much and, not only that, there were about 40 000 [Japanese] troops in our district — they did not take to surrender too easily. Besides, we just wanted to get home.' It was as if the past was already being overtaken by the future in the minds of many prisoners.[8]

Immediately after 15 August, a day that should have stood out forever as The Day in the lives of these prisoners, it seemed that their problems were just as bad, if not worse, than before the news of peace had reached them. Ray Denney recalls those first weeks as a time of 'excitement and frustration'. 'We did not have any news for a week or so and the rations were still the same.' Lieutenant Ralph Sanderson, the senior of those Australians in camp at Niihama, repeatedly asked the Japanese commander, who was still in charge, for an increase in the rations, but Sanderson was consistently turned down. Taking matters into their own hands, the Australians caught and killed a pig, driving the Japanese commandant to fury. But, how times had changed, he took no action, Sanderson joyfully noted. At this camp it was not until 25 August that the Japanese increased the rice ration and issued new clothing. Even then, the men had not been told officially that the war was over. All that the commandant was prepared to say was that peace talks were in progress and that the fighting may begin again at any time. But it was hard to credit this worst possible position when, again on 25 August, a truck arrived at the camp carrying 900 bottles of beer, enough for a bottle for each man. 'First beer for over three and a half years', Sanderson wrote. 'Surprising how many men did not care for it although it was good quality beer. No doubt we would have preferred it to be a bottle of sauce.'[9]

The physical condition of the prisoners continued to alarm the Australian officers and the medical staff among the prisoners. Daisy Keast, a nurse housed near Yokohama, whose normal weight was 11 stone, weighed in at 6 stone on liberation. Douglas McLaggan, at Changi, anxious not to go home in his present condition, was just over 6 stone when he was released. Blair Taylor, a tall man, whose pre-war weight was over 13 stone, weighed just 8 stone on release. Wilfred 'Chicken' Smallhorn, the former champion Victorian foot-baller, was said to weigh 5 stone on liberation. Universally the prisoners were emaciated, their ribs and shoulder blades stood out strongly through their skin, their skinny legs were bowed, and their eyes were sunken in their faces. They knew that they looked dread-ful.[10]

But the human body must be extraordinarily resilient. From 28 August, just on two weeks since the Japanese had capitulated, the Americans began flying in 'POW supplies' to the hundreds of camps all around Japan and throughout Asia. Preparation for these mercy flights had taken some time to organise. Flights of B-29s would overfly the camps, now clearly marked with signs on the roofs and parade grounds as instructed by leaflet. Certain of their targets, the planes would fly so low, at tree-top height many of them, that the prisoners could distinguish the faces of the crew as the planes released their food drops. Typically contained in two 44 gallon drums welded together, the parcels became lethally dangerous, as they were dropped so low that there was no time for the parachutes to slow the fall of the drums. With experience, Allied ground staff would pack wooden crates rather than metal drums, and the pilots would drop them adjacent to camps rather than in the camps themselves, and at a greater height to allow the parachutes to work. But in the first few days lives were lost and men injured in perhaps the most tragic circumstances of all. It shook up the prisoners badly to see these mercy flights go wrong.

One officer estimated that perhaps 40 per cent of the initial drops were badly damaged, with drums exploding on impact and contents scattered everywhere; others might have put the figure higher. At first, though, the men were so desperate for what was coming to them like manna that they would scoop up the fruit salad or the meat from broken tins and eat it, earth and all, right there where the drums had fallen. These flights were a remarkable sight. One of the prisoners, Tom Henling Wade, described them:

> Next day more B-29s came over; blue, red, yellow, and white parachutes blossomed under them and drifted against the backdrop of hills on to the green rice fields. Plane after plane scattered its drifting flowers. Below, over 500 prisoners waved, cheered and skipped with pleasure among the fallen and bouncing boxes. It made a glorious, theatrical spectacle.[11]

Wade estimated that most prisoners put on 25 lbs in weight in two weeks, filling up on bully beef, chocolate, tinned fruit and field rations, all of them luxuries to these starving prisoners. For Sergeant Harold Dwyer, as for many others, part of the marvellous treat was that now they could think of a meal that did not consist entirely or mainly of rice: 'For the first time in three and a half years', he wrote, 'we sat down on the ground in small groups and ate a good meal without *rice.*' Hugh Clarke 'watched the daily transformation of the men around us as their emaciated frames put on flesh and gradually returned to normal'. Many of the prisoners would never again eat rice. One former prisoner, many years later, detected the taste of rice in a bowl of porridge — the oats had been stored in a rice tin — and was quick to spit it out.[12]

In Singapore, as elsewhere, the Japanese suddenly 'discovered' long-forgotten Red Cross food supplies and medicines which the prisoners recognised would have made such a difference and would have saved many lives if distributed earlier. Now well fed and with the new clothing the Japanese had also miraculously located — 'a colossal amount of food and clothing' was the way Douglas McLaggan described it — the prisoners presented to the advance party of Allied troops, arriving at Changi on 30 August, 'in a better way than they had expected'. 'The Japanese were cunning', McLaggan concluded. 'A fortnight before we were in rags and by then at least our skinny ribs were covered up with new clothing.' Plentiful food and adequate clothing, either dropped from the sky or fortuitously found by the guards, might fool the rescuers into thinking that things had not been too bad for the prisoners.

Horrified by the images of Belsen and the other German holocaust camps, where the ravaged bodies discovered by troops and war correspondents were exactly as they had been under the Nazis, many of the liberators of the Japanese prisoners expected to find similar marks of suffering and deprivation on those they were releasing. But everything seemed so much better. Perhaps, the liberating soldiers thought, the rumours of starvation and degradation were exaggerated.[13]

Possibly this was the cruellest aspect of the liberation of the prisoners. Expecting the worst and finding men who had been filling themselves with reasonably good, balanced food for at least two weeks, and in many cases much longer, it was possible to believe that captivity had not been too heavy a trial for the prisoners. It was everyone's job in the Army to make light of adversity, anyway. The prisoners themselves would not want to talk of the horrors they had endured and their starvation and beatings, the memory of which would be a part of their lives for ever thereafter. When the war ended, these men were ashamed of their appearance and horrified at the thought of their loved ones seeing them in such a debilitated state. Writer after writer of contemporary diaries, and later memoirs and recollections, recorded how appalled they were at the thought of presenting their wracked and starved bodies to other Australian troops and most especially to their families at home. They wanted to spare everyone that. So they rejoiced in the return of some weight and in the signs that their bodies were taking on a more normal appearance and they talked up their good health as they talked down their sufferings.

There was a large element of deceit, of turning a blind eye or of wish fulfilment at work here. Indeed this denial of reality is at the heart of the story I am trying to tell. On their return to Australia, from early October onwards, compared with other Australians these men and women looked malnourished and wasted. For many there was a haunted look in their eyes as they turned from too intense a scrutiny, as they covered up their illnesses and made light of their wounds and amputations. Many men came home half the weight they carried on enlistment. One woman, speaking for thousands, remembers that 'Uncle Cec still looked like a scarecrow' when his troopship docked.[14]

Families and friends saw these things and they grieved. But they too would not show it. For the returning men there was a lingering kiss, a firm handshake, a slap on the back, a warm and welcoming smile, and reassurance: 'Oh, you look fine.' Certainly the former prisoners did look much better than, say, in July 1945; they no longer smelt bad and their bodies now carried a little more flesh. But they were not normal and in their hearts both parties to this pretence knew it. With the very best of intentions, wives and mothers and sisters, fathers and brothers denied to the former prisoners what all could plainly see.

There were some, though, who had not had a chance to 'fatten up' before recovery. The story of the discovery of the nurses from the *Vyner Brook* shows how powerfully the obvious sufferings of these terrible victims of the Japanese affected those who first encountered them. These women, cruelly abandoned by their captors, were in the last stages of starvation in August 1945, as were many of the other prisoners in Japan and South East Asia. But the nurses, whose existence was only rumoured, could not easily be found, and they missed out entirely on the food, medicine and clothing drops that the Americans had begun on 28 August. As no one knew where these women were, they had not been supplied from the seemingly inexhaustible American treasure trove. From late August other prisoners were fattening up, to progress from skeletons to badly malnourished, to reasonably healthy in appearance by the time they reached Australia. But the nurses languishing at Lahat, near Palembang on Sumatra, were still deteriorating so tragically that, by 20 August, Jessie Simons, not knowing that the war was over, had reached the lowest point of despair: 'I could see no light at all and remember wondering despairingly how I could possibly manage to stay alive.' 'Young women', she recalled, 'less than thirty years of age, lay in the last stages of exhaustion, haggard, emaciated and incredibly aged by suffering, so that they looked about seventy.'[15]

Although the women could not have known it, the Army had been searching desperately for them since 15 August. They were known to be in Sumatra, but apart from that feeble clue no one had any idea where they were. Attached to the search team was an Australian Army doctor, Harry Windsor of Sydney. With Matron Sage, the head of the Australian Army Nursing Service, Windsor and the recovery team were frantically following up leads, fearing the worst. At Palembang, where the team was received obsequiously by the Japanese, Windsor learnt that the nurses were at Lahat where there was a small airstrip. The flight to Lahat took twenty-five minutes, Windsor remembered, and as the plane landed he could see a group of people sitting under an awning on the edge of the strip. Jessie Simons recalls that Windsor raced towards the group asking 'Which are the Australian nurses?' But Windsor remembers that he stood back to let Matron Sage embrace her nurses first. 'Who are you?' they asked this woman in trousers that they never imagined an Army nurse would wear. 'I am the mother of you all', Matron Sage replied in tears.[16]

Matron Annie Sage, 50 years of age, a dedicated nurse with extensive experience, told these nurses that ever since she had been made Matron-in-Chief it had been her ambition 'to come and get you'. Looking around the dismal airstrip she asked in her anxiety, 'But where are the rest of you?' as she had been expecting to recover 32 women. Apart from those massacred by the Japanese at Banka Island eight of the nurses had died in captivity. The shock of this and the terrible appearance of the women was clearly registered on the faces of the doctor and the matron-in-chief. 'None of us realised', Simons wrote, 'how shocking our appearance was to others'. The nurses walked or were carried to the plane and were soon on their way to Singapore. But the pain of that day was deeply etched in Harry Windsor's mind.[17]

Four days later Windsor sat down to write his official account of the recovery of the nurses, mission accomplished. He typed up four pages, 'a hurriedly written sketch account' as he described it, and he recognised that he might have written twenty pages or more if he was to describe all that he had seen. Harry Windsor was a reserved man not given to exaggeration, a doctor of a gentle and caring nature, and a committed Christian whose beliefs guided every aspect of his life. He might have ignored the enemy completely in his writing, preferring to turn the other cheek, for his report was of medical matters and the future needs of the victims. But Harry Windsor could not contain his rage. He recommended, officially, on the basis of the shocking state of these nurses and other prisoners that he had seen, that the guards, the Kempi, all of them, 'be forthwith slowly and painfully butchered'.[18]

The savagery of this statement would leap at any researcher however drowsy in the hushed quiet of an archival reading room. The words were more dramatic for me as I had known Harry Windsor in his later life; his son is one of my closest friends. The passion, the grinding anger, is entirely at odds with everything I knew of this man or had been told of him. Those few words of brutal and savage retribution, 'slowly and painfully butchered', I have no doubt were precisely what Harry Windsor wanted to order for these Japanese whom he now despised for what they had done. But the words are important evidence too of the wider point that needs to be made about the reception of the Australian prisoners of war. Imagine if all the prisoners had appeared to their rescuers as these nurses did. Starved, emaciated, near to death. What anger and retribution might men less educated, less Christian, less forgiving than Harry Windsor have called down on the Japanese? What sympathy and care might the prisoners themselves have been given to help alleviate their obvious suffering? How might the story have been altered if the prisoners had not had those crucial few weeks in which to lose some of the worst indications of their neglect and deliberate starvation? Matron Sage and Harry Windsor had seen Belsen-like suffering in the faces and on the bodies of the nurses they recovered. The hundreds of members of other Australian recovery teams, and all those who would meet and comment on the prisoners in the first weeks of their recovery, found men determined to make light of their tragedy and men whose bodies were beginning, at least, to recover. 'They are not too bad', one of the war correspondents wrote in an article we will examine more closely later; 'a few weeks' loafing on the beaches will see them right'.[19]

Apart from food, more than anything else the prisoners wanted to be in touch with their families, their loved ones. Many prisoners had not received even one letter or card from their families in the years of their captivity. They could not say whether their wives or mothers even knew that they were still alive. They could not be sure how their families had fared during the war. What had happened to Australia and to siblings in the armed forces? Had they survived, as these prisoners had, or were there fresh trials and sadnesses awaiting them when news started to flow again? Those who were fathers anxiously awaited news of the children who had had to cope without them, to whom they would be, in effect, strangers. The lack of news was one of the greatest frustrations of these early weeks.

Many of the recovered prisoners suddenly had to cope with bad news, although in the years of captivity they had rarely given a thought to the possibility of major change at home. Desperate for a letter from his mother once mail had begun to flow into the camp, one man, Leslie Hall, kept pestering the postal staff. 'Here's the pile', a postal clerk offered. 'Look for yourself.' There were several letters for Les Hall, but none from his mother. Finally, opening a letter from his sister, he learned that his mother had died a year and a half ago. 'How often he had pictured his reunion with her — he would lift his petite mother and swing her in circles, as he had done so many times.' Heartbroken, Les Hall wandered over to a mate but could only point to the sheet of paper in his hands.[20]

Immediately they were free the prisoners had to start exploring for themselves what they would make of their recent past; they had to decide what would they bury or try desperately hard to forget, and they had to sort out what could they say to their families about what had happened to them. Most worryingly, they had to begin to sort out what they might say to the parents and wives of mates who had not survived. Perhaps not every prisoner sat down to puzzle out this issue in the first days of freedom. But all of them, in their own ways, would confront a problem soon enough that few, if any, ever satisfactorily resolved. They would learn, and with sadness, that there was a gulf that could not be bridged between them, as prisoners, and even their most intimate life companions. Many consciously determined that they would never even try to talk about what had happened. In some cases, avoiding talking to a close mate's wife or mother caused terrible, enduring hurt, the woman believing that her grief was of no account. But many men simply could not speak; no one, they reasoned, except a fellow prisoner could ever understand.

But in these first days of liberation there was time for happier thoughts too. Douglas McLaggan, whose book *The Will to Survive* is one of the most honest and aware of those written by former Australian prisoners of war, revelled in the freedom that was now his at Changi. After the surrender ceremony at Tokyo Bay on 2 September 1945, broadcast to all the camp at Changi, McLaggan actually began to believe in his freedom. 'I walked out the gate', he wrote, 'and past the empty guardhouse … It was wonderful to walk out of the camp, a free man, and look at the barbed wire from the outside.'[21]

McLaggan started to think of home seriously, as a place in reality to which he would soon be returning, rather than as an idealised part of a fantasy life. The reality required new understandings and discipline. He needed to write to let his parents and brother know that he had survived and that he was thinking of them. But what could he say? 'There was so much to write about', he recognised, 'and yet at the same time, so much that would not be mentioned at all. Many of the things of the last three and a half years were dead and buried already, if not in mind and memory. I did not want to go raking up the past … I thought it would not be understood and would make me seem a liar.'[22]

Other men agreed, although it does not seem that the former prisoners talked much among themselves about how they would present themselves to family and friends, to Australia. 'In our new-found happiness we wanted to forget the past' was how one of them put it and that seemed to express the unspoken agreement of the vast majority. Could they speak of brutal beatings, of awful, unremitting work, of starvation, of disease so degrading, of inhumanity so remarkable because it was so universal? They could not say, as soldiers before them had said, in telling the sad personal news of a death they had witnessed, that the son or husband had died a hero's or a soldier's death. But they could not say, either, how demeaning in many cases death had been. These former prisoners were beginning to shut down memories even in the first days of peace. When they returned to Australia they would discover an even better reason for amnesia. They would not want to cause pain, to give offence.[23]

For the moment, the issues and the experiences were much more simple — a meal without rice, an unsupervised walk outside the wire, a bottle or two of beer. One man rejoiced when a Japanese policeman, still keeping order in Bangkok, called passing Australians 'Gentle-men'.[24] Others were stunned to be saluted by their former Japanese guards, while many others at first found it difficult to remember not to salute or bow whenever a Japanese guard passed by. The former prisoners revelled in their new, lice-free clothes, they rejoiced in shaving and washing, so luxuriating in the showers that the crew of one American hospital ship had to ask them to take it easy as they would soon run the ship dry of water. And most who wrote or have spoken of the golden days of liberation remember the sheer joy of beds with sheets.

Recovery teams in Japan processed the men quickly and passed them on to Okinawa; typically this was a sea journey for most, although some were ferried across by plane. From Okinawa, where they marvelled at the hundreds of American warships, thousands of planes and seeming millions of men — a war machine they simply could not have envisaged — they were transferred to Manila, the fattening paddock, as they described it. They would be in Manila for some weeks as Australian or British ships had to be found to take them home and ships could not be plucked from the air. They ate well, backing up in the first heady days for more and more again, staggered by the American largesse and organisation. One man remembers living almost exclusively on Hershey bars. Many were goggle-eyed at the profusion of ice cream, when the purchase of an ice-cream 'brick' for consumption at home, pre-enlistment, was a luxury reserved for special days. And so they put on weight and condition and their bodies returned to states they could only dimly remember. A penis rising and swelling was an unspoken relief for the many who had feared, in the absence of an erection during captivity, that they may have become impotent. Malnutrition, exhaustion and brutality had destroyed any type of sexual drive, but the men quickly found out how resilient the body can be.

In Singapore the troops stayed in the camps of their captivity and awaited repatriation to Australia; perhaps their lot was harder as they were not given the change of environment that so invigorated their mates from Japan. To Singapore came former prisoners from the islands and from Thailand and Burma. They spoke of the organisation into whose care they now passed, Repatriation of Allied Prisoners of War and Internees (RAPWI), as 'Retain All Prisoners of War Indefinitely', but increasingly they found it hard to joke about the delays and the stuff-ups. Their camps had too many bad associations that they just wanted to be rid of, but the notion that some had cherished in the first days of peace that ships would simply turn up in Singapore harbour to ferry them home was hardly realistic. The first troops — but a very small number — would leave in mid-September. Mountbatten only took the formal surrender at Singapore on 12 September, and the bulk of the troops would not begin to depart until early October. Perhaps the former prisoners had forgotten that the first rule for soldiers was 'hurry up and wait'; they would certainly have a chance to relearn that art.

War correspondents flooded into Singapore and into Manila and tried to prepare their readers at home for men much changed by their experiences. The correspondents found a level of anxiety among these former prisoners about their welcome at home to which the home-front had perhaps not given sufficient thought. George Johnston, one of Australia's most experienced war correspondents and undoubtedly one of its best, found that the first question put to him by the former

prisoners was not one that he had expected. 'Is Australia ashamed of
the 8th Division for losing Singapore?', men who as boys had been
raised on the heroic stories of the Anzacs repeatedly asked him. 'When
told that such was not the case and that recovery of the 8th Division
had been Australia's Bataan symbol, many broke down and wept.'
Johnston's testimony is supported by others who heard groups of men
wondering about their reception in Australia, fearing that they might
be spurned as apparently General Bennett had been. Writing in early
September, Johnston found that 'almost all' the former prisoners felt
a 'stigma of disgrace and shame' and that they were going back to
Australia 'like a pack of convicts and cowards'. 'A lot of our blokes',
he concluded, 'died in prison camps thinking they were hated and
despised by their own country and people.'[25]

It is hard to know what to make of this testimony. If it was
exaggerated or simply untrue we might have expected howls of
protest from the former prisoners themselves, or from the defence
chiefs and government ministers who were attempting to look after
their welfare. When Charles Bean, in the earlier war, misinterpreted
the mood and behaviour of the First AIF in Egypt, he was threatened
with being tarred and feathered. No one, apparently, threatened
George Johnston, even though the expression 'like a pack of convicts
and cowards' could easily have been misunderstood, and, if untrue,
would certainly have been resented. Johnston's newspaper, the respected Melbourne *Argus*, was not flooded with complaints and
corrections about this stark presentation of the fears of these returning
Australians. Axel Olsen, another war correspondent with the *Argus*,
writing from Manila, described a 'grey-haired, gaunt-faced young
Australian, released last week from a Japanese prison camp, who said,
'I don't know what will happen in Australia, whether my family will
know me'. 'This man', Olsen continued, 'is typical of hundreds of
others who overnight have had to adjust themselves to a world they
had almost forgotten. Many grave and not easily solved problems will
confront relatives of Australians released.' 'I don't want to go back
home until I am fit for my mother to see me', another told him.[26]

Olsen also observed how many things were new to these soldiers.
They gasped at jeeps, the vastness of American planes, and the
staggering quantity of American equipment. Often, he noticed, they

could not understand current army slang, and they often slipped their considerable Japanese vocabulary into their conversation, to the confusion of their listeners. There would be 'a colossal task of readjustment' to be tackled from both sides, Olsen predicted. The national chairman of the Australian Red Cross Society, Dr J. Newman Morris, agreed, basing his views on a three-week tour of the camps housing returning Australians. 'The men were rather nervous about what their reactions would be when they reached home', he reported, and Major-General Cecil Callaghan, in command of the 8th Division in captivity, speaking in Melbourne in early October, confirmed these views. 'Hundreds of prisoners of war', he said, 'who had lived for years in dreadful uncertainty would return to Australia highly strung and with nerves on edge, and the people close to them should realise this and make every possible allowance for mannerisms that would wear off with sympathy.'[27]

Part of the reason for these 'nerves on edge' was the increasing awareness among the returning Australians that they were so out of date that they did not have the language and the knowledge to keep their end up in pub conversations and family gatherings. They did not know that Darby Munro was the winning jockey on Sirius in the 1944 Melbourne Cup or that Balmain and Fitzroy had won the respective premiership flags that year. 'Who won the Brownlow last year', one of them might have asked, not knowing that the award of the medal was suspended from 1942 because of the war. They did not know the words to the hit songs of those years or the names of the 'flicks' [movies] that everyone had seen. Whether Labor or the conservatives were in power in their state was a mystery, and they would need to catch up on the details of rationing and work, hardly realising that their wives and sisters were in jobs that would not have been contemplated when they went away.

To help overcome this huge gap in knowledge, to restart the national conversation between returning prisoners and their families and mates, the *Argus* published a substantial pamphlet, *While You Were Away*, which was to be issued free to each returning man. At least that was the idea, but poor organisation saw many ships from Singapore sail for home without the pamphlets even reaching the wharves. But the pamphlet does help us to understand just how much these troops had to catch up on.[28]

'It is to be hoped', wrote the managing director of the *Argus*, Errol G. Knox, in a foreword, 'that the reader finds no atmosphere of self-glorification in what appears hereafter', because the pamphlet had to tread carefully in describing the winning of the war to men who might fear that they had played no part in the victory. Knowing that 'so many fine young Australians were taken prisoners of war' conditioned the thinking of the troops, Knox suggested, who, although they did it pretty hard, 'particularly in the jungles of New Guinea', were not inclined to boastfulness about their sacrifice. They were too conscious of the terrible sacrifice of the prisoners. 'We are looking forward to a return to ordered life', was the best that Errol Knox could promise, 'and the rehabilitation of every man who served his country.'

John Curtin had come to dominate Australian politics, the pamphlet reported; he 'soon revealed himself as a strong leader, capable of maintaining party discipline and determined to serve the interests of the nation rather than those of party or social class'. Labor won a 'breath-taking' victory nationally in 1943. There were great changes 'in the Australian way of life', with 860 000 men and 47 000 women in uniform and 756 000 workers diverted from civilian production into war industries: 'the cutting down of luxuries, the return to simple foods, and the increased amount of physical exertion made for better health', while 'for the first time in its history [Australia] became a cosmopolitan country [attracting] hundreds of thousands of Allied troops, mainly American, as well as scores of famous people'. The Melbourne Cricket Ground became Camp Murphy, the new Melbourne hospital was taken over by the Americans for two years, and the University of Queensland became the Land Headquarters of the Australian Army.

Popular sayings varied, these returning Australians were warned. Airmen spoke of 'gremlins' and their favourite word was 'wizard'. People 'teed up' a success and 'took a dim view' of a failure. Americans rode around in a 'jeep' or a 'battle buggy' and would approach a woman saying 'what's cookin', good lookin' '. There were then ten pages of sporting news, three pages listing 'notabilities' who had died, and a dozen pages of 'these made the headlines'. The final third of the pamphlet was entitled 'Outline of the War and Australia's Part In It'. A reader who absorbed all 96 pages of news and information could, perhaps, feel more confident in breasting the bar at the local (if there was any beer on) but must have felt wary that some lack in his knowledge of the world would show that he had been locked away in a prisoner of war camp. And, as we will see, many of these returning Australians would soon become reluctant for it to be widely known that they had ever been prisoners of war.

Even a casual reading of *While You Were Away* would have convinced most liberated troops that Australia had changed dramatically from the country they had left in 1940 or 1941. But in the staging camp at Manila, and soon in camps everywhere as they came to be broken up, these men and women began to recognise that their private world had now also changed irrevocably too. As Russell Braddon put it in *The Naked Island*, a book that was to sell more than one million copies world-wide, 'the careful fabric of one's personal life, built up over four years disintegrated at a single blow. One felt curiously alone … all those blokes, Pommies and Australian: all those ties — gone'. For years each Australian prisoner had relied on close mates with whom he could share his stories, his worries, his health, his food, indeed his life. For years each Australian prisoner was in the forced company of other men in the same predicament. They cared for one another and shared what they had. These bonds were suddenly and necessarily broken. Men and women returned to their service groupings, their battalions, their units. Men who lived in Western Australia, for example, were separated from those who lived in Queensland, for administrative ease. 'I was split up from my mates', a man would write. 'I was so upset — I missed them terribly.'[29]

Few of those waiting so impatiently in Australia for the return of the former prisoners could have understood the depth of loneliness and fear that the severing of these ties would cause. There were planted here seeds of future discord and disharmony. In a memoir written not for publication but just to help the man himself make sense of the life he had lived as a prisoner and for all the long years later there is the honest admission that 'I treated my wife abominably … I am not proud of it but at the time I could see no other way to handle my life'. 'Our whole life', this man continued, 'had been dependent on other men; men who had fought with and for us; men who had slaved with us; men on whom we depended on to save us; we needed them again.' Back in Australia this man admitted that 'I began looking forward to the time my leave was over and I could go back to hospital; that was where my life was. That was where my friends were.'[30]

It was with some understandable, if dimly perceived, reason, therefore, that the prisoners took the news of peace so calmly in their camps, as if 'we may well have been told we were to be executed'. They understood that this horrible life was over; but gone, too, was all that had sustained it and made it bearable. As the mighty British aircraft carriers *Speaker* and *Formidable* steamed from Manila, or the hospital ship *Oranje* and the dozens of other ships steamed from Singapore to Darwin and down the east coast of Australia, there were passengers on board increasingly uneasy about their arrival home. Those on the various aircraft heading towards the Rose Bay Flying Boat Base, for example, had even less time to compose their thoughts. On the boat back to Fremantle, one man remembered that 'the talk was all of prison life'; they would tell humorous stories 'but there were things that we could not laugh away'. The talk, too, turned to their welcome in Australia, but even in these last days few were able to talk about the farewells that would soon have to be said.[31]

'Weary' Dunlop was one of the last to come home. There was always something he could find to do, but even he could not delay forever. He was to fly home, leaving Singapore on 14 October, to Sydney for a brief stopover, and then on to Melbourne, to his fiancee of several years and his family. But at Sydney this heroic doctor of the Railway could go no further; 'panic rose inside him; he told the duty officer he had changed his mind: he would disembark in Sydney'. To a doctor friend Dunlop confided that 'he felt that he "wasn't fit to come home", that he "needed to get civilised again" '. The two men lay in the sunshine at Bondi beach for the whole afternoon 'while he worried "Am I the same person I was when I left here eight years ago … Will it work out? I had lost my nerve" '. And yet even though he sensed that the jaws of a trap were about to be sprung, nevertheless duty took over: 'Duty always triumphed with Weary … he rang

Melbourne and murmured some excuses; a civilian was ejected from a seat' and he did finally that night go home.[32]

He may not have known it then, but Weary Dunlop's experience mirrors that of so many other returning ex-prisoners. The evidence is overwhelming. Lieutenant Ralph Sanderson kept a diary once he was free to do so, and with 600 other Australians sailed from Manila on HMS *Speaker*. 'All hands', he wrote as he came to the end of his long account of being a prisoner in the hands of the Japanese, 'are quietly excited about tomorrow — arrival in Sydney. Or are we!?'[33]

CHAPTER 5

'I will turn up like the proverbial penny'

On 14 September 1945 Mrs Greenwood of East Melbourne received a cable from her husband, Flight Lieutenant Cyril Greenwood. He was allowed precisely fourteen words in this first cable and he had measured his words out exactly: 'On my way home about to have first beer. See you soon love both'. Perhaps someone in the Australian reception group arranging the liberation and repatriation of prisoners made a mistake and offered Cyril Greenwood another form, because he cabled again on the same day, writing jauntily that he would 'turn up again like the proverbial penny'.[1]

These joyful cables, still retained in the National Archives, allow us a brief glimpse of first contact between families in Australia and recovered prisoners of war. Our imaginations can fill in some of the rest of the story. Officially we know no more of the Greenwoods, but the joyousness of the moment is in contrast with the fears that the government, the military and even some families harboured for the return to Australia of these prisoners. Naturally the government wanted these men and women back as urgently as possible and War Cabinet directed that the 'matter be given highest possible priority and expense not to be spared'. And yet there was apprehension.[2]

In May 1944 the Directorate of Army Psychiatry in London had issued a paper 'The Prisoner of War Comes Home' in an effort to give some guidance to governments and, ultimately, to families. The report would give any reader pause for thought. It drew on a number of studies, possibly the most influential being that of Lieutenant Colonel A. T. Wilson RAMC on the psychological aspects of rehabilitation. The 'basic problem in all repatriates', the report asserted, 'even where physical illness or disability exists … is of a psychological nature'. 'Emotional problems', the report continued, 'are disproportionately severe in men who have been prisoners for more than 18 months' and 'six months appears to be the minimum period required for a working, even if incomplete, readaption'. An Australian brigadier on the Adjutant-General's staff described the British paper as 'the best writing I have yet seen in relation to this subject', and the Australian Director General of Medical Services (Army) was then required to 'prepare a paper concerning the general treatment of repatriated P.W. having regard to the medical and psychiatric factors'.[3]

The Australian army paper, undated, but obviously drawing on the British report, also asserted that returning prisoners of war would display considerable physical and mental problems. Ominously the Australian doctrine recognised that the British studies and policy related to prisoners held by European powers only. Policy directed towards prisoners in the hands of the Japanese 'will need special consideration later'. By October 1944 British doctrine, and particularly Lieutenant Colonel Wilson's formulation of it, had become standard in Australia. Indeed Naval staff who would be working with recovered prisoners of war 'should be carefully selected now and instructed on the lines of [Wilson's] Report'.[4]

From these small beginnings there followed a flood of documents and statements circulated within the three Australian services about what to expect from the prisoners of war who would one day return to their homeland. It was not comforting reading, as a few extracts will show. 'Their mental attitude is a compound of the attitude of a man long separated from his home plus confinement for an unforeseen, unspecified period in conditions of mental insecurity … coloured by deep feelings of self-reproach (often unrecognised by themselves) and of forsakenness'. The returning prisoner of war 'would be hostile to and deeply suspicious of authority' and also deeply resentful of any suggestion that they were 'different'. Writers recognised that the returning prisoner of war would feel quite 'out of it' and would be embarrassed not to know the hit songs, the sports results and the film news that was such an essential part of everyday conversation. A casual conversation in a pub could become a humiliating and perplexing experience for the recovered prisoner. They should, therefore, be given access immediately to lectures and films that would bring them up-to-date. But, writers warned, prisoners should not be exposed to 'films, lectures etc. which throw into marked relief the contrast between the war-winning activities of certain, especially civilian, groups and the apparent uselessness of the prisoner's period of captivity'.[5]

The Director of Personnel Services (Navy) had absorbed the doctrine comprehensively and his report, written in August 1944 with sensitivity and clarity, must have alarmed any who read it. He stated that 'morbidity from boredom, bitterness at having been left behind, or perhaps guilt at having surrendered too easily' had all exercised the minds of prisoners. 'After repatriation', he continued, 'and the first joyful relief at return has passed, the men begin to realise they are out of date, out of touch and have nothing in common with their fellow men and women and are to all intents and purposes strangers among their own kith and kin.' This doctrine was based on experiences with recovered prisoners in the hands of the Germans; those in the hands of the Japanese, the Director continued, 'will probably present a much more difficult problem'.[6]

As a result of this study, the Navy appointed, on 31 August 1944, Lieutenant Commander Seymour to oversee preparations and to prepare policy in Australia for the recovery of naval prisoners of war. He asked whether, given 'the probability of prisoners of war being in extremely bad physical and mental shape', they should be given leave immediately they returned home or whether they should be retained in a Reception Camp 'to undergo physical and mental reconstruction'. Admitting that families would want to spend as much time as possible with their returned loved one, nevertheless Seymour wondered whether 'an emaciated man's resistance may be lowered to such a degree that he is not fit until partially restored physically to stand up to a comparatively cold climate [after the tropics]'.[7]

An image of the returning prisoner grew among the military planners that built on one piece of bad news after another. It was almost as if doctrine was being developed on a worst-possible-case hypothesis. 'Ex-prisoners of war arrive home', the Navy's Director of Education and Vocational Training asserted, 'with high expectations, but with blunted initiative, brittle self-respect and a load of bitterness'.

No one questioned how this Director had reached these conclusions, but it is possible to see the cumulating strength of assertions across the policy files. 'All prisoners', he continued, 'will present the following symptoms to some degree: restlessness, irritability, disrespect for discipline and authority, fear of enclosed spaces and large crowds in confined spaces, cynicism, embarrassment in society, tendency to quick and violent tempers and rebellious views against any code which tends to restrict their activities'. His branch would prepare a course, he concluded, 'to eradicate the acquired "mental attitude" and to assist readjustment'. A cynic might have observed that it would need to be an especially powerful course to overcome all these disabilities.[8]

Concern about the prisoners reached to the highest administrative levels, as a minute written in February 1945 from the Secretary of the Army to the Secretary of Defence indicates. Writing of the 'emotional and psychological condition of many prisoners' the Secretary argued that 'it is not in the best interests of their early recuperation that all repatriated personnel should immediately be cast on their own resources for a lengthy period of leave before any attempt is made to give them the benefits of medical rehabilitation'. Popular thinking, he conceded, assumed that home life and its comforts would see the men right, but, he asserted, 'medical experience has shown that the members' families, through an understandable ignorance of the psychological problems involved, are able to help the member only to a small extent'.[9]

All of this doctrine was proposing that there was a significant problem for the government and the defence forces. The doctrine assumed that such would be the ill-health of the returning prisoners that massive investment would need to be made in their repair. Whereas family members would expect the immediate return to the homes they had left, the emerging doctrine anticipated weeks, if not months, of recuperation and rehabilitation. At the simplest level, therefore, the return of the prisoners could be expected to place a huge strain on defence medical services. It could also be expected to impose significant conflict between the government, exercising its duty of care to the returning prisoners, and the families, determined to see their men in their homes within hours of Australian landfall.

The prospect of a severe difficulty in managing the recovered prisoners' return to health and the intense newspaper debate it would have provoked ('POWs Languish at Quarantine Depots'; 'Distraught Mother's Plea') must have terrified the government.

Even so, there was within the military medical services a reassessment of the treatment of the 'torpedoed men' in 1944 and early 1945. 'Everyone is agreed that that matter was handled extremely badly', a lieutenant colonel in the Adjutant-General's branch wrote in June 1945. Those who had worked closely on the rehabilitation of these men raised questions about the wisdom of sending them on leave for 90 days shortly after their return to Australia, although it should be remembered that the leave commenced only after three weeks 'readjustment' at the convent at Toowong. A long period of leave without close medical monitoring and assistance, the Secretary of the Department of Air informed the Secretary of the Department of Defence in January 1945 'may have harmful results on [the men] as well as being, in effect, an evasion of the respective Services' responsibility towards their members'. 'After the initial excitement of returning to their homes has subsided', the Secretary continued, 'such members will regress both physically and mentally and, if thrown entirely on their own resources and those of their families, may, in some cases, establish for themselves a psychological disturbance which may never be eradicated, or a breach in family relations which may not be bridged for some time.' This was strong stuff and few desperately anxious wives or mothers would have been prepared to accept it at the time. Later anecdotal accounts confirm much of its accuracy. Few men were able, on their own, to re-establish themselves in society and in their families with ease or sureness.[10]

In view of this, what is surprising, as 1945 unfolds, is that no defined and rigorous program eventuated that would have been the logical outcome of the doctrine on the prisoners' psychological condition. Confronted with the fact of the return of the thousands of prisoners from the Japanese camps, it is as if the belief about the probability of persistent psychological damage was quietly but comprehensively forgotten. It is as if War Cabinet's highest priority was not the return of the recovered prisoners to Australia, but more their immediate return to the homes of the people. It also seems as if the insights gained in the sensitive and careful handling of the 'torpedoed men' were pushed aside. The significant change in direction in the rehabilitation of returning prisoners was never openly discussed, but it appears that there was an underlying view (within the Army, anyway) that the former prisoners should not be treated differently from other returning soldiers.

In early 1945, with the war in the Pacific in a far more satisfactory position, the Australian government began to give serious consideration to the recovery of prisoners of war. In February the Defence Committee established a Sub-Committee to examine issues relating to the release and repatriation of Australian prisoners and to propose action. The Sub-Committee, as John Curtin conceded, would be largely working in the dark. There were, he wrote, 'approximately 25 000 Australian prisoners of war and internees and missing in the Far East distributed in unknown numbers over a wide area. Preparations should be advanced to meet any situation which may develop'.[11]

It was obvious that the military planners would envisage a situation where prisoners would be released gradually as a result of the Allies invading and then securing enemy-held territory. In many ways this was a grim scenario. Planners assumed that individual Japanese commanders would hang on doggedly to their territory and that brutal military action would be required to defeat and eject them. The Allies knew that the Japanese were moving prisoners in Japan to camps adjacent to important military installations as a kind of human shield. It was feared that prisoners everywhere would become a defence for the Japanese or a pawn in negotiations all around the Pacific. Fears for significant further loss of life among the prisoners were widespread among military planners. These fears were realistic.

In this scenario victories in Burma, Thailand and possibly even Malaya required that the prisoners be moved as quickly as possible from the battlefield. Detailed and careful planning envisaged the recovered prisoners in these theatres being moved to India for initial assessment, health checks and early rehabilitation. It may have been months between recovery, stabilisation in India and eventual repatriation to Australia. Although relatives may have objected to these delays, the universal cry 'there's a war on' would have deflected much of the natural disquiet of relatives. In the event, the detailed planning for the

India option was just so much wasted time. Even so, no one could have anticipated the end of the war coming as swiftly as it did, and in mid-1945, within a month or so of the Japanese surrender, plans still envisaged assault troops moving recovered prisoners of war from 'the operational area' to be handed over to the 'Base Sub-area' where reception groups would take over. In June the Secretary of the Army officially advised the Secretary of Defence that it appeared likely that 'Australian PW will be liberated by or as a result of a number of independent operations each of which will present different problems requiring different attention'.[12]

If the nature of the Allied victory could not have been anticipated, nor could the stunning speed of that victory. Planning for the liberation of the prisoners of war, which began seriously only in early 1945, proceeded somewhat languidly. As late as 17 July 1945 a minute revealed that 'final plans have not yet been approved for reception and treatment of liberated prisoners of war ... and it is essential that adequate arrangements be made without delay'. Training for the men who would be responsible for the first contact with the recovered prisoners had not even commenced. Thus the Navy's Prisoner of War Liaison Officer attended the first inter-service 'contact officers training course' only in early August 1945. He found the course, held at Puckapunyal, 'very comprehensive and likely to be of considerable value to Contact Officers'. He recommended, and it was approved, that six RANVR officers attend the second course which was due to commence on 14 August 1945. The trainees, in fact, marched in, jubilantly celebrated the end of the war the next day, and then scrambled for transport for their bases and depots to await orders to begin the work of the recovery of prisoners on the ground. Some training did continue, but it was now in the context of a pressing need for contact officers and recovery teams in all theatres of the Pacific war.[13]

Rudimentary administrative procedures were already in place that seemed to concentrate more heavily on the administrative requirements of the services then on the needs of the men. But before any significant action could be taken the services had to discover the size of the problem that was awaiting them. The most pressing need, still, was for news and information about the men. The Australian government entered this new era of peace with no clear idea of the number of prisoners in the hands of the Japanese, their location or their condition. Indeed a draft circular letter prepared for the Acting Minister for the Army, Senator Fraser, as late as July 1945 to explain to relatives why the mails between the prisoners and their families were still so unreliable revealed the entirely unsatisfactory and continuing situation. 'The Japanese Government', he wrote, 'has notified the Commonwealth Government of the identity of only approximately one half of the Australians known to be in their custody, and we have had to identify others from letter cards, wireless broadcasts and nominal rolls brought back to Australia by escapees. Most of this information is well over two years old and in that time it is believed that the Japanese have transferred thousands of Australian prisoners from their recorded locations to other places at present unknown.' It truly was a dreadful situation.[14]

As we will see, the news of the fate of all the prisoners and the location of the survivors came to light agonisingly slowly and it is hard to believe that the administration could have been much quicker in compiling the all-important nominal rolls of prisoners. Somewhat naively, perhaps, the government did believe that, on surrender, the Japanese would hand over full and up-to-date nominal rolls for immediate despatch to Australia. The Army advised the Prime Minister's Department that 'one of the Japanese surrender terms is that the names and locations of prisoners of war will be transmitted by fastest means. These names will be passed to the next-of-kin immediately they are received in Australia'. However, it soon became clear that the Japanese had not bothered to create or maintain appropriate lists of their prisoners, although in some of the camps Allied officers had kept proper records where they could. Australian administrative arrangements issued before the surrender stressed the importance of the creation of documentation immediately the camps were entered and insisted that full lists of prisoners' names, serial numbers, ranks and so forth be sent by signal 'at the earliest possible moment after recovery'. They should be prepared in the camps and separate rolls should list the names of those who had died or who had been recently transferred to another camp.[15]

There would then be a great deal of work in Melbourne in

matching and confirming these lists and it was insisted that 'next-of-
kin ... should realise that only the official advice to them should be
accepted as final'. Everyone was keen to rush in with the good news
of survival and the first journalists to enter the camps in early
September 1945 began sending lists back considerably in advance of
official notification. The Army, in fact, asked that 'no newspaper or
broadcast reference be made to the names of any member believed
to be dead, missing or wounded. We have a deep obligation to the
next-of-kin of such men'. The widespread dispersal of the prisoners,
the considerable movement of camps and men in the months
immediately before the peace, and the large numbers involved, would
give the three services very real problems in providing quick and
accurate information.[16]

Government ministers also gave considerable attention to the
reception of returning prisoners in Australia. Certainly the newspapers would be quick to leap onto any notion that the prisoners
were being treated shabbily. The acting prime minister, Frank Forde,
wrote to his own temporary replacement, the acting minister for the
Army, Senator James Fraser, in January 1945 about allegations that in
Sydney no real effort had been made to welcome men returning from
Switzerland. 'There will be', he continued, 'in the future many
thousands of these men returning to Australia, and their future
outlook will be greatly influenced by the warmth of the welcome
extended to them'. Forde did not receive an answer to this letter.
Perhaps he was back at Army himself by the time the draft was ready
for signature and realised the silliness of writing to himself. But a
detailed draft had been prepared, marked 'not sent', which set out
considerable reservations about making the welcome home too
public or too elaborate.[17]

The draft letter, like earlier and continuing policy statements, gave
remarkably certain views about what prisoners and their families
wanted and needed. Yet again the officials were speaking for the
prisoners with considerable authority, the source of which is not
readily apparent. The draft deserves to be quoted at length:

The demands by certain organisations and certain sections of the Press
for public demonstrations ... are considered to be contrary to the

interests and wishes of the vast majority of the men and their relatives
… Men who are suffering from the psychological after-effects of pro-
longed imprisonment in enemy hands are pained and embarrassed by
public functions and desire only to be reunited with their families with
the minimum of delay and ostentation … painful and depressing scenes
frequently occur at these meetings and on many occasions female
relatives have become hysterical or have fainted or collapsed. It is felt that
such relatives would find little pleasure in a public reception, particularly
if it delayed or interfered with their reunion with their sons and husbands
… it is impossible to satisfy all critics.[18]

It seemed difficult at least to satisfy the Minister, Frank Forde. He
returned to the issue in July 1945, asking the Army's Adjutant-General, Major General C. E. M. Lloyd, about 'a more public type of
reception on a national basis similar to the American practice'. Forde
had intuited that the returning men might be nervous, expecting to
be blamed for being prisoners and letting Australia down. Warm
public welcoming parades and ceremonies would reassure them of
the people's regard and sympathy. 'Gaffer' Lloyd, as he had been known
at Duntroon because of his serious demeanour, had served in the
Middle East in the first years of the Second World War and was judged
'a staff officer of great quality' who was close to General Blamey.
Promoted Adjutant-General by Blamey as a bluff and plausible man,
another general commented that he appealed to Blamey because
'[Lloyd] could lie to Frankie Forde'. As one of the most senior
Australian military officers, Lloyd would have been aware of the
growing evidence accumulating under the general heading 'Japanese
atrocities'. By July 1945 no Australian in a position of authority could
not have known what these Australian and allied prisoners had
suffered, even though they may not then have had all the detail.[19]

Depite knowing of their sufferings, and perhaps suspecting their
uncertainty, Lloyd sent his minister a response that showed that the
returning prisoners would not have things all their own way. He
explained that the Army had only two aims in the methods devised
to receive and welcome recovered prisoners: reunion with next-of-
kin and departure of the soldier on leave. He wrote:

The actual meeting of the repatriates with their next-of-kin is marked
by emotions which have to be seen to be believed. My own personal

view is that these reunions should be had in the homes of the people ...
such a course would avoid the contagious emotionalism approaching
hysteria. The participation of the Commonwealth Government [in a
public reception] should be carefully considered. There is a feeling in the
Army, anyhow, and I think also in the country generally, that the flap
concerning the repatriated prisoners is a bit exaggerated. The great bulk
of them are fit and well, provided with large sums of money from their
enforced period with no expenses, and now granted discharge from the
Army. On the other hand the soldier who has borne the whole load
comes from the still continuing battle in New Guinea and elsewhere,
tired, diseased and NOT discharged and nobody but his next of kin are
really very interested in him as an individual.[20]

Major-General Lloyd, a desk-bound soldier in Melbourne, prevailed with his minister who did not raise the question of public
receptions again. Lloyd's was not merely a private and personal
opinion, however. An Army instruction, issued in late 1944 or early
1945, set the matter out clearly.

It is possible that the return of P.W. will be accompanied by extensive
newspaper publicity as to their experiences and privations. It is not
desired, however, that more publicity than is inevitable should be given
to them or that they be given any encouragement to believe that they
are entitled to any special privileges not granted to other members
returned from active service.[21]

Of course, the instruction continued, those who had 'borne the
whole load [of the fighting]' deserved the honour and recognition of
their country. But what had not occurred to the Army had certainly
impressed the minister, who had understood quite early on that the
'future outlook [of the returning prisoners] will be greatly influenced
by the warmth of the welcome extended to them'. Perhaps the
doctrine about the psychological damage done to these returning
prisoners of war had been pushed aside because the Army did not
want to make too much of a fuss of the men. Was there lurking here,
too, the suggestion that the Eighth Division had somehow let
Australia down?

But the planners correctly anticipated that the newspapers would
want to make a fuss about the return of the Australian prisoners. Aware
of the logistical difficulties in moving such a large body of men,

nevertheless the papers encouraged an impatience for news and for speedy reunions. An *Age* editorial, 'Speedy Homecoming for A.I.F. Prisoners', published on 15 August 1945, anticipated that the Japanese would 'be obliged to transport these men … to places of safety as directed, where they could be quickly placed on board Allied transports'. It was wishful thinking written in utter ignorance or wilful naiveté. 'Allied transports', including most importantly hospital ships, could not simply materialise overnight and who was to say how conditions were behind enemy lines. There were real concerns about the intentions of the defeated Japanese and the mood among the Imperial Japanese Army; there were also real limitations on the capacity of the Japanese to move large numbers of prisoners.[22]

Did the War Cabinet know that the Army had decreed that there were to be 'no special privileges' for recovered prisoners of war? Did Ministers understand that a Defence Committee directive of 4 September 1945 stipulated that 'rehabilitation of repatriated prisoners of war should be part of the general scheme of rehabilitation of all members of the Forces, and should avoid setting up an exclusive system'? If so, there was some inconsistency in their decisions, because in calling for the return of the prisoners 'at the earliest possible date', in itself a 'special privilege', War Cabinet also directed that 'air transport is to be employed to the greatest extent practicable'. Few other returning soldiers would be flown home. The Governor-General, the Duke of Gloucester, even offered his personal aircraft to the government to add to the number of aircraft available to ferry recovered prisoners home. Yet the military found sensible reasons against the use of aircraft, arguing as late as mid-September that sea transport should be the normal means of bringing the prisoners home. The Army's Director of Prisoners of War cabled from Manila: 'Consider A/C conditions and speed of evacuation unsuitable for personnel so soon after recovery. Air movement does not provide recuperative period similar sea movement.' Indeed, he reported, the recovered prisoners themselves were not anxious to rush home, as they were 'very conscious of their thin appearance and of bodily odor arising from Japanese type diet. Many PW state would prefer spend few days Darwin build up appearance before seeing next-of-kin'.[23]

The War Cabinet possibly did not know, either, that there were those within the defence force who were alarmed that the earlier doctrine about rehabilitation was being so comprehensively jettisoned. On 11 September 1945 Brigadier W. P. MacCallum, the Deputy Director Medical Services for the Army, wrote to his boss about his concerns. He tried to be conciliatory and reasoned, beginning by saying that 'there must be many pressing reasons unknown to this HQ which have led to the decision to return troops as rapidly as possible'. Even so, he argued, 'such a policy is unsound, medically, and should be rigidly opposed'. Those men the brigadier had observed at Morotai and Singapore needed careful supervision and treatment: 'Rapid return to Australia with immediate granting of leave, with its associated lionization, will affect these men unfavourably.' Brigadier MacCallum had also observed the hospitalisation of returning former Indian prisoners of war and had seen the benefits of lengthy treatment, isolation, observation and 'sympathetic yet firm discipline'. If the Australians were treated as carefully, he believed, 'perhaps many future difficulties [will be] prevented'. It was a firm letter from an experienced and senior officer and called into question the process that was already being imposed. Yet the Director General of Medical Services, to whom it was addressed, merely minuted 'DGMS will discuss when meet 30 Sep'. The file was then marked 'PA' (put away). The minute seemed to arouse no further action.[24]

Commanders-in-Chief in each of the Pacific war theatres were made responsible for the protection, maintenance and evacuation of all prisoners of war within their respective zones of operation. The Australian War Cabinet insisted that members of national forces to which the prisoners belonged were to be used in the reception depots at the earliest possible stage of evacuation; in other words, that the prisoners would want to be in contact, as quickly as possible, with their own. Building up quickly after 15 August 1945, the Australian Reception Group eventually comprised 1250 officers and men. The Japanese estimated that they were holding 93 762 prisoners of war. The numbers of Australians have already been noted, but it is worth remembering how widely spread they were. The largest number of Australians, 5549, were congregated on Singapore Island and at Johore; 4830 were to be found in several camps and working parties in Thailand and in remote parts of Burma; there were some 750 distributed throughout the islands of what is today Indonesia and Malaysia; there were about 100 on Ambon; and there were about 2700 distributed between Japan, Korea and Manchuria. The first task of the reception workers was to locate these prisoners; they would then begin to 'process' them, which involved the preparation of nominal rolls, examination by medical staff to determine each prisoner's state of health and, in consequence, the means of travel for his return to Australia; they would then ensure adequate clothing and diet. This was all time-consuming work.[25]

Naturally any significant recovery of Australian prisoners must await the formal Japanese surrender, which was not taken until 2 September 1945. From then on the recovery teams tried to process the prisoners as rapidly as possible, but their return to Australia depended on the availability of transport. In Manila, for example, where all prisoners from Japan were first taken, no shipping had been made available for transport to Australia until early October, and the number of aircraft was 'woefully inadequate'. By 4 October some Australians had been in camp at Manila for 24 days, leading some to conclude that they were being deliberately held there until their condition improved, making them more agreeable to those at home. Many said that they were growing impatient and they wrote of their longing for home. And yet there is plenty of evidence among some of the prisoners, as the Director of Prisoners of War reported, of a reluctance to return home, or if that is too strong, a certain shyness.[26]

To add to anxieties, the planners could not be certain that the Emperor's decision for peace would be observed without exception in all the myriad places where Australian prisoners were still at the mercy of their Japanese captors. Even the entry into Singapore of the Allied Supreme Commander in South East Asia, Lord Louis Mountbatten, on 12 September 1945, was anxiously watched everywhere for signs of Japanese resistance. In more remote locations the dangers were obviously greater. On 16 August 1945, for example, the Australian warship *Bundaberg* arrived at Ambon where there were about 100 Australians awaiting recovery; these men, it would subsequently be found, were in the very last stages of starvation. But without adequate resources to subjugate and control the large Japanese force, *Bundaberg* backed off, the captain fearing that his presence 'might jeopardise the safety of the prisoners'. It was nearly three weeks later before radio contact was established with Australian Land Headquarters at Morotai and the prisoners were not evacuated from Ambon until 10 September, nearly a month after the end of the war. The men were frustrated by the delay, but after the excitement of release they showed little anxiety to get home.[27]

As no one knew with any accuracy the numbers of Australian prisoners in Japanese hands, it was difficult to plan for their evacuation. Teams of military personnel began the work of searching for Australian prisoners, and airmen, mainly American, had, of course, already begun dropping emergency supplies at the camps, particularly food and medicines. The Army minister, Frank Forde, had initially suggested that some 17 500 Australians would be coming home and this led to optimism among the prisoner families, as it would be assumed from these figures that relatively few prisoners had died in captivity. As it became obvious that this optimism was misplaced, Forde admitted to the House of Representatives that officials were still seeking 'the fullest and most reliable information' to pass on to relatives and friends of the inmates of the camps as soon as possible. The minister made this statement on 25 September 1945, that is, some six weeks after peace had been declared. The waiting must have been agonising.[28]

There were warming stories of good news to bolster homefront spirits. There was real relief, for example, for the father and brothers of Sister Kay Parker of Croydon, New South Wales, of whom nothing had been heard since March 1942 when she had been captured at Rabaul. She was reported to be alive in Japan and her brother commented that 'we had almost given her up for lost when a telegram arrived announcing that she was safe'. However, there was a shadow of sadness in the contemplated reunion, as Sister Parker's mother had died in March 1945 and she was not to know the good news. In late August the newspapers reported that there were 7000 prisoners at Singapore whom it was expected would be released 'within a fortnight', but two weeks later Frank Forde was still conceding difficulties in discovering the names and whereabouts of the prisoners and announced rather excitedly that 'a high speed wireless link was flown from Melbourne to Singapore' and was in operation from 1 pm that day, 12 September. At the same time it was announced that a Colonel Williams (the same man who had been so brutally tortured at the Bicycle Camp in 1942), now a prisoner in Changi, was flying home to Melbourne with a list of 4000 names for checking. There were pictures in the newspapers of the Colonel landing at Essendon clutching the vital sheets of paper; it all seemed rather primitive, but was there any alternative? Yet relatives continued to wait, their emotions at straining point, and simply believed that something better could be done.[29]

The search for prisoners dragged on throughout September and into October, even as the atrocity stories began to become more widely known. In a press release in the first week of October Forde announced that of the 17 842 Australians known to be prisoners, 9913 had been recovered, leaving 1409 known to be dead and 3073 of whom nothing was known. Even this figure, which in any case does not add up, was grossly misleading, as eventually it would be discovered that nearly 8000 Australians had died in captivity.

In an age of instant communication it is hard to understand the length of the wait for news; a delay of anything more than 24–48 hours now would be regarded as intolerable. Many relatives waited for six to eight weeks simply to discover whether their son or daughter was alive or dead. With the start of each day relatives must have thought that today, at last, they would know. As each day passed and the atrocity stories dominated the newspapers, hope would be shaken and nerves stretched just a little further. The waiting was near to unbearable. We do know of at least one father who became dangerously ill during the waiting period. His two sons had been prisoners and they were rushed from the *Esperance Bay* on arrival in Sydney to Camden in the hope that they would see him before he died. The Relatives Association recognised the difficulties the government faced, but also knew the turmoil in the hearts and minds of mothers, fathers, wives, brothers and sisters. Sydney Smith pleaded with the military for some sort of official statement. Next-of-kin were pursuing their own enquiries, he reported at the end of September, and they 'attach undue importance to rumours', like a rumour he had heard about the massacre of hundreds of Australians in Borneo.[30]

But the simple fact was that even at this stage the government did not have the information that Sydney Smith and the Relatives Association were demanding. Sandakan, in Borneo, the subject of the rumours to which Sydney Smith had referred, was not yet the confirmed tragedy that it would soon prove to be. Indeed a report to the government on 27 September 1945, six weeks after the surrender, stated that 'it is impossible at this stage to make any reliable estimate of the numbers of AMF PsW who may be expected to be recovered, but new names are being received daily. Based on general reports received the death roll in several areas may be expected to be heavy, but it will take some considerable time to ascertain with certainty the names of those members concerned'. Of course the government could not release this news. Even as late as mid-November there were still 222 men of whom the government had no information what-soever. The real story had only begun to become clear throughout October and many relatives had waited nearly two months to discover if their loved one was alive or dead.[31]

Sydney Smith, broadcasting on ABC radio as late as 2 December 1945, indicated that some relatives were still waiting for definite news about the fate of their men. Of course, by then relatives would be seeking the confirmation of a death, and information surrounding it, but it does seem incredible now that such notification could not have come more quickly. 'There is nothing worse than waiting and waiting', Smith declared. 'I venture to remark that those relatives have suffered more since Japan surrendered than during the whole of the time their men were prisoners of war.' It seems a fair claim. Part of the problem had been that in returning the former prisoners imme-diately to their homes, opportunities for detailed interrogation were severely curtailed. Again there were those who objected to this, and again the pressure to bow to perceived family responses overrode the objections. 'Evidence regarding [the deaths of thousands in the camps] MUST be obtained before those who have the information or knowledge of those who can supply it are dispersed to their homes', a colonel responsible for the records wrote. He asked for an 'urgent re-submission to the War Cabinet' in early September 1945 but no action was taken.[32]

The telegrams and the lists, however, did begin to pour into the service headquarters in October for checking, verification and despatch to relatives. Even today, in the slick and computer-driven archival reading rooms of the nation, a researcher can be moved to tears at the good news and joy the delivery of these telegrams must have caused. Telegram 2 October 1945: 'Advice received that 401737 W/O Bonnice T and crew reported missing 27 Apr 1945 now safe and as at 23 Sept 1945 were at Cycle Camp Batavia ... information supplied by ... recovered RAF PW.' Telegram 8 October 1945: 'Please inform Mrs H Ross Elizabeth Bay that her husband F/O H Ross "is safe in allied hands".' The files contain thousands of similar cables.[33]

The family of Aircraftman Class 1 Donald Wilfred Bruce had not heard anything of him since the brief flurry of news when the 'torpedoed men' had returned home in October 1944. The last months of the war must have been the worst as the Allies edged closer to victory, and then came peace and the highest hopes of all. Yet it was not until 2 October 1945, 48 days later, at 6 pm to be precise, that the family finally had the news they had been waiting for since that first telegram of 14 March 1942 announcing that Don was missing.

With what feelings of terror and expectation did Don Bruce's father take the telegram from the delivery boy? Did the lad's demeanour give the game away? Did the father wait to close the door and to retreat into privacy before he looked at the news he and his family had been awaiting for so long? Did his hands tremble as he ripped open the envelope? The files can tell us none of these things, but it does not take too much imagination and human understanding to enter into the scene that was, of course, being experienced in thousands of homes across the nation. 'A.C.1. Bruce, D.W. Safe', it began. Did the father read on before his outburst of joy? Could he take it in on first reading? 'Pleased to inform you that your son A.C.1. Donald Wilfred Bruce has been liberated and is now at Singapore awaiting evacuation to Australia stop Address communications number rank name Liberated Prisoner of War R.A.A.F. care No. 2 Aust. Reception Group Australia stop further details movements will be conveyed immediately received.'[34]

There was only one further telegram on this airman's file. It was dated 9 October 1945 and it was to tell of the homecoming. Effectively, therefore, from this point on Don Bruce is lost to history.

We do know that he had embarked on the *Highland Brigade* at Singapore on 6 October and his time and place of arrival would be sent to the family as soon as it was known. The waiting was at an end. But all the anxieties of other welcoming relatives would have been played out among the Bruce family, in all probability. They would have wondered about the condition, physical and mental, of their returning hero and son even as they made their preparations for his homecoming. Perhaps it was enough that he was on his way home and they pushed their fears into the recesses of their minds. Possibly too Don Bruce was experiencing the ambiguity that so many returning prisoners felt at the prospect of being among home folk again.[35]

The families of 8000 men and women were to receive cables of an entirely different nature. There never has been an easy way of announcing death in war to the next-of-kin. At the beginning of the First World War the government invited the churches to undertake this work on its behalf, and so searing was the experience for most clergymen that the government gave responsibility to the Post Office in the Second World War. A woman, now living in Bribie Island, Queensland, described for me her family's experience some weeks after peace had been declared. Her brother was a member of the 2/10th Field Ambulance at Singapore. She was living in Mortdale, Sydney, with her parents and was 15 years of age when the Japanese surrendered:

> It was a great day for us when the war ended and we waited for news anxiously … Then came the terrible day, I remember this so well, it would have been about three weeks after the war ended. I was coming home from school and found my father getting off the same train which was strange as it was early for him. He told me that we had to go to the Post Office as a telegram boy had been to the house but he would not give it to my mother (I suppose because my father was next of kin). Naturally my mother was very worried and [had] phoned my father to come home. I remember how grave the Postmaster was (how many times had he done this?) I stood aside and waited and my father soon came to me and as we walked away he said to me, 'He's gone pet'. I could not believe this and all the fifteen minute walk home I just kept saying, It's just a mistake (such an inane thing to say). He had died two years before

in July 1943 and even some of the cards that had given us such hope had arrived after he had died.[36]

The hurt of that moment has remained with this good woman throughout her life; the cost of war is with her even today.

Much of the delay in discovering news like this, or hopefully better news, can be attributed to the speed of the Japanese capitulation. Instead of positioning the recovery teams on liberated territory adjacent to the prisoner of war camps in preparation for the speediest intervention into the prison camps, all recovery personnel had to be moved from Australia along with the food, clothing, stores and, most importantly, medicines that were so desperately needed. A major transport ship, *Duntroon*, could not reach Singapore before 16 September, and although aircraft were flying in small parties of recovery and medical teams, even that was quite hazardous given the chaotic conditions on the island and fears about what the Japanese might have left behind. 'We previously assumed Australian Group would arrive in time to handle recovered PW prior to repatriation', Land-forces signalled to Supreme Allied Commander South East Asia, but, increasingly, this looked unlikely.[37]

There were many problems associated with the recovery of prisoners and many of these were caused by a lack of preparation and planning. But there were successes, as the report of Commissioned Gunner Blatchford makes clear. He was aboard the *Shropshire* in Tokyo Bay and was soon working ashore at a variety of places. The first group of prisoners he met were British, and they told him something of the work and conditions on what would soon be known simply as the Railway. Then he came across a party of Australians. Nothing can improve on Gunner Blatchford's own account:

> [My duties] were very simple. Trains bringing in repatriates had to be met with a smile and a welcome. Easily the most pleasing duty ever imposed upon anybody … It would be a very hard man indeed who had no lump in his throat and tears very close to his eyes as he surveyed the scene. These were tremendous moments, charged as they were with tense feeling which beggars description. They will live forever in the minds of those privileged to experience them. The repatriates' relief and pleasure knew no bounds and if the vigour with which they shook hands was any indication of their happiness at seeing us, they certainly have never been happier.

It was not possible to get detailed information from these men as our object was to shake hands with and talk to as many as possible and clear them from the station in ambulances and trucks with minimum delay … Reactions vary little. Nearly all wanted to (and did) vent their pent-up feelings by talking. Some asked questions such as 'How are things at home', 'Tell us about the atomic bomb' … One or two appeared quite unable to realise that they were free and one Australian in particular jumped and looked startled whenever he heard any Japanese speak in loud tones. Not a pretty sight.[38]

On 10 September the RAAF recovery team, 'Firstaf', cabled to 11 Group RAAF Headquarters with first impressions of the prisoners at Singapore: 'General condition of prisoners improving many suffering recurrent malaria and malnutrition. Morale and discipline of all troops seen very good.' The recovery teams would naturally begin to impose a new, or at least different, order and discipline on these troops, though with the best intentions in mind. Thus in August the RAAF directed its Liaison Officer: 'Every possible endeavour should be made by the RAAF Liaison Officer to accommodate RAAF POWs separately from A.I.F.' Men who had been brought together by tragedy and disaster and who had forged the closest bonds of mateship would now be pushed apart by the services. In the rush to help these men whose suffering was so clearly visible to all, did anyone stop to ask them what they themselves might want? Most of the recovery teams encountered chaos in the first few weeks, and chaotic conditions were not conducive to careful thinking about the needs and interests of the men and women for whom everything possible was to be done. A handwritten note attached to a file from Lieutenant W. R. Smith RANVR to Lieutenant Commander W. J. Seymour, the Navy's liaison officer, written on 21 September, perhaps a week after landing, reports: 'Busy as hell — first week just chaos — no stores etc. Having much success, but some disappointments.'[39]

Roy Smith was a good writer and keen to let his superiors know the score. Another handwritten letter, again fortuitously attached to a file although it appears to be a personal letter, is addressed 'Dear D.N.I.' (Director Naval Intelligence) and was written on 14 October, when Smith had been at work with the prisoners for about a month. He reported:

> We have not had a particularly happy time on this job. The organisation was appalling and I'm afraid I could never boast having been attached to 2 APWRG. The vessels carrying clothing and other very necessary stores were for some strange reason sailed to arrive here long after the first two batches of P.W. departed — it was really tragic to see hundreds of recovered P.W. leave for home in a pair of Jap shorts, Jap shoes and a torn blanket or bag over their shoulders to protect them from the rain; many of them had no shoes but very noticeable was the fact that almost to a man they had retained their Australian hats — very dirty and very much patched with bits of rag — but still their original hats. I have given most of my clothing away to them; one Army Captain burst into tears when I was able to give him a shirt and a pair of khaki socks … he had not owned a shirt for over three years … It has been an interesting but very uphill job — no blinking organisation — but I think we have sent most of our men away reasonably happy; unfortunately mail dated Aug/Sept is only now arriving for chaps already sent home; the Post Office has lived up to its reputation to the last.[40]

The earlier doctrine that these men would need to be treated with kid gloves and that any snarls in the system would send them into rage or depression becomes deeply worrying in the light of this and similar reports. Lack of organisation could have placed a severe strain on the recovered prisoners and might have badly affected their health. Back in Melbourne, the doctrine still prevailed. Recovered prisoners, the Deputy Adjutant-General 2 had written in June 1945, 'have a more than usually keen resentment of being mucked about, and are extremely anxious to know exactly what is in store for them'.[41]

Commander Long, the Director of Naval Intelligence, received another account of the chaos surrounding the recovery and treatment of prisoners, this time from Manila. His informant here was Lt A. G. Steele RANVR who wrote on 12 October (that is, two days before Roy Smith). Steele had arrived at Okinawa on 7 September and had reached Nagasaki on 12 September. After evacuating the camps, the contact teams departed for Okinawa on 4 October and reached Manila on 8 October. 'After being pushed from pillar to post we eventually arrived [at 1st Australian PWRG Headquarters]. After waiting for some time whilst NCOs argued whether we could be billeted in the camp or not, we were eventually given a camp stretcher in a tent and then had to borrow blankets.' There were hundreds of Australian recovered prisoners in the camp, many of whom had already waited long weeks to reach Australia. Major N. S. Thomas, who was with 1 Australian PW Contact Group in Japan, complained that 'the forwarding of completed nominal rolls was slow and in many cases PW arrived in Manila before GHQ (Manila), who was responsible for advising the various Governments, had been advised of their recovery'. This meant that chaos was simply being transferred from Japan to Manila. The reason for the foul-up, Thomas believed, was that the recovery teams came in too late and there were too few of them; these errors were due, he believed, to 'a lack of foresight and true appreciation of conditions'.[42]

Reports from members of recovery teams commented on the mood and health of the men. Lieutenant Shaw, for example, although complaining that the teams needed to work 24 hours without a break to 'handle the large numbers of PW in the time laid down', conceded that 'the task was simplified by the excellent co-operation from the PWs themselves who at all times appeared in very high spirit'. Lieutenant Winter-Irving, from Recovery Team 45, reported on 9 October that at Yokohama the Australians looked 'in fair condition' but the majority were suffering from malnutrition. 'In spite of their condition', he continued, 'the Australians always seemed in the best of spirits in comparison with the average allied PW.' Even though they appeared malnourished to Winter-Irving, the prisoners themselves explained that the food dropped by the American aircraft had improved their physical condition greatly. They asked Winter-Irving about rates of pay and 'naturally, about Home conditions and how the war had affected Australia. Many questions were asked about rumours they had received from Japanese guards etc. Most prisoners from Singapore were interested to know what the Australian Public thought of the Eighth Div., and General Gordon Bennett'.[43]

Roy Smith was less certain about the health of the men. But, again, he was writing personally and not for an official report. 'Most of what we were told at the school we went through at Puckapunyal was wet', he told Commander Long. 'These men are mentally sick and it's just a case of common sense dealing with them. I'm afraid it will be many months before they are again normal — if ever, in some cases. They have been starved and brutally beaten, almost to a man, and they tell some heart-rending stories of their captivity.'[44] Perhaps everyone was too busy to listen to news confirming what the planners had suggested would be the case several months earlier.

Good food, rest and the removal of anxiety about the future was, however, producing a significant change in the men's bodies. It should be remembered that, although the Supreme Commander entered Singapore, for example, on 6 September 1945, regular air drops had been giving the prisoners access to food and medicine from late August. This was true for most prisoners, regardless of the theatre or camp, although it was not so for the nurses found at Palembang who were still in the condition many men would have displayed on 15 August. The improvement in many of the prisoners' physical appearance by mid-September, while greatly pleasing them, did mask some of the problems that physicians would need to be alert for. But the impulse to return the men as quickly as possible to Australia allowed for little more than segregation into 'stretcher cases' requiring transport by hospital ship and 'walking wounded' who could come home by ship or aircraft as availability dictated. The prison camps were not the place for sophisticated medical examination, and the recovered prisoners, fearing military red tape, had a strong incentive to avoid disclosing too much of their condition for fear of detention in some hospital or rehabilitation centre on arrival home. Even so, their health was foremost in their thoughts, as a directive from Allied Land Forces, South East Asia, Headquarters, anticipated: '[A prisoner] will have seen much illness around him and for this and other reasons, he may be unduly concerned about his health state'. The directive required that 'an impressive medical overhaul' be given 'as early as possible [and] be thorough enough to reassure the man'. This directive, it seems, did not establish common practice. The concern about the impact of 'too much leave — too much home life' for the 'torpedoed men' had been quietly forgotten.[45]

Even as the recovered prisoners were on their way home, the military forces were preparing to wash their hands of them. Again, what might seem callous behaviour was being designed in the name of what the men themselves would want. The Army's Queensland commander advised Melbourne Headquarters that 'in many cases [the recovered men] are restless and do not readily conform to even simple forms of regimentation'. Since this was written on 12 September before any prisoners in Japanese hands, except the 'torpedoed men', had returned to Australia, Headquarters might have asked how this man could possibly know. 'It is felt', he continued, 'that they would be more readily readjusted if released early to their home and friends.' Of course, those who were regarded as requiring serious medical attention and nursing could not be sent home immediately as this officer was proposing, but the Army's Director General of Medical Services had the answer there. 'The less time spent by PsW in military installations other than in hospitals or convalescent depots the better', he wrote in late September. If a man did require medical attention and he were fit enough, it was best that he live at home, but if that was not possible then 'it seems desirable that such patients be held in Red Cross Convalescent Homes rather than convalescent depots or other Army installations'.[46]

Cyril Greenwood had drunk his first beer in Singapore and after champing at the bit in camp for the next few weeks he was eventually processed for return to Australia to turn up 'like the proverbial penny'. We cannot know what his expectations were, because like many of the people in this story, he is known to us briefly and serendipitously in government files and is then lost to sight. Cyril Greenwood cannot have known about the fears for his health that so many well-qualified people had held, nor can he have known how comprehensively those in authority had rejected proposals arising from these fears. Rejection of the advice from psychologists and others came about partially, it would seem, from a desire not to build an artificial barrier between recovered prisoners and other Australian servicemen and women, and partially because of the sheer weight of numbers of those coming home. Sending the recovered prisoners to their own homes immediately they returned was the easiest and most obvious solution to the issues their return raised. It also accorded with the strongest wish of the prisoners themselves and their families.

CHAPTER 6

'It wasn't as I had expected'

'All hands are quietly excited about tomorrow — arrival in Sydney', Lieutenant Sanderson had written, and then had wondered, 'or are we!?' There was, indeed, ambivalence among those whom the ships and the planes were now bringing home; there was ambivalence, anxiety and apprehension among those who were waiting at home. Starved of news for so long and alarmed by reports — however fleeting — of the dreadful conditions in the prison camps, relatives at home simply did not know what to expect.

We now know that the Japanese captors instigated and tolerated a regime of such barbarity and brutality that it is difficult to comprehend. In thinking about the problems of return from captivity we need to remind ourselves of just how much these men had, in fact, suffered. We will not understand the difficulties they encountered in civilian life if we do not face up to the tragedies they suffered in the camps. Each man's story is different, but there is a common thread of vile inhumanity in each recounting of the years of imprisonment.

Sitting in a quiet and elegant Canberra home with Lloyd Ellerman and his wife, joint survivors of the post-imprisonment years, I am offered coffee and home-made cake. Lloyd, a successful banker in later years, tells of his hard and dangerous work in the shipyards of Kobe, and later of working as a coal-miner, a job he detested. He tells too of brutality. For no good reason on one occasion, he tells me, he and five other Australians were picked out by their guards and ordered to lay into one another. It was to be entertainment for the guards, we suppose, as together we try to understand their motivation. Each of the Australians was reluctant to go in too hard on his mate, Lloyd says, so a guard intervened to show how it should be done. He knocked

Lloyd to the ground with a blow that might have broken his jaw and
then indicated that that was the way they should fight. And so the
prisoners started again. A tiny incident, no doubt, but exquisitely
cruel, attacking the very mateship that sustained these starved and
exhausted men. And this was repeated, in endless inhuman variety, in
camps throughout Asia and Japan.[1]

John Curtin and his ministers had begun to learn something about
these atrocities long before there was any prospect of the prisoners'
recovery or war's end. And the government struggled to know what
to do with the information. Some argued that full publicity of the
conditions of the camps and the brutality of the treatment would
bring about an improvement from an enemy increasingly likely to
lose the war and which must recognise that it would soon be brought
to account for its actions. Others, the British government included,
argued that 'further official statements regarding Japanese atrocities
against prisoners of war would, at the present juncture, merely cause
distress to relatives without achieving any compensating benefit to
the prisoners themselves'.[2]

The Americans had a different view, at least in early 1944, and when
they did release some of the atrocity stories, John Curtin tried to put
the American reports in context: 'The constant aim of the Government has been to seek to reduce the period of [the prisoners'] ordeal,
and it is hoped that the increasing weight of military assaults will
bring to the Japanese military leaders a realisation of their account-
ability and an amelioration of the lot of the prisoners of war.' If we
win the war, he was saying, these atrocities will stop; if we look like
winning the war they will stop too; Australians, he counselled, should
re-dedicate themselves to the war effort.[3]

In any case there was some concern within the military forces that
these stories of atrocities were a bit far-fetched, or, if true, were merely
a part of what war meant. Colonel Wilson writing to the Secretary
of the Department of Defence in November 1944 described a
statement about atrocities as 'a horror statement with a highly
sensational trend'. 'The reference to bamboo huts', he continued, 'and
beds improvised from bamboo poles, whilst no doubt statements of
facts, could be said of our own camps in New Guinea.' The horrible
account of the sinking of the *Royko Maru* and the subsequent

sufferings of the prisoners in the sea for four days, in Colonel Wilson's view, 'is such as could no doubt be told in regard to the crew of any torpedoed merchant vessel with added privations in the case of cold water'.[4] Stories of atrocities were bad for morale, some believed; they unsettled the relatives of prisoners, others argued; and some in the military wanted to minimise any discussion of the sufferings of prisoners, as if they were merely a hazard of war.

For the sake of the relatives, and for the sake of the men still fighting, there were very good reasons to keep news of the atrocities quiet. But the government intended to punish the perpetrators after the war ended, and in June 1943 had appointed a Queensland Supreme Court judge, Sir William Webb, to report on Japanese atrocities and breaches of the rules of warfare. Webb's initial report, presented to the government on 15 March 1944, showed that there was a need for an ongoing watching brief and Webb continued to compile what evidence he could in the expectation that it would be made available to the war crimes trials after the war. Very little of what Webb discovered would be made known to the public while the fighting continued, but as the Chief of the General Staff had written in May 1944, 'at the appropriate time publicity should be given to the atrocities committed by the Japanese'.[5]

The government tabled a summary of Sir William Webb's findings in the House of Representatives on 12 September 1945, in response, possibly, to the increasing frequency of reports of atrocities that began appearing in Australian newspapers in late August and early September. With the war over, the Government now had a different problem; it needed to show that it had known of the atrocities, that ministers had imposed censorship for good reasons, and that they would now assist in the fullest measure in the prosecution of war criminals. Indeed, they could claim correctly, Webb had already gathered much of the evidence. Ministers might not have been able to do much then, the reasoning ran, but at least they had been keeping an account that would now be used to bring the criminals to court. But as Attorney-General H.V. Evatt noted, '[The Webb] report relates only to part of the whole field of Japanese terrorism and criminality'. Webb had begun his work too late to investigate some of the most gruesome episodes of Japanese brutality.[6]

In September 1945 the story of the treatment of the Australian nurses aboard the *Vyner Brooke* focused Australian attention, more than anything else, on the criminality and brutality of the Japanese. The ship had left Singapore Harbour on 12 February 1942 and included among its passengers 64 Australian nurses from the 2/13th Australian General Hospital. The *Vyner Brooke* was bombed and sunk off Banka Island near the east coast of Sumatra on 14 February; two of the nurses were killed during the bombing, another nine must have died at sea; the remaining 53 reached land at various points around the island. Near Muntok, on the north coast of Banka Island, 22 women surrendered to the Japanese, along with a party of men. The Japanese marched the men around a small headland, and the women were horrified to see the soldiers returning alone, wiping their bayonets clean of blood and reloading their rifles. The soldiers then ordered the nurses to walk into the sea. When they were knee-deep, holding up two of their number who were badly wounded, the Japanese turned a machine-gun on them, killing all but one, Sister Vivian Bullwinkel. Badly injured, she regained consciousness to hear the murderers running up the beach, laughing over the massacre. Her survival meant that this story would be known. The subsequent treatment of the surviving nurses, who made landfall at other parts of Banka Island, would drive the rescuing doctor, Harry Windsor, to rage and recommendations of revenge. Likewise, the story of the preceding massacre outraged millions of Australians in the first days of peace.[7]

'The cold-blooded murder of [the] Australian nurses … represents a depth of sub-human brutality which cannot but arouse fresh anger and abhorrence beyond the power of words to express', the *Age* editor wrote. 'We do not know yet the full record of Japanese bestiality in this war', he continued, '[but] gradually the record of Japanese atrocities is being pieced together, with successive revelations of massacres, torturing and unspeakable humiliations of Australian and other victims.'[8]

Journalists, some of them former prisoners and others who were quick to get to the camps, were providing this evidence. Rohan Rivett, caught at Singapore and forced to work on the Railway, wrote that he 'had been sitting on what I felt was a tremendous story for three years and naturally was not anxious to be kept tied up in military red tape while scores of Allied correspondents poured in and picked up the story'. Rivett was ambitious: 'Having been "in the bag" while dozens of other war correspondents were winning fame and fortune in many theatres, I had the journalist's craving to get more story out before it was scooped.' Like many former prisoners now facing the need to restart their lives, Rivett feared that professionally he was either forgotten or well behind his colleagues. He started to tell the story as soon as he possibly could, and was syndicated to newspapers in every Australian capital city. In 1946 he published the 'first complete chronicle' of Australian captivity, *Behind Bamboo*.[9]

Private Maurie Ferry, aged 24 on release and described as 'a former Sydney newspaperman', talked of the Railway to the Sydney *Daily Telegraph*, which headlined his story 'AIF Men Beaten with Bamboo. Repeated Floggings Caused Many Deaths'. Described as 'looking fit and well again' and having put on a stone and a half in six weeks, Ferry spoke of his experiences as 'an unforgettable nightmare'. The *Daily Telegraph* also reported the indiscriminate execution of Australian and British prisoners and noted that 'all the prisoners were either permanently or temporarily unfit'. The *Sydney Morning Herald* correspondent Guy Harriott, described by the *Herald*'s historian as one of its best war correspondents, interviewed returning prisoners on their ships at Darwin. He wrote of the deaths at Tavoy of eight Australians from the 4th Anti-Tank Regiment who had been tied to stakes and shot. Harriott's informant said that he had buried the men in graves freshly dug and that 'the bodies were still warm' as he placed them in the graves. Other men told Harriott 'tales of dreadful individual brutality'.[10]

George Johnston, of the Melbourne *Argus*, was one of the few Australian war correspondents to win the type of fame normally reserved for the leading American correspondents. He already had five books behind him, and in front of him was the Australian classic *My Brother Jack*. The *Argus* gave Johnston as much space as he needed to tell the story of the prisoners he met in Manila and of the war criminals they named for him. 'Captain Sibata', for example, 'was the inventor of a whole series of terrible tortures, which brought about many deaths and caused men who did not die to be maimed for life or rendered insane … [Sibata] himself lashed a British officer and a British padre so shockingly that both men are now incurably insane.' In this one article Johnston proceeds to name and describe the actions of another seven Japanese war criminals.[11]

News from the camps, once so scarce and so treasured, now came very fast and in such quantity that some editions of the major Australian newspapers were literally swamped with stories from the prison camps. On the front page of the *Argus* George Johnston told of the brutality of the guards, of the 'pathetic stories' of the Australians, of brutal floggings and starvation, of 'rat and disease ridden hovels', of 'meagre food allowances'. Athole Stewart, also in the *Argus*, wrote of 'wizened, prematurely old men suffering from malnutrition and tropical diseases … of heart-breaking work by [men] who gave their life-blood to build the central Sumatra railway'. The men he saw were 'hardly better than skeletons covered with skin. They were listless and motion-less the only movement being their eyes'.[12]

It was nearly impossible to find the words to describe the reality of what the prisoners had endured. 'Sub-human' and 'brutal' tend to lose their edge when repeated constantly and repetition dulled the senses. There were some stories that could not be told; as the *Daily Telegraph* reported, 'Allied authorities in Singapore consider that many horror stories are too obscene for publication'. But the journalists tried: 'Many of you in Australia have recently seen pictures of the horror of Belsen camp. On Saturday I saw those pictures repeated in the flesh.' An air force nursing sister spoke of 'two Australians lying on stretchers [who] croaked and whispered their tale of horror to me … on their skeleton frames were the scars of cruel beatings'.[13]

Such reports stirred up the editorial writers. 'Mr Rivett does not write from hearsay', the *Argus* remarked, 'he learned [the Japanese] devilry at first hand. The brutality, arrogance and dishonesty … an expression of the innate savagery of a race of sub-human brutes.' 'There can be no thought', the *Argus* concluded, 'of treating the Nipponese race as an honourable defeated foe.' 'Throughout the war', another *Argus* editorial remembered, '[we] have stressed the need for realism … realism demands that the Japanese be treated as the inhuman, semi-barbaric creatures that they are.'[14]

'Enough', cried letter-writers to the *Daily Telegraph*. 'What good purpose is served by publishing stories of Jap atrocities?' a plaintive father asked. His son was a prisoner of war at Amboina and, although there had been no letter from him since he had become a prisoner, the parents and their daughter-in-law, the McEvoys of Marrickville and Stanmore, had been writing regularly. 'You can imagine the feelings of his mother and wife when they read these reports', Mr McEvoy continued. They were still waiting for news, for any indication that their special soldier was alive and safe, yet all that they could read about were accounts of executions, beatings and brutality. For Hilda and Bert McEvoy and their son's wife, Lilian, the news when it came was dreadful. Corporal Herbert Stanislaus McEvoy, aged 32, of the 2/12th Field Ambulance had been murdered at Laha on Ambon on 20 February 1942. For all those years this family had been living with a false hope that only the coming of peace could expose.

'Bring the boys home first', Mr McEvoy had written hopefully on 11 September 1945, before he had known of his son's death, 'then, if the stories [of the atrocities] are true, be just as diligent in seeing that the malefactors are punished'. The newspaper to which he had written took not the slightest notice of this sensible plea. Two days later the *Daily Telegraph* carried the story 'Japanese Brutality in Amboina Camp', telling that 17 Australian soldiers had been executed there, that the guards had tortured other prisoners, beating them with steel wire and pushing lighted cigarettes into their ears and noses. 'Members of our family are nearly crazy with grief and rage', Mrs J. Kinch of Rushcutters Bay reported. 'The Japanese must be humiliated before our blood will cool … we must refuse to trade with them for a thousand years.'[15]

'For two months', wrote Charles Bean, the First World War official correspondent, 'the Press has been full of the details of atrocities so shocking and continuous that many readers have opened their newspapers with dread and then thrown them away in horror.' Perhaps Bean, a gentle man, was describing his own reaction. But he was at Pozieres in 1916 and had seen what the massed artillery had done: limbs, body parts shattered or scattered randomly; men's minds deranged. Bean had talked to the survivors of the fighting at Lone Pine and had been told that the trenches had become so crowded with the bodies of the dead that men had to stand on the dead bodies, even on the faces of their mates, to keep on fighting. Was war less vile, less horrifying when at least there was the chance of men fighting back, when the brutality was not directed as if personally to individuals? Did Charles Bean revolt, finally, when the punishments and starvations were so meaningless, so unnecessary? When the deaths were not to win some contested ground, however minuscule, but merely for the pleasure of watching caged men die.[16]

Bean argued that Australians should not brand the Japanese as sub-human, for that was to say that the problem of the Japanese was so hopeless that there could be no cure. Bean wanted Australians to face up to the atrocities openly — there had been atrocities throughout history, 'even perhaps one or two black events in the Australian bush'. Only in openly confronting the atrocities would Australians derive the 'will and power of planning to prevent them'. There was purpose, therefore, in publishing these stories, Bean believed; they would commit Australians to creating a better world and commit them to assisting Japan to turn away from its militaristic culture that was such a part of its history to a better understanding of its place in the world.

Few Australians can have missed the stories of the terrible things done to the prisoners of war, and everyone, it seemed, had an opinion about whether these things should be published. A churchman would speak of the 'mental anguish' the stories caused; a government minister would say that all Australians were 'horrified at the terrible news'. In the *Bulletin* Malcolm Ellis, a journalist with strong Army connections, condemned the money motives of those who published the stories of atrocities and brutality and recounted how the news affected some of the relatives of prisoners: 'the collapse of an old man whose son is in some south-east Asian prison camp; the fainting of a girl-wife who hours after was still hysterical; the breakdown of a poor soul who sobbed her heart out on a morning tram with women passengers trying to comfort her'. 'One anguished mother', he wrote, 'for two or three days could not pick up a paper without seeing a picture of a blind-folded Australian being executed.' The stories that were coming from Sandakan, Ellis wrote, 'doubtless struck the heart of every relative of a prisoner in Borneo with a chill of fear and horror'.[17]

So even while they waited for definite news, a time described as being worse than the war itself, the families and friends of the prisoners had to cope with new fears and anxieties. From the newspaper reports, which none could avoid except by flinging the paper away in horror, they would now know that the prisoners had suffered starvation and malnutrition. They would know, too, that the prisoners had been forced to work in hard and demeaning jobs and in terrible conditions. They would now know that their own loved one had suffered individual and personal brutality: beatings, possibly torture, or perhaps even worse — obscenities that could not even be published or spoken about. Perhaps, they hoped, it might have happened to the other fellow, perhaps it was possible that my son had been spared the worst excesses. They would see it in their men's bodies though, they feared, on first encounter, and in their eyes, and they would know then that there were things that could not ever be spoken of. They would need to be brave, they told themselves, and not let on that they suspected what might have happened. It would be wrong, they reasoned, to ask too many questions, to pry. They would let their boy work it out in his own time. But it would be tough, this first meeting, this searching the soul of a boy they had known so well but who now knew things that they could never know. It would be tough, but it was his homecoming to be celebrated and they must be brave and show him that life would go on.

The first prisoners of war of the Japanese to arrive in Australia came by flying boat to the Rose Bay Base in Sydney, on Sunday 14 September 1945, almost exactly a month after the war had ended. They had beaten most of their fellow prisoners home by more than a month. These returning men were the fittest of the recovered prisoners, all 132 of them, and they needed to be fit to withstand the rigours of a long flight. They came to the flying base in a flight of eight Catalinas, the ubiquitous, twin-engined aircraft beloved of pilots, uncomplicated to operate, simple to maintain, dependable. What a dramatic sight that must have been and with what keen anticipation the watchers would have been scanning the skies and straining their ears for the first indication that the flight was soon to arrive. There were 50 000 people packed into the area near the flying base. Along the driveway to the wharf the crowd stood 12 deep.

'Thousands more', the *Daily Telegraph* reported, 'crowded the adjoining park and surrounding hills and lined the water's edge. Many families brought their lunches.' It was a long wait; no one could be certain when, precisely, they would arrive. As these men of the Eighth Division stepped from their aircraft, 'no human noise ever surged over the harbour like that which swept out from the shore to greet the first men ... freed at last from the long captivity as they came home ... rousing cheers and coo-ees went up, car horns were tooted and a spontaneous roar of welcome greeted the men as they stepped ashore.' But this is as we would expect it. There are no surprises here in this warm and generous welcome.[18]

Many of the soldiers looked 'pinched and travel weary' to one journalist or 'not very demonstrative' to another. 'One man stood in his launch and looked on his native land, tears pouring down his cheeks. Another sat down and stood up and sat down again.' They did not wave or look about searching the faces of the crowd for relatives because they had been told that their relatives would be waiting to meet them at Concord Repatriation Hospital, for greater privacy. Each man focused on his own thoughts. Perhaps the returning men were embarrassed and surprised by the reception or they may have been overawed by the size of the crowd and its noise. They looked uncomfortable and ill-prepared for the welcome and hurried to the buses that would take them to their families.[19]

Most journalists scampered for their cars to follow the buses from Rose Bay to Concord where the men would be finally assessed before being sent off with their families. One wiser journalist, writing for the *Bulletin*, remained and recorded a different scene from the one the recovered prisoners had found:

> They were gone in a minute. What followed seemed as touching as themselves. The composure of group after group along the footpath seemed to collapse. The writer has seen many poignant and dreadful scenes around the world but he cannot remember any which moved him more than the spectacle of these silent people, standing on the edge of a Sydney pavement in the dusk, their faces crumpled, their hands grasping bags, hat, little children as their tears fell unashamedly.

They had been holding themselves together for the sake of the returning men, but they had worried about them for so long and had feared for them that their emotions broke through at the sight of these gaunt and subdued Australians. They now knew something of what these men had endured although they could not speak of it to them. They wept for them.

These first men home made a triumphal procession from Rose Bay to Concord; they could have no doubt of the warmth of the people's welcome and the depth of their interest and sympathy. Martin Place in the city was packed with well-wishers as the Eighth Division men drove by. At Leichhardt a shopkeeper passed in packets of sweets and cigarettes to the men, saying that his son was a prisoner too whom he hoped to see home soon. A young woman, evading police who were trying to keep some order, jumped on one of the lumbering buses, and moving through it embraced each of the former prisoners in turn.[20]

It was the same in Melbourne when the first arriving Victorians reached that city on 19 September 1945. There were 119 'lean, wan-faced men' who arrived by train at Spencer Street station to face a crowd at the station in places 10 and 20 people deep. Driven through the city in cars, not buses, to an Army depot, the soldiers gazed in amazement at the thousands of people who lined the streets: 'Roar after roar of cheering broke out.' An *Argus* journalist, Crayton Burns, travelled with the soldiers from Albury to Melbourne and the men admitted that they enjoyed the crowds and the cheering all the way along the line, 'not of any love of applause for its own sake — they were past that — but because here was evidence that Australia understood the inevitability of the surrender at Singapore'. It was still there then, that nagging fear that perhaps the people would dismiss them as men who had betrayed the Anzac legend. Burns found that they did not talk readily about their sufferings; 'there was no need, for it was apparent in their faces', even though 'these men are among the fittest and youngest of the survivors'.[21]

There is an intimacy and a privacy surrounding these first moments of reunion that writer and reader should want to respect. The Services attempted to do so by limiting the number of relatives who could be present at the first reunion and by ensuring that the reunions were not held under the full glare of publicity and public curiosity. One woman imagined that she would greet her returning fiancé 'all alone'. She played out the moment in her mind many times: 'I pictured he would get off a train and walk towards me, and I would hurry to him'. The reality was utterly different: 'Hundreds of soldiers were unloaded from buses at the Showgrounds in Flemington and we all milled about in confusion till we bumped into the one we were seeking.' Many other spoke of frantically searching for their loved ones, desperation threatening to cloud the long-anticipated joy.[22]

Reunions would best be held, if we recall Brigadier Lloyd's view, in the privacy of people's own homes. As this was not practical, the Army, in April 1945, devised proceedings that were generally adhered to when the prisoners began returning in October. The Army plan provided for a band to be playing on the wharf while the ship was berthing and 'until the returnees leave the wharf'. The band was then to proceed to the Army depot at which the returnees would be processed, 'where it plays again throughout the proceedings'. The ex-prisoners of war, once disembarked, were to be escorted to waiting buses or cars for transport to the Army depot; they were to be given cigarettes and a card of welcome from representatives of the Australian Prisoners of War Relatives Association. Relatives, who had been advised a few days before of the likely time of the arrival at the depot, were expected to be on hand to welcome the former prisoners there: 'A period of half an hour is made available for the personal welcome.' A suitable hall was set aside for this part of the proceedings and members of the Australian Red Cross Society were on hand to provide refreshments, cigarettes and so on. The Army noted that the Red Cross made 'excellent efforts in this regard ... the atmosphere created ... is one of great warmth and friendliness'. At some stage a message of welcome from His Royal Highness the Governor-General was to be read out and then returnees would be given a medical examination which might take up to an hour. If certified fit for leave, the soldier would receive some pay, items of clothing if necessary and leave passes and would then be free to go. It was all rather bureaucratic in the planning.[23]

That, then, was the Army plan, but of course the reality was different. The hospital ship *Oranje* reached Melbourne on 30 September on its journey from Singapore via Brisbane and Sydney. A large crowd gathered at Princes Pier to welcome the soldiers in defiance of instruction. There were 50 000 people at the wharf and along the road to the city. It was a Sunday, and people were happy to wait up to three hours for the merest glimpse of their heroes. The police said they had never seen anything like it before. A young wife had waited patiently for several hours for her lieutenant husband. 'I shan't cry, I shall greet him with a laugh', she had said. 'But when her husband walked towards her, limping, she sobbed and nearly fell.'[24]

At some stage an official had opened an iron gate at the head of the pier to let out an Army car and the crowd rushed forward — 'about 1000 cheering screaming people'. They swept the guards aside and 'raced madly across the wharf to the long line of RACV cars … in a second cars disappeared beneath a tidal wave of emotional humanity'. It was chaos as 'sprigs of wattle, flags, kisses, hugs and handshakes were distributed indiscriminately'. Perhaps the planners might have foreseen the public interest.[25]

Melbourne eventually abandoned the cars for buses, which meant that the public could actually see the men as they were driven to the depot and this increased the crowds on the streets, even though, as the days went on, the arrival of returning prisoners was no longer a novelty. The Army chose the least frequented route for the drive from Port Melbourne to Royal Park or the Showgrounds, avoiding 'main city thoroughfares'. 'It was considered that returning personnel would be in a marked state of nervous excitement in anticipation of their imminent reunion … anything in the nature of a public parade or public welcome is irksome to them', the Army assured the Relatives Association. Depite the difficulties, the returning prisoners still aroused great public interest and excitement. Their sufferings had been so universally accepted by the public that the clamorous welcomes seemed, in some part, to be a kind of reparation, a way of saying sorry. In mid-October, as one of the convoys of buses made its way through Melbourne, crowds threw 'confetti, flowers, fruit, beer, chocolates and money' at the men, 'eager to give the boys a royal welcome'.[26]

It was the same in the other cities around Australia. The nurses from the *Vyner Brooke* made Australian landfall in Western Australia and spent some days recuperating at an Army hospital in Perth. The

matron, Sister Eileen Joubert, appealed over the local radio for flowers
to brighten up the wards: 'The response was overwhelming. The large
forecourt of the military hospital was covered in blooms, some of
them brought hundreds of kilometres, others carried locally in
wheelbarrows.' Everyone wanted to do something to make the nurses
feel welcome.[27]

On board the British aircraft carrier *Speaker*, the men 'debated
endlessly how we would be received in Australia'. They remembered
what they had heard on the secret radios in Changi of 'the harsh and
bitter reception given to General Gordon Bennett in 1942', and they
reflected that his only crime had been to escape, whereas 'our far
graver sin was that we had actually directly helped the enemy for
three and a half years'. But the warmth of the public welcome, 'the
tumultous, emotional welcome … swept away all our doubts and
fears … It was more, far more, than we had ever dreamt of'.[28]

Newspapers printed dozens of personal stories, and reporters kept
a lookout for returning soldiers whom readers would recognise, such
as the Australian wicket-keeper Ben Barnett, who was welcomed by
Victorian Cricket Association players and officials. Barnett had re-
placed Bert Oldfield as the test keeper in 1938, and his failure to
stump Len Hutton on 40 at the Oval is regarded still as one of cricket's
most costly misses, as the England batsman went on to make 364. 'I
will play cricket again', Ben Barnett told the reporters, claiming to
feel '100%', 'but what I want to do right now is to get to know my
small son. He was five months when I left in July 1941, now he is a
young man.' Barnett was selected for the Victorian team within a few
months of his return, but he played only one more season in Australia
before settling in Britain.[29]

There were some stories that the newspapers would not tell,
however; stories of men who came home to betrayal or abandonment
from wives or girlfriends who, hearing no news for so long, had
assumed that their man must have died. 'It was a very relaxing trip to
Perth', wrote Ron Winning of the voyage on *Circassia*, 'weather good,
and the knowledge that we would soon be home was wonderful. We
reached Perth and were able to phone our families. After a day in
Perth we sailed again. However, there was a tragedy. One of the men
phoned home and was told his wife had formed a liaison with another

man. After we sailed he slipped over the side. He wasn't missed for a while. The ship hoved too but the search was hopeless. After all he had been through.'[30]

For every man singled out for attention by the newspapers, thousands of others simply went home with their families and their stories are lost to us. But a few have described what it was like. Take Les Read, from the 2/19th Battalion. Les and his father, who had fought in the First World War, had enlisted together from Wagga Wagga, but whereas the father went to a training battalion, the son went to Singapore and then to Thailand where he worked on the Railway. Les was later deeply ashamed of his behaviour on the day of his homecoming and has blotted out of his mind much of what happened.

> I cannot recall any details of us entering the heads or Sydney Harbour nor actually disembarking. We were allocated to numbered or lettered double-decker buses … [at Ingleburn] I disembarked and then I saw my mother, my father and three sisters. I cannot recall what transpired I think I was just overwhelmed. I think we went into the YMCA hall for a cup of tea. I cannot recall details of what happened next. It just seemed that all which had gone before me over the last five years had suddenly evaporated … I seemed to have a great feeling of insecurity and just wanted to be alone … I don't know what I said to mum and dad but I made some excuse that I had to report for leave passes etc and that I would come to Parramatta tomorrow ready for the trip home to Wagga.[31]

Amazed and no doubt extremely disappointed that their son and brother would not come with them when all around them happy parties were setting off for their homes, Les's family left the camp. Les himself wandered around the camp aimlessly, the Army appearing quite indifferent to his existence.

> Somehow or other I found my way to a railway station and on to Parramatta … My mother, father, sisters and friends were just washing up after the evening meal. I only remember them saying that they hoped there was something left for me. It was then that I realised that they had all gone to a great deal of trouble in preparing a welcome home dinner with decorations etc. I think I just felt numb … These thoughts have bugged me for years and more so since my mother's death having since

learnt from her few belongings and little notes, the anguish she must
have gone through alone [while he was a prisoner].

Les Read's younger sister Rosemary has also described what
happened, from the perspective of those who had been waiting at
home for Les's return. Although she was only five years of age when
her father and brother enlisted, Rosemary saw the daily cost of the
war to her mother, ground down by her worry for her son. She wrote:

> The fall of Singapore and Les's capture was a devastating blow — Mum
> baked for Les, with lots of T.L.C., fruit cakes and Anzac biscuits which
> were packed into tins and wrapped in hessian — I can remember helping
> to sew them with big curved bag needles — Once Mum included a little
> figure of Donald Duck to bring a smile to Les and his fellow captives'
> faces. Les told us years later that the Japs got it and fought over Donald
> Duck! I doubt if the boys ever got the benefit of the parcels.
>
> Mum prayed a lot for Les's safe return. She had adopted a saying …
> 'This too will pass'. Mum would tell Les in her prayers 'Hang on for this
> too will pass' … When it was time to go to Sydney for Les's return there
> was great excitement and lots of joyful tears — Mum was beside herself!

Rosemary remembers that she was left at Parramatta while the rest
of the family went off to Ingleburn to meet up with Les for the first
time, and she recalls her disappointment that her brother was not with
them when the family returned, dispirited, to the Parramatta house.
She concluded:

> Some time after we had arrived home in Wagga, Les was standing on our
> front lawn looking towards the street — As I approached from behind
> he swung around and I thought he was going to throttle me! He said
> don't you EVER sneak up behind me again or I might harm you. He
> then gave me a hug. This jolted me. I realized the fearful life he had
> experienced.[32]

There is something in Les Read's honest account of his homecoming that touches an issue that hardly any of those I talked to could
comfortably discuss. It is an issue that was important to both former
prisoners and their families and yet for lack of evidence cannot be
studied closely. But it is present, understated, in the memories of a
daughter and her father, a son and his mother, a husband and a wife.
Relatives had suffered grievously during the war from the lack of

news, from the fear of death or horrible beatings befalling their loved ones, from anxiety about rehabilitation and adjustment. Their sufferings, they believed, would be recognised and understood by the returning former prisoners, who would see that they too had been grievous victims of the war; that they had been partners in the horror that war had brought them. Those on the homefront awaited the return of their prisoners eagerly but with some reserve and trepidation, as if they sensed already the inability of those returning to understand that partnership. What these people at home found the hardest to understand, therefore, was the sense of rejection that was a part of many family stories of the return of the prisoners of war. Former prisoners felt out of place at home, ill-at-ease, strangers in the midst of those whose mere existence had sustained them in the camps. They missed their mates, but it was more than that. Their families could never share their experiences, enter their minds, understand their fears and depressions, and in the hurt that this realisation brought, in many cases they pushed their families away. Those who loved them the most, and had suffered so terribly in their absence, had now to deal with a sense of rejection, which may have been the greatest suffering of all. And they felt, too, that the prisoners did not understand their own suffering, making the rejection of them even harder to bear.

The misunderstandings and ambiguities multiplied. One former prisoner, returning from captivity on his troopship, made Australian landfall at Fremantle in Western Australia. He was a Tuncurry man from northern New South Wales and knew no one in the West. With a couple of mates, he decided to catch the train into Perth — there were only a few hours of leave granted — and maybe have a beer or two on Australian soil for the first time in more than three and a half years. On the train into Perth a young woman inquired whether the three were indeed returning prisoners of war; the newspapers had been full of the story of their arrival. She then invited them to her home; her parents, she said, would be honoured to look after men who had suffered so much. The prospect of a brief glimpse of Australian family life delighted the men and soon there was beer in a welcoming house, good food, neighbours, yarns, laughter and much contentment.

The next port of call was Melbourne, where the former prisoner again believed that he knew no one. But from the wharf he heard his name being called and to his astonishment he saw his sister. Quickly granted leave, he soon learned that she had married and now lived with her husband in Melbourne. The world, as all the returning prisoners quickly had to accept, had not stood still during their years of captivity. The returning soldier's sister had arranged lunch at a Melbourne hotel to celebrate the homecoming; they had known that he was on his way home and they had made their plans. Relaxing with his sister, her husband and a few of their friends, the former prisoner asked the small group what they had thought when they had heard that Australia's 8th Division had been captured at Singapore. 'We were ashamed', one of the group replied. 'We thought you chaps had let us down.'[33]

The returning soldier was stunned and deeply hurt. 'My stomach knotted up. I lost my desire for food … I withdrew into myself … I was shattered … I asked myself the question, does everyone think the same way?' He found it hard, in the future, ever to admit that he had been a prisoner of war. It is a terrible story, to be sure, but is it true? Had this man merely heard what he had been expecting to hear? Had someone with an inelegant and clumsy reply fed on his own fears for his homecoming? The Japanese captors had constantly told the prisoners that they were disgraced in the eyes of their own people. The Japanese themselves had treated the prisoners as beneath contempt for the fact of them being captives. The prisoners had heard a little of the mixed reception, to put it at its mildest, accorded their commander, Lieutenant-General Gordon Bennett, on his flight from Singapore and return to Australia. Reports from the reception teams — the very first Australians to meet the prisoners after liberation — tell us that the first and most urgent of the questions the recovered prisoners asked was how they would be received in Australia. The prisoners worried that they may have let Australia down, or be thought to have let Australia down. Whenever the conversation of groups of prisoners was overheard as they came closer to Australia, one of the most earnest topics of conversation was the nature of the reception they would experience. There is no doubt that the returning prisoner who told me this story has believed ever since that day in the Melbourne hotel that Australians were ashamed of the Eighth Division and its failures. It must be asked, though, whether anybody could really have been as insensitive as to tell this man that he was a failure or something of a pariah. The story needs careful interpretation and context if we are not simply to gasp at the pretty scene in Perth and the tragedy in Melbourne. Can we ever know the truth of it?

Neither the former prisoners nor their families and friends at home were well-prepared for the homecoming, but with time, and sensitivity on both sides, people would fit back into the groove of life; they had to. Parents and wives had been warned not to ask too many questions. One man, who had managed to keep a diary account of his life as a prisoner, handed over his writings to his sister. 'It's all in there', he said, 'just don't ever ask me about it.' Les Read's sister wondered whether silence was the best policy. 'Les has never spoken much of his ordeal', she wrote, 'and none of the family has forced the issue for fear of opening old wounds. Perhaps that was a mistake.' Even after so many years people are still wondering what was the right thing to do.[34]

Pretending that all was well was perhaps a normal human reaction, 'not forcing the issue', and remarkably, with the prisoners of war now in their readers' homes, the newspapers dropped the prominence given to the atrocity stories and began what seemed to amount to a campaign to convince readers that these men were alright. This campaign surely stretched credulity given the horror stories that had preceded it. The new approach was no more absurd than in a report from Guy Harriott as he sailed the last leg of a voyage home on the *Highland Chieftain* with some of the returning prisoners. Harriott had already written of the atrocities and brutal treatment prisoners had suffered. Now he had a different story to tell, and his assessment was likely to have been believed by Harriott's *Herald* readers as he had lived with and reported on Australian troops since 1940, first in the desert war, then in Greece and later in the Pacific.

The liberated prisoners as Harriott found them were 'indistinguishable from any other contingent of Australian soldiers'. 'That is the way they want it to be', he continued, 'they don't want anyone's pity. These men are not broken, even battered, in body or spirit. Their scars have healed fast.' Harriot found the former prisoners cheerful but perhaps leaner, quieter, more thoughtful than other Australian men of their age. He found that they were bitterly disappointed that their war had been of such short duration and that they 'savagely resented the Malayan surrender'. There was nothing wrong with them, he advised his readers, that a month's 'loaf on the beaches won't cure' and he found that even the 'amps'— amputees — were cheerful, 'as nimble on one leg as many men are on two'. Harriott had heard the advice to relatives and friends that they should humour the returning prisoners, 'agree with everything they say, discourage any conversation which will recall what they went through in captivity'. This, in Guy Harriott's view, was 'dangerous rubbish'. The prisoners were, he concluded, 'perfectly normal'. A case of wishful thinking? Or what the recovered prisoners themselves wanted him to write?[35]

Encouraging the idea that these young Australians were 'perfectly normal', the newspapers began to publish 'happy snaps' from the camps where the men were waiting to come home. 'All the prisoners looked remarkably fit' became a constant theme in the newspaper accounts. 'Why you're not bald at all', the *Daily Telegraph* quoted a young woman joking with her fiancé. 'I was certain you'd have no hair and no teeth.' There were pictures of men eating well in Singapore, pictures that showed that they really were quite fit and healthy. Star Fitzroy footballer 'Chicken' Smallhorn, who was in such a dreadful condition at Changi, was pictured cooking eggs and stew and was reported looking forward to more football. But could a man whose weight had reportedly fallen to little more than 5 stone ever seriously consider playing football again? He did not, although he would enjoy a long career as a football commentator on radio and television. There were now many reports of men putting on weight, and despite the tragic stories that the newspapers did still print there was greater interest in finding a positive side to the bad news: 'Despite the harrowing nature of the story', the *Age* commented on the story told by Lieutenant Colonel J. M. Williams (see Chapter 1), 'some comfort may be drawn from [the story-teller's] condition ... yesterday he looked in good condition' and he did say that 'only those blessed with a sense of humour could come through what we went through'. This from the man who had been brutalised in interrogation to the point of death.[36]

The Australian commander at Changi, Lieutenant Colonel 'Black Jack' Galleghan, broadcasting from Singapore before the first men returned home, emphasised the strength of their fighting spirit: 'I want to say to the parents and loved ones of the troops I have commanded that they have men of whom they may be justly proud. The men have borne hardship and oppression with a spirit that could never be broken. It is the spirit of their fathers of Anzac. With it we shall build a great Australia of the future.'[37]

Letters from the camps had tended to reinforce this message: 'I am in tip-top health and condition', a father wrote to his daughter in September 1945, but even so he anticipated some of the difficulties they would both experience when he returned home. 'You are wondering what I'm like and I'm trying to build a mental picture of the people in my little family. Well this is sure, if I find you as fit and as full of pep for the future as I am myself, life should be very rosy at our place.' 'What a lot we have to find out about each other', he admitted in his next letter. 'I am dying to know what you and the little ones look like and what your hobbies are and your likes and dislikes.'

This girl, Nola, was thirteen years of age when her father came home and she remembers all the details with a freshness and clarity which highlights how important these days were for her. She would often come across her mother in tears during the years of captivity. 'Mum might have heard some news on the radio to start her off' and she missed her husband dreadfully. So too did Nola miss her father. When the news of peace came, Nola was at school and she remembers throwing streamers from the bus on her way home in her joy at what the news meant for her family. She remembers, too, how excited her mother was when she got home; and her little sisters were racing through the house shouting 'Daddy's coming home, Daddy's coming home'. When they heard that he was safe, and in Nola's memory this was very soon after the news of the peace, 'I don't think we stopped crying for two days'. Nola's mother went alone to Sydney to meet her husband and they were away for three days 'to get to know each other again'. Nola went to the station alone to welcome her mother and father home and might have been apprehensive at meeting the man whom, in truth, she hardly knew.

Her father was gaunt and thin, she thought, but 'didn't look too bad to my eyes ... I thought he looked alright'. He held her hand all the way home from the station and kept saying to her, 'You're beautiful, look at your beautiful skin'. His sisters got together 'and made him a party when he came back. I suppose a couple of days after. They were all fantastic cooks, my aunts. I'll never forget it. I've never seen so many sponges ... Dad was absolutely overwhelmed because all the [relatives] came to that party'. But Nola also remembers that she was 'a bit of a problem' when he got back, because she resented the loss of her position with her mother and because her father did not really know how to treat her. Her father did not believe that she needed a say in the running of things at all and 'their personalities clashed'. 'I was petrified of Father actually', she concluded. 'I was scared stiff of what he'd do if I did something wrong.' He was a stern man, much given to lectures which Nola and her sisters found 'boring'. And he never talked about the war. 'I wanted to be very close to Dad and I never was. I tried ... I wanted a piece of him and he couldn't give it to me.'

It is not hard to imagine this father of three, 37 years of age when he enlisted, dreaming of his family, forever in his thoughts, in all the years of his captivity. He would have missed them desperately and he would have cursed the fact that he would never regain all that he had lost of their growing years. 'You will know Janice and Wendy so much better than I', he had written to Nola in that first letter. 'I'll get you to put me through a quick catch-up course.' But that was too optimistic. He could find out about 'the latest news and the music, movies and school doings, books and topics of the day', as he asked that Nola be prepared to bring him up-to-date in all of these. But there could not be a 'quick catch-up course' in the lives of his children. They had lived a significant part of their lives without him and those years would remain forever lost, making this father, and possibly many others like him, somewhat remote and unknown to his children. More than a decade later this man, who had resumed his work as a teacher, would have the first of his 'nervous breakdowns': 'he was morose, he couldn't cope with work'. Possibly the seeds of the illness were planted in those first days at home when the high hopes and dreams of the prison camps clashed with the reality of lives that had grown apart.[38]

Each man and the circle of family and friends to which he would return would need to make adjustments. There might have been a better way, a more leisurely and a more structured way of assisting the accommodations that needed to be made, but in their haste to make it normal again all sides to these issues minimised the difficulties. Most would soon admit, however, that 'it wasn't as I had expected'.

CHAPTER 7

'You are not going home as prisoners'

Frederick ('Black Jack') Galleghan was the commander of the AIF in captivity in Singapore and deputy commander of all Allied prisoners in Malaya. Awarded the Distinguished Service Order for his brilliant ambush of Japanese forces at Gemas, Malaya, on 14 January 1942, and for his organisation of the withdrawal of Australian troops to Singapore, Galleghan was to achieve lasting fame at Changi. He realised that survival depended on morale and discipline, and as one soldier admitted, 'We were more frightened of BJ than of the Japanese'. 'You are not going home as prisoners', he had told his men, 'you will march down Australian streets as soldiers.' Home in October 1945, Galleghan refused to associate with prisoner of war organisations and he urged his old battalion to follow his example. 'In taking this stand', his biographer and a former prisoner wrote, 'he probably did the survivors of the 8th Division a disservice.'

Galleghan had started life as a post office messenger boy, but he had always dreamed of being a soldier. After seven years in the cadets of the 'Boy Conscription' he had enlisted in the First AIF in January 1916 and had served on the Western Front, twice wounded in action. Resentful that he had not been made an officer, Galleghan persevered in the militia after the war, gaining the promotion he sought. He had joined the Second AIF in January 1940, now 43 years of age, and was immediately appointed commanding officer of the 2/30th Battalion, 8th Division. When his men had returned to Changi from their time building the Burma–Thailand Railway, Galleghan was so moved by the toll of death and the desperate condition of the men huddled on parade in front of him that he was unable to speak and moved through their lines silently and in tears. But this was not soldierly, this captivity and its atrocities, he seemed to be saying on his return to Australia, and he wanted, above all, to be known as a soldier. There was conflict for Galleghan between being a soldier and being a prisoner; the commander was in denial.[1]

Not so Brigadier Arthur Seaforth Blackburn. Never a sturdy youth, and a solicitor by training, Blackburn nevertheless enlisted in the First AIF in October 1914, and was on Gallipoli on 25 April 1915 at the Landing. Charles Bean concluded that Blackburn and another had penetrated further inland on that first day than any other Australians, at least among those who survived. At Pozieres on 23 July 1916 Blackburn commanded a party of fifty men who destroyed an enemy strong point and captured 400 yards of trenches, in the face of fierce opposition. For this Arthur Blackburn was awarded the Victoria Cross. Severely wounded, he returned to his native Adelaide, married, resumed his professional life, and was a prominent member of the Returned Services League. He re-enlisted in 1940 and was given command of the 2/3rd Australian Machine-Gun Battalion and fought in Syria. Promoted temporary brigadier, he commanded 'Blackforce', with orders to assist the Dutch against the rapid Japanese advance through Java. Despite his reluctance, the Allies surrendered on Java after three weeks of fighting and Blackburn became a prisoner. He would be released at Mukden, Manchuria, in September 1945.[2]

Prominent again in the RSL, Blackburn became something of an advocate for the cause of former prisoners and, badly broken down in health himself, he was quick to recognise the special problems that the returning prisoners would face. Blackburn did not waste any time in pushing for the special and different treatment of returning prisoners. In fact he first spoke out about their special needs in the middle of September 1945 well before many of the prisoners had returned home.

'Nearly All Neurotic' was the *Herald* headline and for once the sub-editor had not exaggerated the story. What, in fact, Blackburn did say was very close to that. 'Nearly every man returning from the prison camps', he reported, 'is a neurosis case.' Conceding the trials and sufferings of the fighting soldier ('We know just what the fighting men went through'), Blackburn called for justice for the ex-prisoners, and demanded that something be done for them without delay; 'it must be remembered', he continued, 'that the fighting man did have his comforts, his letters from home, his mental and physical relaxation between spells of bitter fighting'. Blackburn described some of the privations the prisoners had suffered and also described what he had heard was being done for former American and British prisoners. There was nothing like this in Australia, he explained; no country chalets or trained psychologists, no special hospitals or timeless care. In Australia 'our men are sent to ordinary hospitals, to convalescent camps — not rest homes in the country — and are then subjected again to the routine of discharge depots'. Putting his case on 21 September 1945, within days of his return home, Blackburn called dramatically for prompt action: 'The nation must realise today that it has an extremely urgent problem on its hands. We have had no experience of it before and we must begin to understand it before it is too late.'[3]

Two senior Army officers, Galleghan and Blackburn, two experienced and highly decorated fighting soldiers and two totally different responses to the problems of the returning prisoners. The first response of denial asserted that the prisoner needed no special assistance; they were not prisoners at all but should see themselves as returning soldiers. The second response was a plea for understanding that would bravely confront the differences between fighting soldiers and prisoners and would assert that the prisoners needs were special, different, and of a higher priority than those of the returning soldier. This fundamental difference of opinion about the recovered prisoners would bedevil responses to them for many years yet.

There were at least two problems with treating returning prisoners with special care and consideration, as Brigadier Blackburn was suggesting. First, his recommendation ignored the esteem that fighting soldiers expected and deserved and turned a blind eye to the stigma that captivity implied. Second, as military and political leaders would discuss privately but hardly openly, the lavish treatment of former prisoners of war could influence the minds of those who would be called on to fight the next war. Governments would seek to protect themselves from the idea that it was better to sit out a war in a prison camp, secure in the expectation of a hero's welcome on return and lavish compensation, than to engage in bitter fighting. To reward the returning prisoners of war now could well impair Australia's fighting capacity later.

The Royal Australian Air Force had much earlier adopted King's Regulations and Air Council Instructions applying to the Royal Air Force, and recognised, as did their British counterparts, that flying aircraft in battle was much more a matter of individual determination and choice than was available, for example, to the infantryman being led into battle. Strategists had for long feared that men, given the option in situations of extreme danger, might choose not to fight. It had been observed in the First World War, though not much commented on by official historians, that a proportion of men simply would not leave the trenches when the whistle blew. Flying Corps pilots then were not always provided with parachutes lest they abandon their aircraft too readily.

It was the same in the Second World War. Strategists developed techniques to ensure that crews did not turn back from bombing missions with the ready excuse of a suspicion of engine failure and there was monitoring over enemy targets to ensure that crews made every endeavour to reach their targets and actually bomb them. The maintenance of morale was seen as a key ingredient in aircrew completing their assigned tasks, even in the face of enormous odds. As we have seen, Australian commanders demanded the censorship of atrocity reports in case aircrew, so worried about their prospects in a prison camp, failed to press on with their missions. In this climate of concern about individual decision-making in the face of the enemy, it is hardly surprising that King's Regulations required that 'a court of enquiry ... be convened in every case [where an officer or airman had been taken prisoner] to investigate the conduct of the individual concerned and the circumstances of his capture'.[4]

In view of the numbers of aircrew becoming prisoners, the RAF accepted that KR 1324 had become 'an impractical counsel of perfection' and it was agreed that no court of enquiry would be needed if the air officer commanding 'was satisfied that no blame attached to the individual'. The Army in Britain reached a similar conclusion, again with more than a nodding acceptance, presumably, of the impracticability of a court of enquiry for every one of the many thousands of British soldiers captured. The Air Board in Australia in 1944 accepted the British amendments to regulations and few Australian captured airmen would thereafter be called upon to explain the reasons for their captivity. It was a sensible decision; courts of enquiry on top of what was known of the sufferings of the returning prisoners would most certainly have inflamed popular opinion and would have caused great anguish to the returning ex-prisoners. Nevertheless, the original regulations and the debate over the amendments does show that the authorities felt they had to ensure that soldiers and airmen would not simply seek to avoid their duty by going over to the enemy. Treatment of the prisoners on their return home had to be arranged, the authorities believed, with at least some recognition of the future requirements for morale and for the fighting capacity of the services.

Today, knowing what had happened in the Japanese prison camps, we find it incredible that those in authority could believe that anyone would willingly put themselves in the way of such a terrible ordeal. We likewise look for the utmost generosity and liberality from the government in the treatment of returning prisoners. But we need to recognise that an understanding of these problems dawned only slowly on those responsible for the health and rehabilitation of these Australians. All too soon after their return to Australia the 'tough it out' spirit of 'Black Jack' Galleghan triumphed over the more generous and anxious approach of Arthur Blackburn. Most people today with any knowledge of what had happened would have sided with Arthur Blackburn in this debate, if they saw any need for a debate at all. But there were a whole series of issues that the government had to resolve following the release of the prisoners beyond the first impulse to bring them home as quickly as possible. At one level we would expect to find government ministers treating the prisoners with unprecedented generosity to compensate them for their sufferings, but we should recognise the danger inherent in such a policy. Government files show the extent of the concern from officials and the military about how far the generosity might extend. Officials and ministers debated, in very great detail and for some issues over several years, the amount of leave, the question of pay and back pay, issues of compensation, the nature of bravery awards to prisoners, standards of health care and support, and questions of employment. Many former prisoners criticised the outcomes of these debates as being mean-spirited and churlish, believing that their sacrifice deserved better from the nation.

Potentially the former prisoners were in an advantageous situation. They had accrued pay and leave at the same rate as others in the services, but they were unable, of course, to access their entitlements while they were prisoners of war. Each recovered prisoner, therefore, had large banks of leave and pay on which to draw. To load them up, for example, with additional special leave, as some sought, in compensation for their sufferings would exaggerate their entitlements and force comparisons with those who had been fighting and who would now enjoy far fewer entitlements. The government was in an invidious position. All Australians would want to reach out to these damaged, brutalised men and women and to do whatever was needed to ensure their speedy return to health and to normal life. And yet some sort of line needed to be drawn to prevent jealousies and embittered comparisons arising. Had the prisoners needed immediate and long-term hospitalisation, had they come home looking like Belsen survivors, perhaps the line might have been placed further along the spectrum of generosity. As it was there were many people ready to attack government parsimony and niggardliness. The issue should never have been 'What can the government get away with?' Rather it should have been 'What do these former prisoners need in all the circumstances?'. There was too little work done to find out what the prisoners really did need, while there was plenty of anecdotal evidence, within the circle of families and friends and perhaps more widely, that these men and women needed long-term and generous support.

'If it is politically expedient for prisoners to be sent back to their homes without proper preparation, sent back they will be', the *Bulletin* predicted, even though 'thousands of prisoners will not benefit by being decanted into civil life without preliminary reconditioning'. The writer continued: 'Anyone who has been in constant contact with prisoners of war has had the experience of seeing some of them turn from apparently well and normal men into nervous wrecks.' Hugh Clarke wrote of a 'sense of deflation' at being home. He wrote

of the ordeal of a family welcome-home party. There was no deceit
or turning a blind eye here. Although Hugh Clarke knew himself to
have recovered remarkably in weight and appearance since his time
in the Manila 'fattening paddock', he found that his aunts burst into
tears on seeing him again. He could not cope with that. 'I do not
know what I expected', he wrote, 'but whatever it was, it was not in
Brisbane.' Instead, Hugh Clarke 'shot through' with a mate, a former
prisoner of course, to the Warrego River and 'lived in almost monastic
solitude'. 'Week after week', he reports, 'we absorbed the calm of
endless flat plains, the stolid sheep and the cloudless star-studded night
sky.' Clarke and his mate moved on, first to Sydney and then to
Melbourne: 'As long as we were moving we were happy.' Tom Uren,
later a politician and senior Australian government minister, went to
a family homecoming party in Five Dock, Sydney, where the 'whole
of the Uren–Miller clan had gathered to welcome me home'. 'I
couldn't talk about what I'd been through: I just wanted to forget
about it and get on with life. After a few days at home I decided to
go and visit my brother Les [in camp at Mt Morgan in Queensland].'
Like Clarke, like thousands of others, Tom Uren just wanted to get
away.[5]

A former nurse, Phyllis Briggs, simply could not face being alone.
'I was so accustomed to being surrounded by hordes of people that
it was frightening to be alone — even to be in a bedroom alone …
I was afraid even to cross a road alone, to go into a shop or on a bus.
It required a lot of courage to do any of these things.' Dozens of other
former prisoners have written of similar fears.[6]

Others reported that they could not yet sleep in beds, ending up
on the floor, and that their sleep in any case was ruined by nightmares.
Lloyd Ellerman vomited, and his wife Muriel did too, most mornings
for the best part of a year, so awful were the nights. 'Are you pregnant?',
the concerned father asked this daughter, because the regular morning illness could not be disguised in that cramped, shared house. 'If I
am, Lloyd is too', Muriel laconically replied. Some former prisoners
told of being unutterably lonely. For Australian Army Nursing Sister
Jenny Greer, 'It seemed a very lonely time. So much so that we used
to try to meet the others from the camp for lunch or for drinks after
duty every day until we got used to being among civilians'. Every day.

For others simpler pleasures were enough. One man, a prisoner on Ambon, who had dreamed of doing this for years, 'went to the local corner store and bought a pound of broken biscuits'; he was just happy to eat his biscuits as he wandered the family garden 'smelling, picking and even eating the flowers'. Some encountered family tragedies, the death of a parent, the collapse of a marriage, that they had never expected in their dreams of a triumphal return that had sustained them in the camps. Devastating though these major traumas must have been, for the majority it was Hugh Clarke's sense of emptiness, 'a kind of hopeless hope', that was the most difficult aspect of readjustment. 'Everyone was established, their lives were running smoothly, and you were an intrusion. I'd say the first twelve months or so was a very difficult time.'[7]

Douglas McLaggan was hardly well when he returned to Australia in October 1945 from his hospital bed in Changi. After a few weeks at the Concord Repatriation Hospital he was placed in the care of the Red Cross, first at Gordon, Sydney, and then at Bowral. His convalescence and rehabilitation were limited compared with, say, the 'torpedoed men' or what Arthur Blackburn understood was being done in America. Even so, with the country life seemingly doing the trick, in early 1946 McLaggan was back at his old job in Martin Place, in an accountant's office. Douglas was living at home, sleeping in a bedroom that had been preserved exactly as he had left it when he went to war; not a chair or lamp, not a book or a cushion was out of place. His parents were kind; his employer could not have been more considerate, even suggesting that he might leave the office whenever he felt the need; the boss did not seek explanations or permission. He might take an hour off, or the day; he was not to feel under any pressure, his boss told Douglas. Taking advantage of that freedom, on 31 January 1946 Douglas McLaggan got up from his desk and made a short walk to the Registrar-General's office: 'I was crazy enough to change my name by Deed Poll from Douglas Ormiston McLaggan to Douglas Ormiston', he wrote. 'I told Dad [that night], who was a bit surprised to say the least. Anyway I changed it straight back again and it was never registered anywhere. Mad.' McLaggan has no explanation for this behaviour, but is it too simple to say that he just wanted to be another person? 'No man', McLaggan concluded, 'who was on the Burma Railway would, for the rest of his life, be free of psychological and physical scars, suffered under those conditions.'[8]

It would be wrong to exaggerate the difficulties of those returning from the prison camps and there must be many stories of the success of those who quickly settled back into the life they had left. And yet even the success stories seem to raise some questions. 'So your father picked up his life with no apparent difficulty?', I asked a woman who had volunteered to tell her story because her father had suffered so few difficulties in readjustment. He had taken up his old job again, she told me, and had done well; promotions followed and a heavy level of responsibility; he was a good and loving father and an attentive husband. Well, he liked a drink, she conceded; a glass or two of scotch each night after work. 'But on Sundays', she reported, 'he would take a bottle of scotch into his study and sit there drinking steadily all day until it was finished.' Apparently this successful business man could not bear idleness and time on his hands; his mind returned inevitably to what he had seen and experienced and he would drink to oblivion, to forget. Yet the world saw this man as remarkably well adjusted, one of the success stories.[9]

For Godfrey Taylor the homecoming could not have been more agreeable. His family, in the tiny outpost of Quaama, New South Wales, had heard nothing during the years of captivity except what he was able to communicate on two printed cards. The postmistress, receiving the telegram saying that Godfrey Taylor was safe, drove out to the homestead 'blowing the car horn all the way. There was no doubt at all to the villagers and at home that it could only be good news'. His family was waiting to greet him in Sydney. 'Without a doubt', he wrote, 'this was the happiest day of my life.' And yet, back home, 'happy as the occasion was … it was tinged with sadness'. Others had not made it home, good mates, and the happiness seemed wrong. And so, after discharge, Godfrey stayed on in Sydney for a few weeks. 'I wasn't fit, emotionally or physically, to cope with a job at that stage, as well as life in a big city.' The weight of evidence was with Douglas McLaggan: 'No man who was on the Burma Railway would, for the rest of his life, be free of psychological and physical scars.'[10]

In November 1945 Brigadier Blackburn wrote to Eric Millhouse, South Australian President of the RSL. He was worried about the government's leave provisions and by a requirement that former prisoners move too rapidly, as he saw it, back into their former jobs. Either start work now or lose the job seemed to be what employers and the government were demanding. They needed more time, Blackburn argued, before they could make life-forming decisions. 'Many prisoners', he wrote, 'are in the mental state of "Bewilderment".' Again Blackburn called for urgent help for these men and women as he recognised the difficulties they faced. But did he at the same time recognise the problems that special treatment might cause?[11]

Some, no doubt, wanted too much when Australians were still subject to rationing and an extreme shortage of a wide range of consumer goods. A patient writing to *Smith's Weekly* from the Heidelberg Repatriation Hospital on behalf of four former prisoners of war argued that the government 'should make our allowance of cigarettes and beer a little more than the ordinary serviceman's issue. For three and a half years we were deprived of the pleasure of a smoke and a drink. As it is we have to eke out our issue … and after being home for six weeks we have not yet been allowed to buy even one bottle of beer'. That might have been seen as mean-spirited rationing, and certainly *Smith's Weekly*, the digger's paper, took up the case, but for the government there were wider issues that would not be spoken of openly. 'Experience has shown', a military report stated, 'that ex-PW are particularly susceptible to the effects of intoxicating liquor and it is most essential that every effort be made to restrict, as far as possible, all opportunities of access to alcohol, except on medical recommendation.' Men in their own homes were, of course, their own masters and everyone wanted to 'shout' the returning prisoners. Deferred pay, time on their hands, and the desire to restart a normal life saw many former prisoners spending too much time in the nation's pubs. With good reason, perhaps, authorities were keen to see the men back at work.[12]

Many seemed to think that there were heavier issues than smokes and beer. By the middle of 1946 the former prisoners would have been expected to be back at work and getting on with their lives. Many of them had married in the few months since their return or were at least engaged. Lloyd Ellerman advised his intended, Muriel, that he had changed because of his prisoner experience and he suggested that she might want to take a new and close look at him before committing herself to marriage. Their previous understanding should not bind her now, he told her, in what he thought were the changed circumstances. This was sensible and mature, although Muriel needed little time to confirm their intention to marry. Many other marriages may have been entered into less thoughtfully and were rushed affairs.

Many former prisoners had started courses, part-time mostly, seeking to better themselves, very conscious of time lost. Many others feared that a breakdown in health would set them back again. Some had not been able to return to the workforce at all. An ex-member of the 2/29th Battalion started a letter to *Smith's Weekly*: 'All my money is gone. It was 10 months before I could work; 10 months in which I had to keep my wife and two children.' That was as far as he got; he was too upset to continue. The man's wife took over the letter: 'His nerve is gone. His eyesight is bad and he can't settle down. Meanwhile he has to work every day and each day I see him going down and down.'[13]

Soon the government files started to accumulate letters from individuals and organisations calling for financial compensation for those who had been prisoners of war. Even before the former prisoners were on their way home there were suggestions that their future needs should be the responsibility of the Japanese. A father from Glen Huntly, Melbourne, wrote that the Japanese Government should be forced to pay 'reparation to them at the rate of £1000 per man … give them enough cash, extracted from the Japanese, to enable them to buy a home for themselves and live in comfort in case they are unable to compete and earn sufficient for themselves'. There were other letters, too, asking for a pension of £500 each year per prisoner, or £5000 for the dependants of those who had died. These sums were simply unrealistic, but they are evidence, nevertheless, of the depth of sorrow and concern that many in the community felt for the returning prisoners. Perhaps there was an expectation, in the first days of peace, that the Japanese would be levied with 'reparations' as the Germans had been after the First World War, effectively being required to pay a significant proportion of the entire cost of the war.

The treaty of Versailles saddled Germany with intolerable war debt and has been seen as one of the crucial elements in the coming of war again. While 'reparations' was a dirty word for those making peace a second time, there were many in Australia who expected the former prisoners, at least, to receive some financial compensation.[14]

It quickly became apparent that reparations were not now to be a part of the victors' demands and former prisoners themselves began to campaign for the back payment of a just wage from the Japanese for all the work that they had performed during their years of captivity. This became known as the 3/- a day claim, but it would be some years yet before this relatively modest demand for compensation was agreed to. Earlier claims were much less modest. In late 1946, for example, the 8th Division Sub-Branch of the Australian Legion of Ex-Servicemen and Women began talking of a claim for £5000 for each ex-prisoner. Within a very short time the Legion received 'more than 600 letters supporting the claim'. Writing to the prime minister to justify that level of compensation, the secretary of the Sub-Branch explained that 'our members feel their health is fading fast and many have had to give up working through bad health. We don't want to be a burden on Our People. We as Victor ask you to take up our claim'.[15]

Individuals wrote to government ministers also seeking financial assistance. P. M. Tully from Chatswood, Sydney, for example, wrote to the External Affairs minister, H. V. Evatt, outlining the diseases and illnesses which he had suffered since his return to Australia. 'I wish to make a claim for two thousand pounds against the Japanese', he continued. 'Should you think this amount is unreasonable I would be pleased to receive advice on the matter. Trusting that this is not an inconvenience to you at the present busy time.' A note for file on a similar claim shows a lack of urgency or attention to detail in the work of the public servant responsible for moving the paper around ministers' offices: 'This file was recovered by me today from a disused drawer in the back of my desk in which apparently it was put when I was moved to the second floor some weeks ago.' Perhaps the claims were seen as so fanciful as not to merit serious consideration.[16]

But *Smith's Weekly* quickly took up the call for compensation of £5000, and having studied letters sent to the 8th Division Sub-

Branch by former prisoners concluded: '[This is] one of the most shocking stories of the age — of men wasted and burnt out almost beyond redemption, living in the perpetual shadow of fear; of broken lives and broken homes; of tormented minds and maimed and obscenely mutilated bodies.' Was this newspaper comment just hyperbole or was there some truth here that the government could not afford to disregard? 'When I came home', one man wrote, 'my health was in a very bad way. The mental strain was such that at night I used to wake up in a lather of sweat, sometimes screaming and moaning after having dreamed of the nightmarish ordeals we passed through. My wife stood it for a few days only and cleared out ... She says I am mad.' 'I was never in bad health before but since I came home I have one dread always that I will lose my memory', another man wrote: ' ... I cremated 160 of my mates who died of cholera ... It worries me to think what would happen to my wife and family if I had to knock off work. That worry, I think, is half my trouble.'[17]

Exaggerated? Isolated cases? We would like to think so. £5000 per man was indeed an exaggerated and unsustainable claim when the average weekly wage for a male in 1946 was around £3–£4. The claim, so out of proportion with reality, colours our understanding of the condition of the men making it. It would be too easy to dismiss the case and lose the file. If they have grossly exaggerated the money sought, the argument runs, they must have exaggerated their sufferings too. Possibly it suited some people at the time to think so. Australians have never warmed to 'whingers'. Yet soon after *Smith's Weekly* had taken up the cause of the ex-prisoners, Dr 'Weary' Dunlop wrote to the newspaper to add his voice. Weary Dunlop was already a hero to many of the prisoners who had worked on the Railway and he would become one of Australia's most highly regarded and best loved citizens. The Doctor of the Railway. For many he came as close to a secular saint as Australia ever knew. Weary Dunlop supported the campaign: 'I cannot speak too highly in praise of *Smith's* action.' He believed, he wrote, that the brutality the men had experienced at the hands of the Japanese has 'shortened their life expectancy by at least 25 per cent'. Bravely he then outlined his own circumstances and they were reported thus: 'Since he returned to civil life he has suffered 20 attacks of malaria; the effects of amoebic dysentry's terrific drain upon his constitution is still felt; and the tendons of one leg have been seriously weakened by tropical ulcers.' And Weary Dunlop did not even mention the emotional and psychological traumas that he and his wife suffered in the early years after his release. His biographer, Sue Ebury, tells us that 'he continued to fight the war in his subconscious' and that 'the frenzy of his dreams terrified Helen [his new wife]'. 'He would kick and lash out, and she feared going back to sleep. One night she awoke to find his hands around her throat … it was beyond his control.' If Weary Dunlop was prepared to testify that he struggled to return to a normal Australian life, it cannot be assumed that others were exaggerating their difficulties.[18]

There was still plenty of evidence in the community of the pain and sadness caused by the capture of Australian prisoners and their suffering and death. A father seeking compensation for the death of his prisoner son on behalf of his wife and himself wrote that 'we have never had one happy day since we heard of his death … it is not the loss of the boy that hurts so much as the rotten conditions he died under'. A man writing from Alphington, Melbourne, of his mother's grief stated that 'my mother became a hopeless invalid through worry and anxiety and the ultimate news of his death … as it is now I have to stop home from my employment to take care of her … I am paying a debt for the Japanese [and there are] many cases of people too heart-broken to do anything'.[19]

This pain and suffering was bad enough and widespread, but there was a hard edge entering the demands for compensation from the Japanese that exceeded even this. Men did expect some difficulty in an orderly return to their civilian lives in Australia, but they expected, too, that time would help to heal their scars. It was their continuing medical condition and their fears for their medical future that now began to alarm many of them as they recognised that they were not healing easily. Weary Dunlop had now told them that their life expectancy had fallen by 25 per cent and they themselves were still experiencing trauma and illness well into 1947. It was no longer a question, it seemed to so many former prisoners of war, that they must take their chances in the way that all returned men were taking their chances. Yet still the government insisted that it was wrong to try to make a distinction between classes of returned men. That may have been a feasible position, they began to believe, when people were pushing for first-class rail travel for returning prisoners in October 1945. 'It is desired to treat returning ex-prisoners of war with every sympathy and consideration', the government replied, 'but members of the AMF who have spent a considerable portion of the past six years in operational areas also deserve consideration.' It was also a defensible position when former prisoners of war sought a special payment to compensate them for the lower 'subsistence conditions' they suffered compared with what they should have been entitled to under the Geneva Convention on the treatment of prisoners of war. 'It would be illogical and unjust to give consideration to the payment to prisoners of war', the government replied, 'and not consider payment to all members of the Forces while under active service conditions.' Perhaps these minor pinpricks should be shrugged off, the former prisoners reasoned in the early months of their return. No one could really understand what had happened to them.[20]

But was it reasonable to seek to treat with equality and even-handedness all returned Australian veterans when there was considerable evidence emerging that the former prisoners were suffering acutely and in ways that were certainly not the norm for most other former servicemen? There was emerging among returned prisoners of war a wide variety 'of health and personal problems', a conference on health issues reported. Red Cross delegates to the Melbourne conference, held in June 1947, revealed that they had dealt with 2600 ex-prisoner cases in 1946 and 462 cases between 1 April and 11 May 1947. Most of the cases involved physical or mental sickness, family troubles or difficulties with employment. It was beginning to dawn on people at this conference and elsewhere that the former prisoners might have been in a class of their own and might have deserved different and special attention.[21]

Stan Ringwood was born at Albury in 1914 and was a 'bootmaker, repairer and mechanic' when he enlisted in the AIF in July 1940. He joined the 2/30th Battalion, 'Black Jack' Galleghan's battalion, and soon came to worship the old man. Galleghan got to know Stan Ringwood personally, recognised his worth and had him promoted sergeant. Stan, who had lived most of his life in Junee, New South Wales, a railway town, married Jean, a Junee girl, in April 1941, just

three months before he left Sydney for the war. A son, John, was born
after Stan had left for the war. Stan fought at Gemas in Malaya and
had some really worrying times and then became a prisoner with the
defeat at Singapore. Soon he had dysentry and was in the Changi
hospital for twelve months. A tall man, with a magnificent military
bearing evident in the photographs his son proudly shows me, Stan
Ringwood lost more than half his body weight in hospital — he was
down to six stone. During his time as a prisoner he received only
three cards from home. In June 1943, after 15 months of uncertainty,
his wife finally heard that Stan was at least alive — he was a prisoner.
Her reaction, expressed in her letter in return, was typical of those
who had suddenly been released from the terrible fear that their
soldier might have died:

> Well, sweetheart, I am walking on air … I am so relieved to know that
> you are safe and well. So you can understand why my feet haven't touched
> Earth since last Friday night when the news arrived … I had nine Phone
> calls, Stan, when the good news of you passed round Town, you can just
> imagine how it went, like Wild Fire … [John] and I will be waiting for
> you at the Station as we have arranged over and over again. It will be
> wonderful won't it Stan … when you come home darling all our worries
> will be over.

Jean Ringwood and their son John lived with her parents in Junee
through all the years that Stan was a prisoner. It was a great day when
he was to return home, a day for all the town. John's grandfather, the
captain of the local voluntary fire brigade, spruced up the fire truck,
and with bells ringing proceeded to Junee's magnificent railway
station to see the train arrive. Jean, of course, had gone to Sydney, but
John stood on top of the truck straining to see the train approaching.
When a Mrs Myers called to him that he must be excited to know
that his father was coming home, John was perplexed: 'My father?
He's not my father. This is my father', he yelled, pointing proudly to
his grandad. That comment set the tone for much that would follow.
They had built a sleepout at the back of the house for Stan, Jean and
the little boy; it was just one room really, but with a small stove so
that they could live as a family when they wanted to. But Stan was
difficult, nervy and moody; he smoked incessantly and got on the

grog. There were shouting matches between husband and wife, with the in-laws joining in. John had never heard cross words in that house before. There were plans to build their own home but somehow that never happened. They all rubbed along together and his parents continued to live in the sleepout until 1961 when Stan became fire chief himself and the family moved into the newly built station house. There had been no more children after John; illness and malnutrition in Changi had seen to that. Stan had set up as a boot repairer when he started to work again after the war, but the shop had burnt down in 1947. Then it was the railways for Stan, first at The Rock and later, and until he died, aged 55, at Junee.

The worst times, John recalls, were when a mate died. Stan would read obsessively the death notices in the newspapers, scouring the columns for any bloke he had known. But they depressed him, these constant reminders of his own mortality. 'I'm living on borrowed time', he would say. The words became a refrain, a mantra. It was always there, this fear that his life had been brutally shortened, and that death was just around the corner, as indeed it was. Stan Ringwood could not forget the war; it was with him and his family constantly. A death would set him on a binge and he would drink olive oil to line his stomach to allow for more determined drinking. John learned to hate Anzac Day which would put his dad out of action for a long while.

If the papers reminded Stan Ringwood of his mortality, the publicity soon being given to the war crimes trials forced many of the former prisoners and their families to confront the horrors of the camps once more. The atrocity stories had shocked Australians before the prisoners had returned home, and now the war crimes trials brought the horror of captivity and the brutality of the captors squarely back to the former prisoners. What did families do now as they read the papers that featured so prominently the stories from the prison camps? Dad still would not talk about it and there was another worry and barrier for them all. Something in the papers might set Dad off; he was so unpredictable now, and could we just pretend that we were not every day reading about his life?[22]

The regional War Crimes Trials opened in early January 1946, just as most of the former prisoners in Australia were struggling to get back to their old jobs. Australian military courts in Singapore, Morotai, Labuan, Darwin, Rabaul and elsewhere convened throughout 1946 and 1947 to judge and to pass sentence on the Japanese defendants, but the trials dragged on until early 1951. Every day for months the newspapers featured stories of brutality and evil, and then after that only the really sensational stories made it into the press columns. The accounts did not spare their readers' sensitivities and there were many pleas that the stories be censored. One former prisoner demonstrated a couple of the common tortures used at the prison camp housing Australians on Ambon, the 'Lockheed' and the 'stones'. The 'Lockheed' torture required the prisoner to balance for long periods on the ball of one foot with the other leg raised, and his arms raised level above his shoulders. In the other torture prisoners were made to hold heavy stones above their heads until they weakened and, arms collapsing, the stones fell on their heads. Then came the story of the Sandakan Death March in which 2000 Australians died. 'Prisoners on falling out from the march' the prosecutor claimed, 'gave their rice ration to comrades and shook hands before meeting certain death'. The two Japanese officers on trial 'calmly and unemotionally admitted crimes which shook the battle-hardened Australian troops listening'. The evidence of 'callous murder and studied cruelty unequalled elsewhere' convinced the Australian Military Court and both Japanese on trial were promptly sentenced to death.[23]

Day after day the Courts heard horrible stories of pain and suffering. One witness gave evidence that Private Robert Farley of Petersham, Sydney, had been beaten by guards until his face was unrecognisable and he later died. The report so boldly published shocked one reader almost beyond bearing: Private Farley's mother had been told by the army authorities that her son had died from disease. She appealed to the RSL to have these reports stopped or censored; Mrs Farley did not want another mother to have to endure the horror she had lived through. The RSL took up the cause and extracted promises from some newspapers that they would at least suppress the names of the deceased.[24]

But it still went on. In November 1950, four years after the trials started, the prime minister, Robert Menzies, agreed with a further RSL representation seeking to limit publicity: 'The publication of such gruesome details is unwarranted and particularly distressing to all concerned.' Menzies pledged that the minister for the Army would renew approaches to the newspapers, although the trials were taking place in open court, 'in the hope that the next-of-kin and relatives may be spared any further anguish'. The trials had stalled after 1948 and it was only on Australian insistence that they be allowed to continue that trials were still continuing in 1950. Senator Denham Henty wrote to Arthur Fadden, the Commonwealth Treasurer and deputy prime minister of complaints he had received: 'The relatives in Tasmania of our boys who were apparently slaughtered in agony, feel that no good purpose is served in upsetting the wives, mothers and sweethearts of these lads by rehashing the details they are striving to forget. Could you suggest in the right quarters that enough has already been written.' The former prisoners remained very sensitive to this. They were uneasy, to put it at its mildest, about those who, like Rohan Rivett or Russell Braddon, had broken the prisoners' unspoken vow of silence. When he published his *War Diaries* in 1986, Weary Dunlop wrote in the Preface: 'I have shrunk from publishing these diaries for over forty years. It seemed that they might add further suffering to those bereaved, and add to the controversy and hatred.'[25]

The publicity surrounding the trials was of special concern to Charles Huxtable. He was an Australian war hero, a term that should not be thrown around lightly; like many of the others he is little known today. Huxtable was a doctor and for a non-combatant to be awarded a Military Cross was unusual, but to be awarded another on top of the first was remarkable. In the battle of Arras in 1917, noted for the fury of the artillery bombardments from both sides, seven of Huxtable's stretcher-bearers were buried by the explosion of a shell; he at once organised a party of men and dug out all of the stretcher-bearers while shells continued to fall all around. At Cambrai later that year he was awarded the Military Cross again for rescuing wounded men under heavy fire. Born in Sydney in 1891, Charles Huxtable might have thought he had done enough, but when world war came a second time he joined the 113 Australian General Hospital and after five months in Singapore he became a prisoner of the Japanese. Waiting for him in Australia were his wife and four children. He worked as a doctor throughout his imprisonment at

Changi, and, although less famous than Weary Dunlop, Charles Huxtable was equally beloved of his men for his tender care and his devotion to their well-being, despite the almost total lack of medicines and any assistance from the captors. He saw in the bodies of the survivors and heard from them of the terrible sufferings on the Railway. Writing to his wife as soon as the war was over he noted that 'the light of life will seem to have gone out when the lists [of the dead] from this country reach Australia', and he wrote of 'that accursed railway ... that is where most of our losses occurred from disease and starvation and overwork'.[26]

Yet in May 1948 Charles Huxtable wrote to the newspapers appealing for an end to the war crimes trials. It was a provocative letter because Huxtable justified his position by claiming that bad things had been done on both sides. 'The Pacific war', he wrote, 'was bitter, racial and merciless and the cruelties of which the enemy were guilty did not exceed those practised by us'. War, this man who knew war so well claimed, was always evil and it was time to forget the past in the hope of learning to live a better way in the future. His letter provoked a fury of response, but Charles Huxtable would not be deflected: 'The Allies, in my opinion, have forfeited the right to sit in judgement upon Japan as a nation ... [for] the Allies' policy in the Pacific seems to have been a policy of ruthless extermination of the enemy.' Of course, Huxtable conceded in another letter, 'tragedies like the Burma railway, Sandakan ... Palembang ... all such things are stories this country must not be allowed to forget. But there are other and more permanent ways of honouring their memory than by the punishment and recrimination of the enemy'. One of those who came to Charles Huxtable's support was David Griffin, whom Huxtable had cared for in Changi. Griffin wrote of a quality 'which [Huxtable] possesses to an extraordinary degree — that of Christian toleration'.[27]

It was probably a counsel of perfection to call on those who were still reliving their sufferings through the war crimes trials, either as former prisoners or as still grieving relatives, to see the Japanese as no worse than the Allies, their cruelties 'relatively small in scope ... beside the mass cruelty of the white man in Europe'. To a man still in the grip of his demons, convinced that he was living on borrowed time, and worried about his health and his continuing ability to hold down a job, the Japanese were a hated and evil enemy. For Charles Huxtable, release from his demons would come through forgiveness and toleration and he would soldier on in the toughest conditions of Australian medicine as a member of the Flying Doctor team. For others there might be many years yet before they could learn to forgive their enemies and do good to those who had so hurt them.[28]

CHAPTER 8

'Stirring up trouble by segregating POWs from their fellow servicemen'

In October 1947 the Chairman of the Repatriation Commission, George Wootten, wrote to the Secretary of the Public Service Board in Canberra to arrange payment for doctors and others who would be involved in a making a survey of the health of 10 per cent of those former prisoners of the Japanese who had returned to Australia. Although rising to the rank of major-general in the Second World War — he was a graduate of Duntroon's first class in August 1914 — Wootten was an unlikely soldier: 'fat, perspiring, bespectacled' was how the official historian Gavin Long described him in New Guinea. He was, in fact, a mammoth man of 23 or 24 stone; he was domineering and 'it was virtually unknown for any member of his staff to oppose him'. But, despite his rough ways and an inefficient administrative style learned in his army days, at the Repatriation Commission Wootten was 'immensely compassionate towards his huge clientele, anguishing about what he could do to help a class of returned soldier or particular individual'.[1]

In 1947 Wootten had set up a committee of medical men 'to ascertain what is the problem in re-establishing prisoners of war in civilian life, and what measures are suggested to solve it'. In the sometimes disappointing way of government files, Wootten does not say why he had established this committee. In fact, he had been pressured into it by a band of ex-prisoner doctors. Since his return from captivity, Weary Dunlop had remained an icon for his former patients; they came to his consulting rooms for treatment or just for conversation; and wives called too, 'to understand the health problems — the constant diarrhoea, recurrent malaria — and the changes in

behaviour in their husbands which only families saw'. Dunlop knew
that there was a problem with these men. He had also formed the
view that the examination of former prisoners prior to discharge
from the services had been perfunctory and that their health now
needed to be closely monitored. Other doctors who had survived
captivity were coming independently to the same conclusions and
nineteen of them, meeting in Melbourne, decided to press for action.
They selected a committee of seven and resolved to offer their
expertise to George Wootten at the Repatriation Commission. It was
on the basis of their representations that Wootten had then established
his own expanded national committee.[2]

Weary Dunlop wanted the health of all former prisoners of the
Japanese to be investigated; instead, the committee decided on a
preliminary survey of 10 per cent of the men who had been in the
camps. While Wootten accepted this recommendation from his medical advisers, he was very keen, nevertheless, to avoid any publicity that
might indicate that there were real and long-term problems with the
health of these men. Indeed the committee itself was unanimous in
resolving that 'publicity in all these matters [was] to be avoided as far
as possible'. When Wootten had earlier arranged for the printing of a
pamphlet for local doctors who might be unfamiliar with the special
health needs of former prisoners, he insisted that the title should not
attract attention: 'Some Aspects of Medical Investigation and Treatment' was all that the title disclosed. As he advised the minister, 'it will
be noted that in the title of the booklet, any reference to Ps.O.W. has
been avoided … it is the intention of the Commission … that [they]
should not be treated as a class apart and that there should be complete
avoidance of any publicity concerning them'.[3]

Indeed when the men selected for survey came face to face with
those conducting it they found that the work was being carried out
by the Commonwealth Employment Service 'with a view to avoiding
any pension or medical treatment complications'. The questions these
10 per centers were to be asked fell into two main categories, those
that related to the general re-establishment of the former prisoners
in their homes and in their workplaces, and those that related to their
health. A CES officer conducted the first part of the interview, a
medical officer the second. Men would attend various offices in the

capital cities and regional centres — the bush would have to come later, if at all — between 7 and 10 at night so as not to interfere with their work. Attendance would be voluntary and the organisers hoped that each interview could be completed in about 30 minutes. That was asking a lot.[4]

Instructions indicated that the interview should cover all of the following points: date of capture and age at capture, length of captivity; theatres of service before and during captivity; work while a prisoner and the period in months of each type of work; education and training; employment history; reasons for changing jobs where changes appeared to be too frequent; and how the interviewee was coping at work. The interviewer was then to move to family issues such as whether the man was married before captivity, the quality of housing, and home circumstances (in a situation where about one in five Australian families were sharing accommodation with in-laws or others). The medical officer then took over the interview and investigated health during captivity and checked height, weight, vision, hearing and present condition, and looked for symptoms like 'depression, anxiety, memory defect, sleep disturbance, emotionalism, shakiness, feelings of inferiority, phobias and general malaise'. However, the interviewers were instructed that 'symptoms should not be emphasised, but treated casually, so as to prevent the interviewee subsequently dwelling on them'. The whole exercise was not to raise questions or alarm in the mind of the interviewee. Indeed the letter of invitation that the 10 per centers received indicated that the 'check-up' intended 'to bring to light difficulties that may have become apparent' but that 'it was just as necessary to know how many are satisfactorily re-established and well in health as to know those who are still having difficulties and have been slower in getting back to full fitness'. The targeted man was asked to consider that 'by sparing a few minutes to talk over things with us you might be able to help your former comrades if not yourself'.

Despite this 'softly, softly' approach, a couple of senior former prisoner doctors were angered by what was being done. In Sydney Dr W. E. Fisher led the charge against the Repat and his Melbourne colleagues. Ted Fisher was born in Sydney in 1901 and was not a doctor to leave a trail of paper records or an account of himself. He died in 1965. As foundation chairman of the 8th Division Council there is no doubt that Ted Fisher placed a high priority on the rehabilitation and continuing good health of the men with whom he had served. Yet he had 'a haughty manner which was used to cover a sensitive and somewhat self-conscious character' and he was 'aggressively intolerant of inefficiency and sham'. He never married and after the war lived with his mother until his death. A doctor wrote of him that he was 'shy, reticent, retiring' and of an 'unusual character'. The opposite of Weary Dunlop. And yet so passionate was he for his former comrades that 'his private-practice was largely sacrificed [to] his public-spirited zeal'.[5]

Fisher looked at the survey form with disdain, as did Dr Bruce Hunt in Perth. The son of the first head of the Department of External Affairs, a gunner in the First World War and a doctor afterwards, Hunt was an expert in diabetes: 'To see and hear the massively corpulent Hunt berating some benighted diabetic for weight gain was to be privy to a most awesome tableau credible only to its participants.' A prisoner himself, with a fearsome reputation for standing up to the Japanese in the interests of his men, Hunt would work tirelessly for former prisoners in Western Australia, yet in a letter to Fisher he described the proposed survey form as 'fantastic, as unlikely to produce accurate information and therefore, as valueless'. 'Personally', he continued, 'I don't think any questionnaire is necessary or desirable.' On the basis of his experience with former prisoners, he thought that medical officers should look for signs of a small number of medical problems. Hunt had no interest in any possible psychological damage, but raised, instead, the question of holidays: 'A number of these men started work very shortly after their discharge without having a decent holiday. They have been going flat out ever since and badly need a spell.' This call for a holiday was almost a reminder of the journalistic simplicity of Guy Harriott, whose view was that all these men needed was to loaf on the beach for a few weeks.[6]

Ted Fisher had completed a survey of his own in which he failed to find the nervy, moody men of whom some families were now speaking. Perhaps the way *Smith's Weekly* was presenting the problem was exaggerated, as if all returned prisoners were observably mentally disabled. Perhaps the call for compensation of £5000 had further shown the need to be wary of an extreme response. Ted Fisher wanted to convince his patients that any medical condition they had was treatable and minor. If they were confident of their underlying good health, he reasoned, they would be capable of living normally; but if they were constantly in fear of major breakdown or disease, their fretting would hamper their rehabilitation. We would do well to remember that it was, for some at least, the fear of illness that was as much a problem as illness itself. Dr Fisher understood that.

As Visiting Physician to the Repatriation General Hospital, Concord, Fisher arranged to have all the former prisoners attending the hospital, except the surgical and psychiatric patients, admitted to two special wards under his care. Other doctors questioned and even resented this segregation, but over a twelve-month period Fisher would be able to study these patients closely. While admitting, for a range of good reasons, that his survey was not perfect, nevertheless Fisher concluded, 'it is reasonable to assume that the body of patients admitted to the main R.G.H. of the State over such a twelve month period represents fairly the current, active and most serious morbidity occurring in the group from which that body of patients is drawn'. Dr Fisher examined 435 men from an estimated 5200 returned prisoners in New South Wales, a higher proportion of patients to returned men than among other groups of returned men, but even so, in his mind, given the diseases to which they had been exposed and the limited medicines available in the camps, a 'gratifyingly small' number.[7]

He found other good news in his work at Concord. That only 36 individuals were admitted to the psychiatric wards from a population of 5200 failed to support the claim, he believed, that the ex-prisoners 'as a class are the victims of "war neurosis" '. Almost all the diseases he treated he described as 'on the wane', although hookworm was the most prevalent disability and difficult to eradicate. As to sexual disability, 'a very small number of patients, not amounting in total to double figures, has come to notice complaining of impotence or of sterility'. 'The impotence', he reported, 'appears invariably of psychological origin. The rarer cases of sterility need further and more detailed investigation.' Overall Dr Fisher concluded that the reasons for admission to Concord 'in many instances are trivial, that the incidence of disorders attributable to the tropics or to captivity is waning, that many of the responsible conditions are those to be [found] in any similar group of ex-service personnel and that the incidence of significant "war neurosis" is negligible'.

Yet an interim report about the 10 per cent survey in the Melbourne metropolitan area produced different results. Some 497 ex-prisoners had been invited to attend for interview and 368 had responded. Nearly half of those interviewed (165) were advised to lodge new claims with the Repatriation Commission or to seek further medical treatment. It might be concluded from this that only a proportion of ex-prisoners who needed medical treatment were presenting themselves to their doctors. Dr Fisher, in other words, was seeing only a proportion of those who really needed medical help. The others were holding back. In looking at men beyond the examination couch, in looking at their lives rather than simply at their bodies, the survey came to some worrying conclusions.[8]

In suburban Sydney the picture was much the same. Of 350 men examined, defect in vision was noted in some 32 per cent of cases, and 30 per cent complained of lack of appetite for food or that food did not appeal. 'As to sleep — it seems it was difficult to get off and many were light sleepers — nightmares very often woke them and the wife complained of loud talking and screaming.' And yet for the majority there was no evidence of disease or disability in their bodies. These were men, therefore, who would not have presented at Concord or to their own doctors, even though the majority, it seemed, were suffering, at least, from disturbed and broken sleep. Although all of the men examined seemed to be in some type of work, 'ability to perform as [prior to enlistment] was lacking'. Sport was a 'dead letter': 'Almost all now looked over the fence at the other fellow, and although many of those questioned were still below 30 they had lost all interest and enthusiasm for strenuous sport.' Very few of the men were undertaking any course of study, unlike many other ex-servicemen who had rushed to take advantage of the Commonwealth Rehabilitation and Training Scheme which opened universities to many classes of Australians for the first time. 'In most instances' the ex-prisoners rejected study because they were 'too tired or simply

[had] no ambition'. 'Memory generally, at least in half the number, was impaired, more or less.'[9]

Statistics were one thing, but the anecdotal commentary of several Melbourne doctors amplified the figures. The senior Repatriation medical officer in Melbourne, A. H. Melville, identified various factors affecting the health of the men surveyed, particularly the standard of education of the ex-prisoner, his domestic circumstances and his age. Dividing the interviewees into three age blocks — under 23, 24–40 and beyond 40 — Melville suggested that

> the older men, being already well set in their jobs and domestic circumstances [before enlistment], did not worry unduly about their future [while they were in the camps] while the "youngsters", being less well set in employment and having no domestic worries, and maybe considering that what they were undergoing as captives was what might be normally expected in war, considered that the future could well look after itself or would be looked after for them.

The marital status on enlistment was also of importance 'since the married member, particularly the comparatively recently married, would be expected to worry much more than the unmarried man. In some cases the wife, having given up her husband as lost, has made other domestic arrangements, with consequent ill-effect upon the health and rehabilitation of the husband'.

Several of the doctors commented on the inability of the former prisoners to put on weight and 'many [stated] that their appetites generally are still poor'. One doctor looked closely at the emotional state of the men he examined. 'On release and return to home life', he wrote, 'there was naturally a period of exhilaration. During the next few weeks they were more emotional, and a period of irritability followed, as they tried once more to adjust themselves to family and social life. In nearly all cases this period of irritability and heightened emotional state generally has passed off.' Many of these men were 'friendly, happy and contented' but 'unfortunately domestic strife is largely responsible for a considerable number of Anxiety cases. The main problem is housing. Very few of these men have their own homes. Many with wives and children live with relatives'.

Another doctor concentrated on the unhappy middle group in age.

'A number were dissatisfied with the set-up of their lives ... many were married [prior to enlistment] and some have found difficulty in settling back "into the bosom of their families" after the long absence. This is aggravated by the lack of housing ... this group complained of being less able to do their work, and that they tire more easily and sooner than formerly'. So while this doctor found the physical condition of the men he examined 'surprisingly good', their 'mental outlook and nervous condition' was sharply affected by issues such as housing, domestic conditions and employment. Another reported: 'Rehabilitation has on the whole been satisfactory; [yet] there are a fair number of men mainly aged between 30 and 40 years who are not well rehabilitated. These are mainly men of poor educational standard who prior to enlistment drifted from one unskilled job to another and who are doing the same now with the added handicap of not being quite 100% fit.' 'Nearly all suffered from a definite anxiety state trend', another doctor reported, 'though most did not wish to labour the point. This anxiety state would be expected to occur in those who had undergone the experiences of prisoners of war.' 'A large proportion', another doctor claimed, 'undoubtedly sustained nervous trauma but they are on the whole recovering quite well.' This doctor estimated that less than 5 per cent of the men he had seen 'showed permanent severe nervous trauma'.[10]

The picture was a mixed one, with some reason for confidence about the return to full health of many, but an awareness that other men were still suffering trauma to a greater or lesser degree. It should be remembered that all these investigating doctors were returned men themselves. Whether this made them more sympathetic to the plight of the men they were examining, or more eager to find them recovering and on the path to health, cannot now be known. But it does seem strange that one or two non-prisoner doctors were not inserted into the survey, for the purpose of checking whatever preconceptions the investigating doctors might have brought to their tasks. It may be, for example, that the doctors were expecting to find greater difficulty to adjusting to life in Australia than in fact they found. All emphasised that Australian conditions, particularly the chronic shortage of housing, were putting a strain on the men. None seemed prepared to argue, although of course they had not been asked, for special conditions for the returning prisoners. It does seem that special assistance with housing might have gone a long way to helping with the ex-prisoners' recovery, but this would have made a special case of them.

In December 1948 the Repatriation Commissioner informed the Minister that 'as a consequence of the facts disclosed in the survey it was deemed advisable to go ahead with a complete overhaul of the remaining cases'. In other words, indications from the 10 per cent survey were so worrying that the Commonwealth would now examine the remaining 90 per cent. Surprisingly, however, the expanded survey would be completed by doctors only and would concentrate only on conditions 'which may call for medical treatment and war pension'. Wootten argued that the expense and the time taken for the 10 per cent survey had made repetition on a much larger scale impossible. The 10 per cent sample had shown how extensive the personal problems of ex-prisoners were, but many of the problems identified were beyond the reach or assistance of the Repatriation Commission. The Commission could not induce a renewed interest in playing sport and it could not drag unambitious men to study. The Commission could not make work more fulfilling nor heal the silences or gaps in family life. The Commission could not find houses for families making do with in-laws nor could it make sleep easier for grossly disturbed men. If a hundred, or even a thousand, had needed assistance in these ways, it may have been possible to help them. The 10 per cent survey indicated that thousands more needed assistance and that was beyond the Commonwealth's resources. Better, therefore, to treat only what the medical men could perhaps heal.[11]

As the remaining survey got under way, *Smith's Weekly* continued to hammer away at the problems ex-prisoners faced. The public airing of these problems was probably not helpful, because a man who is constantly told that he is sick will often begin to accept that perhaps, after all, he is. *Smith's Weekly* infuriated Dr Fisher, who attacked the claim that ex-prisoners 'have neither the will nor the resistance to fight their way back into civil life' as 'grossly untrue'. 'An impartial survey', he insisted, 'has shown that Australians who were prisoners of the Japanese have been better rehabilitated than any other section of ex-servicemen.' Whatever the survey showed, it certainly did not show that. 'I bluntly disagree with the sob-stuff which has been published', he continued and that blunt disagreement led Dr Fisher to some exaggerated statements: 'One of the things we pride ourselves on is that p.o.w of the Japs have come back better balanced very often than when they went away'; 'One of the striking things about p.o.w. life was that men had no neurotic manifestations'; 'I don't believe for one minute that having been a prisoner of war of the Japs has anything to do with the sterility of the few.' 'P.O.W. health is not detriorating', Dr Fisher concluded. 'Continued statements to that effect are damaging', not least, he suggested, in the employment of former prisoners whom employers might treat warily.[12]

It was strong stuff to assert that the former prisoners were better balanced now than they had been before they became captives. It was possibly top-of-the-head stuff, written in a moment of considerable anger. There was too much anecdotal evidence that Fisher seemed to be ignoring: evidence of morose men, moody men, men breaking down. And if Fisher was right that the 10 per cent survey had produced such benign responses, why had the Commonwealth, at considerable expense, extended the survey to cover all returning prisoners. Fisher's position was illogical and it angered Weary Dunlop. 'A deuce of a lot of people', Dunlop wrote to Fisher, '[were] damned irritated for the intemperate vigour with which you state your views … and which appear to imply "why the heck should we worry any more about a bunch of boys who are really doing better than any other service men".'[13]

Weary Dunlop's concern for the men with whom he had served never lessened, and yet, at least in the early 1950s, he seemed to find it difficult to pinpoint precisely what the medical problem was with these men. He complained of men 'slipping through' the Repatriation 'safety net' and of 'vague symptoms' of ill-health. A Repatriation officer tried to put his finger on Dunlop's concerns: 'I think Mr Dunlop must have some definite points to discuss and he, being of a somewhat reticent nature in personal conversation' is anxious for the Committee to reconvene. Few, perhaps, in later life would notice this reticence in Weary Dunlop, but his concern for the health of the men would never abate. There were, he knew, continuing and troubling problems. It was just that no one could closely define them.[14]

The health survey showed how remarkably resilient is the human body. Australian prisoners of the Japanese had suffered malnutrition to starvation, they had been beaten, they had fallen sick with a variety of diseases, and they had worked as slaves for long hours in appalling conditions. Yet three years after their release the doctors could report a reasonable level of health. Their patients tired easily at work, their vision was affected by malnutrition and their memories were not as good as they once had been, but in general they were fine. And that was as far as most of the doctors, and ultimately the government, were prepared to go. A single man, living with his mother, and a leading specialist doctor in the highest income earning group in Australia, might not readily have understood the problems troubling Stan Ringwood, for example. Returning to a home owned and organised by his father-in-law, consigned to a single-room sleepout with his wife and son, Stan was not the independent fellow of his prison camp dreams. Nor was his work anything but drudgery. Stan Ringwood would be dead, aged 55 years, in 1969. Sixty-five ex-prisoners of the Japanese had committed suicide between 1945 and 1960, and a further 900 had also died in that 15-year period, all of them relatively young men. The health survey could have predicted these things.[15]

There were, apparently, thousands like Stan Ringwood, as the health survey disclosed. Doctors could do nothing to improve these conditions and few of them understood the problems in the minds of their patients that domestic and work circumstances could throw up. At an ex-prisoner of war reunion in the 1980s one of the wives shyly sought help from the table of women, stating that her husband had suffered from violent nightmares ever since his return home. She was now finding his anguish hard to cope with after all these years and she wondered aloud if any of the other husbands had ever been afflicted with the terrors of the night. There was silence and some tears for a long moment. Every woman at the table had a similar story to tell and yet all had kept the nightmares and worse to themselves, never dreaming how near to universal this experience was for former prisoners of war. It was a moment of release for all the women. The health survey might have started that conversation forty years earlier.

In the minds of many of the former prisoners concern for their health was related to the question of compensation from the Japanese.

The war crimes trials sought to punish those who had most abused the prisoners, but compensation would show that the Japanese people, as a whole, accepted responsibility for what had been done. Compensation was something that Australians understood: a grievous wrong that was done would be made right by the payment of money. Compensation would confirm for the former prisoners, even if only in their own minds, that they had suffered a great wrong. Compensation would also restore their dignity and sense of self-importance. It was hard for others to understand this; a former prisoner, more than forty years after recovery, wrote to the Japanese ambassador in Canberra asking for restitution of a valuable watch that had been taken from him in captivity. The ex-prisoner did not want his watch back — that was hardly realistic; he wanted acknowledgement that it should not have been taken; that he was a person with rights and with dignity and that he could stand up for himself. The matter had obviously been preying on his mind for many years. Calls for compensation were closely linked to questions of self-worth.

There was also a sense that as the prisoners had been forced to build assets of enduring value for their captors, these assets, the Railway, airfields, wharves and so on, should be added into the calculation for compensation. As the member of the House of Representatives for Fremantle, Kim E. Beazley, wrote to the minister for External Affairs, H. V. Evatt, in July 1947, 'During their period of enforced labour … Prisoners of War played a large part in constructing in Singapore the aerodrome, said to be worth £3m and the Singapore–Thailand Railway … they consider that a claim exists … for these assets.'[16]

The high, even exaggerated, claims for compensation of the first years after the war were politely ignored by governments and soon enough the former prisoners fixed on a campaign for the Australian government to give what amounted to back-pay, three shillings a day subsistence allowance, that the soldiers would have received if they had been on active service. In the minds of the former prisoners the payment was not really compensation but a restitution of what was actually owing to them. Soon after winning the election in 1949, and as a consequence of an election promise, the Menzies government appointed a committee of three to examine the question of the subsistence allowance. Chaired by Mr Justice Owen of the New South Wales Supreme Court, the other members were Lieutenant-General Sir Stanley Savige and Dr W. E. Fisher. In 1915, at just 16 years of age, Bill Owen had run away from school and enlisted in the AIF; he served as an under-age soldier on the Western Front until near the end of the war, being wounded and gassed. As a judge he was described as 'conservative', preferring 'what in legal principle is well-established to that which savours of experiment'. Savige, who had served on Gallipoli from September 1915 and then on the Western Front, had demonstrated his practical concern for the dependants of soldiers by founding Legacy in Melbourne in 1923. The official historian, Gavin Long, judged that Savige lacked 'a brilliant mind — his staff invariably beat him badly at checkers' but noted his 'gift of leadership, knowledge of men, great tact and much commonsense'. Dr Fisher we have already met.[17]

Appointed in May 1950 the committee was to examine two issues: whether the enemy powers had failed to fulfil the duties and obligations towards prisoners of war imposed by the Geneva Convention and, if so, whether a 'moral responsibility' rested upon the Commonwealth government to make a special monetary payment to the servicemen who suffered such hardships. Committee members had no trouble with the first question, and nor should they have had; the war-time Labor government had consistently stated that the Japanese, in particular, had flouted the Geneva Convention; it would be difficult for a government committee to rule otherwise. The Webb report into war crimes confirmed that the Japanese saw themselves as under no obligation to act under the terms of the Convention. Two members of the committee, however, then decided that the Australian government had no moral obligation to make any special subsistence payment by way of compensation to the former prisoners. In his bland press release the prime minister, Robert Menzies, claimed that any compensation 'should be made by the defaulting power and not by the power to whom the prisoner belonged'. In fact the committee's majority report was much harsher than this. 'Capture was one of the hazards which every serviceman must face', the judge and the soldier stated, and a claim for 'hardship money' was 'without just or logical basis'; 'it would be unsound and contrary to the national interest to create a precedent which would, now or in the future, place a "monetary premium" upon becoming or remaining a prisoner of war'. There it was again, the notion that any special treatment given to former prisoners of war might weaken the resolve of future soldiers and encourage them to hand themselves over to the enemy, no matter how brutal the consequences might be.[18]

When Cabinet considered Owen's report Australia was at war again, in Korea. Was it likely, knowing the fanaticism of the North Koreans and the Communist Chinese that Australian soldiers would relish the prospect of imprisonment in return for the possibility of future largesse from their government. Such an argument says little for the committee's perception of the intelligence of Australian soldiers. Dr Fisher disagreed with his colleagues, although he did not specifically comment on this nonsense; instead he submitted a minority report saying that the three shillings per day should be paid out of reparations, if any, that might be levied on Japan by the peace treaty.

The government accepted the majority report rejecting the claim, but, concerned that the public might see the decision as unduly harsh, at the same time established a Prisoners of War Trust Fund of £250 000. Payments would be made to former prisoners considered by the Trustees 'to have suffered special disability not common to other members of the Services' and as a direct result of their war-time imprisonment. Again the prime minister's statement did not tell the full story; Cabinet had decided that the money to be contributed to the Fund would 'include war reparation moneys'. The effect of this was that only those ex-prisoners of war suffering a 'special disability' would have first call on whatever money would be received from the defeated enemy. The government had turned from compensation payable to all on the basis of hardship suffered and unconscionable behaviour by the enemy and would now only assist those whose special need was obvious and provable.

The prime minister himself invited Brigadier Arthur Blackburn to chair the Board of Trustees that would be established to manage the fund, but before Blackburn felt that he could accept the appointment he raised a number of concerns about the proposed fund. One of the Brigadier's major worries was how the fund would operate alongside the pensions paid by Repatriation. As Blackburn was quick to deduce, those suffering the greatest 'special disability' were probably already receiving a full repatriation pension, the total and permanently incapacitated (TPI) pension. Blackburn asked, 'Are the Trustees to have the power … to make grants under the plea that the War Pension is inadequate?' A Treasury officer commented on the same point: 'I think it should be accepted that the Government has made adequate provision by way of Repatriation benefit … the Trustees may find that they are placing themselves in the position of passing judgement on the Government as to the adequacy of its provision for totally incapacitated ex-members.'[19]

There were other critics of the Trust Fund. Ex-servicemen's organisations complained about the suggestion of charity that surrounded the Fund, when repatriation payments had always to this point been seen in the context of rights and obligations. In Parliament Labor's Leslie Haylen denied that former prisoners had 'emotionalised what might be described, in the crudest terms, as a sob story', saying that it was in fact 'one of the most tragic historical incidents of the recent war'. Haylen deprecated the stigma of the 'dole depot' surrounding the Fund.[20]

Regardless of all this, the Prisoners of War Trust Fund commenced operation in March 1952, the Trustees having earlier determined that the fund would assist only ex-servicemen prisoners and neither their dependants nor members of the Merchant Marine who had become prisoners during the war. In April 1952 the Trustees sent a letter to 14 128 ex-prisoners of the Japanese and 7826 prisoners of war in Europe, inviting them to apply for assistance if they believed that they could make a case. A year later the Trustees had received 4289 applications for the assistance that had been set by the Trustees at a maximum of £250 per applicant. Approximately one half of the applications succeeded and the average payment was £72. The Fund ground on into the 1970s propped up by small injections of capital.[21]

Events had overtaken the Fund, an election promise that had taken more than two years to implement. In February 1952 the government received £730 000 from the sale of Japanese assets in Australia and arranged to have this money divided equally between surviving ex-prisoners and the dependants of those who had died. Each

recipient received £32 and a further £54 in December 1954, after
the sale of further Japanese assets. No doubt £86 was well received
by most ex-prisoners — one doctor referred to it as 'a small but
welcome cheque' — but it was little enough, in truth, compared with
the original expectations for compensation. Each man, at some stage,
must have recognised that he would have to make his own way
without much help from the government. Their extraordinary lives
in the camps should not, the government seemed to be saying, entitle
these people to any special privileges or treatment. As Robert
Menzies wrote in October 1952, 'Although we are sympathetic
towards [the ex-prisoners] for the sufferings and privations which
they endured, I can see little prospect of obtaining further reparations
from the Japanese government to augment the benfits that have
already been, or are to be, provided for them.'[22]

The anger of these men would not subside easily and they would
have resented the suggestion that they deserved 'special treatment'.
They wanted justice, as they saw it. Take Dr S. E. L. Stening, like Ted
Fisher, a Macquarie Street, Sydney medical specialist. In 1947 Dr
Stening wrote to the minister for External Affairs, Dr Evatt, with a
claim against the government of Japan 'for malfeasance to me whilst
a Prisoner of War'. Dr Stening, a surgeon lieutenant in the Royal
Australian Naval Reserve aboard HMAS *Perth*, was taken by the
Japanese from the waters of Sunda Strait on 1 March 1942. He was
released from captivity on 15 September 1945. He itemised his claim
carefully: 'for failure to provide medical treatment when wounded —
£250' (fractured skull, fractured nose, lacerations to face and scalp,
penetrating wound of left knee joint, traumatised thumbs); 'for
incarceration for 127 days in Ofuna Interrogation Camp, Japan @
£10 per day — £1270' (here communication was forbidden and
oppression was very grim); 'for a most severe beating with clubs in
front of the entire camp and Japanese staff — £1000'; 'for 8 other
camps 1101 days @ £3 per day — £3303'; 'for most severe beating
at Taisho Camp on an occasion when I had objected to sick men in
camp being forced to unload a lorry load of coal — £1000'; 'for
being deprived of medical books and periodicals ... for this reason
my skill and knowledge decreased ... that for at least 10 years my
income will be lowered by £1000 per annum — £ 10 000'. This last

item included 'for residual mental and physical disabilities … persist-
ing into civilian life'. The grand total came to £16 823. There is no
record on the file of Dr Evatt's reply, but the claim might have been
seen as a terrible cry of anguish and a strong plea for justice. Dr
Stening then disappears from the pages of history; his response to
£86 in compensation can only be imagined.

Life moves on, of course, and in the pattern of these things, by the
early 1950s the former prisoners of war were finding the need for
organisations and journals that would bring them together as men
began to drift apart. 'The days roll by, the months pass on … the hustle
and bustle of "Peace-Time" existence, the calls of business, the ties of
family life all tend to limit contact with our fellow P.O.Ws', the editor
of *Barbed Wire and Bamboo* wrote in December 1951. If time took its
toll, could their story remain in the forefront of the nation's consciousness? Probably not. The real meaning of the health survey would
begin to recede as national attention went elsewhere.

Writing an account of the work he had done a POW Liaison
Officer recognised what was needed: 'My own view is that unless
propaganda is comparable with the propaganda put out by General
Eisenhower about Belsen and other horror camps in Europe: unless
it is of the highest order we will not achieve our object [of impressing
the story on the people].' Some tried. Rohan Rivett's *Behind Bamboo*
had been published in 1946 and sold very strongly. Russell Braddon's
The Naked Island, published in 1952, also sold very well. The question
arises about the impact of these books. Was Australia's orientation still
too deliberately European for these books to enter the national
consciousness in the way, for example, that the hugely popular P. R.
Reid's *The Colditz Story* did?[23]

Colin Simpson, a respected Australian storyteller, worked as a
journalist before joining the Australian Broadcasting Commission in
1947 'as a writer of travel documentaries', as the ABC's historian put
it. Simpson did, indeed, turn to travel stories at the ABC, but his first
project with the national broadcaster was to prepare a documentary
on what had happened to Australian and British prisoners at Sandakan and on the death march. Simpson had a budget of about £1000,
a significant sum that would allow him to travel to Borneo, and the
program would be broadcast jointly by the ABC and the British

Broadcasting Corporation. 'They feel', Simpson wrote, 'that it is part of the function of national radio to do such a job which is, in a sense, a record of history, and something for our war archives.' But Simpson immediately recognised the difficulty his work represented: 'In telling the story I am anxious to avoid undue distress to the relatives of men who are dead.'[24]

In Australia, among the former prisoners particularly, the entire story about prisoners of the Japanese was not being told precisely for that reason; the telling must inevitably cause distress. 'Dad never talked about the war', they all told me. The story was inseparable from the brutality and there were so many examples of men hiding the truth. Where a mother had been told that her son had died of disease, as we have seen, it was simply too distressing to reveal the truth — that he had been beaten so badly that his face was unrecognisable. The former prisoners, who might have told what had happened, were reluctant therefore to speak for fear of offending still-grieving relatives. Writers and documentary makers decided that they must observe the same constraints. There was little that was gallant in the story of the Japanese camps, where the heroism lay simply in endurance and in living a life for others. Simpson told his wife that Sandakan 'is a terrible story I have to piece together'. 'There is a book in it', he continued, 'but I don't think I could bear to write it, though it should be written.'[25]

Colin Simpson recognised that the story of Sandakan could not be 'fully and properly told without bringing in the survivors' — there were six of them, from the 2000 Australian dead — but it is remarkable and somewhat disturbing to see the difficulty Simpson had in 1947 in finding the addresses of these men. Men who had suffered so much should surely not have been left completely to their own devices and yet they were lost to the Army, even possibly, it seems, to the Repatriation department. Simpson wrote to 'Mr Botterill' a little more than a year after this remarkable survivor had attempted to settle down again in Australia, asking, 'Do you have an address for Owen Campbell in Brisbane whom I am trying to contact so far without result?' When he did find that address, he wrote to 'Dear Owen Campbell', saying that he was trying to find Private Short or rather that 'the Army is trying to trace him for me'. Within a couple of years since their recovery, these men who had suffered so disastrously had been surrendered by the Army to their privacy, to their families and to their own resources. The authorities could not even say where they were.[26]

Gunner Wal Blatch was married before he embarked for service overseas, but, of course, his wife, Joyce, had no idea where he was or of the conditions at Sandakan. Blatch's best mate was Gunner J. R. 'Dick' Braithwaite, and on the march to Ranau the two of them had spent time planning an escape. Just to drop off the track and into the jungle was, however, perilously dangerous and it became obvious to the men that Blatch, the stronger of the two, would make it to Ranau while Braithwaite would not. Tragically believing that Ranau represented salvation, where the Japanese would at least feed and care for those who completed that appalling trek, Braithwaite dropped off into the jungle to die, and Blatch struggled on in the expectation that he would ultimately survive. Rescued by the local people, Braithwaite was taken to the Americans at sea and, remarkably, survived. Wal Blatch may have reached Ranau — we will never know — but he died there or on the track as did all the other Australians. Soon after the war, in 1946, his widow remarried. 'Dick' Braithwaite had come to tell her about her husband's life as a prisoner and to tell her as much as he could about how he had died. It was Dick Braithwaite that Joyce married in 1946: 'I was expecting that Wal would come home', she told me, 'and I knew I would have to work hard to care for him after all those years as a prisoner; I felt then that I should just look after Dick in Wal's place; he needed a lot of help.' There were many difficult years for them both, as Braithwaite suffered greatly in health and was not able to work consistently. He died in 1986 and this loyal and devoted woman was widowed again, her duty done.[27]

'Six from Borneo', Colin Simpson's radio documentary, was broadcast on the ABC on Friday 30 May 1947 at 9.15 pm. 'More Australians died in North Borneo than on the building of the infamous Burma–Siam railway', the narrator explained in introducing the program, 'yet the story has never been fully told to the people.' 'I take it you heard "Six From Borneo" ', Colin Simpson wrote to Dick Braithwaite two weeks later. 'Quite honestly I thought you stole the show, on the actuality end, anyway.' Simpson's was a fair assessment. Describing hunger at Sandakan, for example, Braithwaite had said, 'I suppose most of us lost weight mentally as well as physically. Some men went mad.' Bill Stipcewicz, another survivor, said that he was pleased that the ABC was 'telling the story of what happened. It should be known and never forgotten. It's all fact, all of it. It's grim and terrible, I know that. But it's a lesson that ought to be part of the history we teach in schools'. It never was.[28]

The ABC 'has had a few letters' about the broadcast, Colin Simpson told Dick Braithwaite, and 'all comments have been approving'. There were also a few letters forwarded to the six survivors. I'm sorry to give you trouble,' said Simpson. 'I'm afraid it was inevitable, and of course natural that relatives of those who did not survive should still seek information.' Could Owen Campbell have told the family of his closest mate that both of them had escaped from the death march into the jungle and that their loved one had later cut his own throat? He was too weak to go on, Campbell recalled, and, recognising that Campbell would never leave him, as he must do if he was to survive, this man had taken his own life to save his mate. Were these the sorts of things that the former prisoners could now tell those still wanting to know? It seems unlikely.

Colin Simpson had walked the track from Sandakan to Ranau; he had talked with the six survivors and some of those in Borneo who had helped them and the other Australians. He had seen a tree against which five Australians had been shot; he had seen two skulls in the jungle and numerous other collections of bones; he had seen cutlery and other evidences of lives once lived. 'If only paper lasted like glass or even leather', he had written in his notebook on the track, 'how much more we might know of the death march story.' Colin Simpson never did write the book he thought the story deserved; that would come from other pens much later. And Sandakan did not become one of the defining stories of the nation. The six survivors, like all the other surviving former prisoners of war, were left to get on with their own lives: counselled, at least implicitly, against 'stirring up trouble by segregating POWs from their fellow servicemen'.[29]

Conclusion

We leave these men and their families somewhere there in the 1950s — the health survey completed, some minimal compensation paid, a few of the stories in print or in the archives, but with the nation's attention now directed elsewhere. There was no malice in that shift of focus and no deliberate decision to turn our backs on these men. It was simply ever thus.

When Charles Bean wrote the last words of his monumental history of Australians and the First World War in 1941 he could hardly have known that it would be more than a generation later before historians would return to the sites and the themes with which he had been living since 1914. Bill Gammage was one of the first to rework Bean's territory. His book, *The Broken Years*, reawakened an interest in that war for students and teachers of Australian history. And *The Broken Years* found perhaps more general readers than Bean had ever won, ex-servicemen excepted.

In a final chapter that Bean could not have written as he laid down his pen in 1941 Gammage tried to look at 'the outbreak of peace'. He traced, however briefly, the return of the AIF to Australia and assessed some of the problems the returning soldiers faced. He also tried to tell us that the returned men did not have everything their own way. Governments, employers and the general community urged the men to get on with their lives, but it was a cruel generation to be born into, with the Depression coming to knock the stuffing out of men who were just, perhaps, getting back on their feet after the horrors of the Western Front.

'None of my friends like returned soldiers', one insufferable young man born in 1913 had written in 1931; 'what we actually see every day till they have got on our nerves are crippled, blind and battered wrecks, with brass badges on, begging in the streets, howling about pension reductions, while their women and children are in dire straits.'

Safer by far to keep these wrecks off the streets and out of the sight of those whose compassion had closely defined limits.

Imagine the outrage if such a letter were published now about the few surviving Anzacs. The last man to have been at the Landing at Gallipoli was accorded a state funeral when he died and the few remaining veterans of the Great War are treated as living national treasures. To some extent this can be explained by an understandable veneration for extreme old age, and to some extent by a sentiment of wanting to be in touch, personally, with an important aspect of Australian history.

When the eminent Australian historian Ken Inglis joined a party of returning Anzacs in 1965 on the occasion of the 50th anniversary of the Landing, he reported that the veterans were met, on landing at Anzac Cove, by a group of about 100 people:

> Camermen, reporters, [Turkish] war veterans, men in uniform from the army base at Gelibolu, men in suits from Istanbul, women in shawls from villages on the peninsula, and four Australian hitchhikers in parkas and jeans … [these four young Australians] were welcomed by the old men as unexpected living evidence that *some* young people cared about the Anzac tradition.

On Gallipoli in 1990 for the 75th anniversary of the landing, some 7000–8000 young Australians joined with the veterans, and the looks of awe and love on their faces as they watched these old men go about the place they had made their own was inspiring. Each year since 1990 the crowd, predominantly of young people, at the Dawn Service at Gallipoli has continued to grow, reaching bursting point in 2000, although at a different venue to accommodate the crowd of perhaps 15 000 people.

'Australia Remembers' commemorated the 50th anniversary of the end of the Second World War just six years ago, and if we followed the Inglis chronology for Anzac we would just be at the turning point in our interest and compassion for those of that war. So it is not impossible, by any means, that those who suffered in the Japanese prison camps will yet be admitted to the ranks of Australian heroes, nor is it impossible that their story will eventually become one of the defining stories of the nation.

That story is one of endurance, heroism, compassion, of mutual support called mateship, of terrible suffering and vile degradation. It is a story of death on a large scale and of illness and injury that was near universal. Like the story of Simpson, the 'man with the donkey' at Gallipoli, the prisoners' story has brought forth a man — Weary Dunlop — whom many people began to recognise as a hero towards the end of his life. If there was more to the story of Anzac than merely Simpson, as of course there was, there was more, too, to the story of the prisoners than Weary Dunlop, as he was the first to insist. Australians have been happy to let Weary Dunlop stand for all the others, as Simpson stood for all the myriad acts of kindness and bravery at Anzac Cove. Weary Dunlop's story is one we can comprehend as we try to understand the awful issues that the story of the prisoners of war forces on us.

A more mature understanding of that story will tell us that heroism was not confined to the few but was a quality that every prisoner needed in his or her own fashion. In the many stories told here and in the thousands of others sadly lost to history there are qualities of nobility, goodness and heroism that can inspire us. To recall but one of those stories, for Les Bolger, still, Bill Scarpello is a hero of the Railway in his compassion and gentleness, in his concern for his mates, in his endurance. That Les Bolger later took on the awful task of telling Bill's mother exactly how her son had died shows that he would not shirk his duty and would honour, as best he could, the memory of a man he loved. Each individual prisoner would have similar stories to tell. Many of them came home still thinking that they had let Australia down. We could not tell them then, but we do know now, that in their story 'there is faith enough for all of us'.

This book has been based on the assumption that the homefront cannot be separated from the battlefront and that history is not best understood as a series of actions and activities isolated and separate from each other. The brother and sister, 56 years after the event, still grieving for a father who never came home, and a mother who could never comprehend why his mates who did survive could not come to talk to her about him, are part of Australia today. For them that war and his life are not history; they are part of a present reality. For them, as for so many others, 'this war never ends'.

Notes

1. 'Tragedy after tragedy'

1. *Age*, 23 January 1942.
2. Gavin Long, *Six Years War*, Australian War Memorial, Canberra, p. 148.
3. John Barrett, *We Were There*, Penguin, Ringwood, p. 227.
4. John Barrett, *We Were There*, pp. 167–69.
5. *Argus*, 15 October 1945.
6. Rohan D. Rivett, *Behind Bamboo: An Inside Story of the Japanese Prison Camps*, Angus & Robertson, Sydney, 1946, p. viii, p. 245; George Munster, *A Paper Prince*, Penguin, Ringwood, 1985, p. 39; Rivett, *Behind Bamboo*, p. 257.
7. National Archives of Australia (NAA), A705/15 item 166/6/796.
8. Statement by the Prime Minister, 24 April 1942, NAA, A5954/69 item 672/5.
9. A. J. Sweeting, 'Prisoners of the Japanese', in Lionel Wigmore, *The Japanese Thrust*, Australian War Memorial, Canberra, 1957, pp. 512–15.
10. 'Football Behind Bamboo', *Football Life*, September 1969.
11. A. J. Sweeting, 'Prisoners of the Japanese', pp. 541–44.
12. Hugh V. Clarke, *A Life for Every Sleeper*, Allen & Unwin, Sydney, 1986, p. xv; Peter Dennis et al. (eds), *The Oxford Companion to Australian Military History*, Oxford University Press, Melbourne, 1995, p. 129; A. J. Sweeting, 'Prisoners of the Japanese', pp. 568–69.
13. Peter Dennis, *The Oxford Companion to Australian Military History*, p. 129.
14. Linda Goetz Holmes, *Four Thousand Bowls of Rice*, Allen & Unwin, Sydney, 1993, p. 17.
15. A. J. Sweeting, 'Prisoners of the Japanese', pp. 555–56.
16. A. J. Sweeting, 'Prisoners of the Japanese', pp. 541–92; see also Hugh V. Clarke, *A Life for Every Sleeper*, Sydney, 1986.
17. Lloyd Ellerman, Monash ACT, interview with author, 15 June 2000.

2. 'If only I knew what has become of him'

1. Note from the War Office, London to Australia House, 18 August 1942, NAA, A2908 item P26/9 pt 4; *Argus*, 5 March 1942.
2. Cable from High Commission, London, to PM, 19 February 1942, NAA A816 item 67/301/79.
3. *Daily Telegraph*, 5 March 1942; cable from High Commission, London, to PM, 18 February 1942, NAA, A5954/1 item 671/1.

4. *Argus*, 12 March 1942.
5. High Commission, London, to PM, 9 July 1942, NAA, A2908 item P26/9 pt 4; High Commission, London, to PM, 10 April 1942, NAA, A1608/1 item A20/1/1, pt 2.
6. Letter, Randwick North to H. V. Evatt, 6 July 1942, NAA, A981 item TRE751.
7. F. J. MacKenzie, Sydney, to PM, 13 March 1942, NAA, A981 item TRE746; Mrs Grace Harrison, South Melbourne, to PM, 4 November 1942, NAA, A981 item TRE755. It is probable that Mrs Harrison's son did survive his captivity, as his name is not listed on the Commonwealth War Graves Commission's 'Debt of Honour' register.
8. High Commission, London, to PM, 12 September 1942, NAA, A981 item TRE755; Australia's response, 16 September 1942; *Sydney Morning Herald*, 18 May 1942.
9. PM to High Commission, London, 16 September 1942, NAA, A981 item TRE755; 'Conditions of Australian and New Zealand Prisoners of War in Japanese Hands', NAA, A5954/69 item 672/1.
10. Alison Todd, manuscript account, 'The capture of M.V. *Hauraki*' and interview, Alison and David Todd, interview with author, 2 June 2000.
11. Alison Todd, family papers.
12. Frank Davidson to L. G. Wigmore, 3 March 1943, NAA, SP112/1 item M60.
13. War Cabinet papers, NAA, A5954/69 item 672/1; and for Conlon's committee, NAA, A1608/1 item B20/1/1 pt 1.
14. Telegram to Mr M. Bruce, 14 September 1942, NAA A705/15 item 166/6/796.
15. PMG's Department to PM's Department, 27 May 1943, NAA, A989 item 1944/925/1/3 pt 1.
16. Mrs E. Burton to PM, 30 October 1942, NAA, A981 item TRE772 pt 2.
17. Geoffrey Serle (ed.), *Australian Dictionary of Biography*, vol. 11, Melbourne University Press, Melbourne 1988, pp. 661–62; Richard Cashman et al. (eds), *The Oxford Companion to Australian Cricket*, Oxford University Press, Melbourne 1996, p. 484.
18. Sydney Smith to PM, 13 April 1943, NAA, A1608 item A20/1/1 pt 3; *P.O.W.*, 14 March 1942.
19. *P.O.W.*, 28 January 1942; 15 April 1942; 14 March 1942; 15 May 1942; 15 October 1942.
20. *P.O.W.*, 16 November 1942; 15 July 1942.
21. *P.O.W.*, 15 September 1942; 15 July 1942.
22. *P.O.W.*, 15 August 1942; *All In!*, p. 141; *P.O.W.*, 15 June 1944.
23. Australian Red Cross Society Publicity Service, Circular 304, NAA, SP109/3/1 item 329/01.
24. E. G. Bonney to H. Eather, 3 November 1942; CCT to Bonney, 16 July 1942; Bonney to Tasmanian Censor, Professor C. S. King, 30 November 1942, NAA, SP109/3/1 item 329/01.

25. Memorandum to Bonney, 17 December 1942, NAA, SP109/3/1 item 329/01.

26. Sydney Smith to PM, 27 July 1944, and E. G. Bonney to Secretary PM's department, NAA SP 109/3/1 item 329/09.

27. High Commission, London to PM [lost date] and SEAC Weekly Intelligence Summary, 16 June 1944, NAA, A705 item 32/6/60.

28. Mrs D. H. Wallace to PM, 2 February 1944, NAA, A1608 item A20/1/1 pt 4; it would seem that Mrs Wallace's son survived.

29. Mrs E. M. Evans to PM, 24 March 1944, NAA, A1608 item A20/1/1 pt 4.

30. P. Timmens to PM, 8 August 1944, NAA, A1608 item A20/1/1 pt 4; Mrs R. Murison to PM, 2 April 1944, NAA, A1608 item A20/1/1 pt 4.

31. Mrs Bodah Quinn to Mr E. Ward, 14 December 1943, NAA, A1608 item A20/1/1 pt 4.

32. Mrs J. A. Lyons to PM, 2 June 1943, NAA, A1608 item A20/1/1.

33. Minute, DPW&I, 4 October 1943, NAA, B3856 item 144/20/23.

34. *Hansard* (House of Representatives), 17 November 1943; Linda Goetz Holmes, *Four Thousand Bowls of Rice: a Prisoner of War Comes Home*, Allen & Unwin, Sydney, 1993, p. 7; *Argus*, 24 March 1945; *Herald*, 20 March 1945.

35. High Commission, London to P M, 18 February 1942, NAA, A5954/1 item 671/1; message for Censors from Chief Publicity Censor, 2 June 1944, NAA, A5954/1 item 671/1.

36. *Sydney Morning Herald*, 7 October 1943.

37. Curtin to Drakeford, Minister for Air, 7 October 1943, NAA, A5954/1 item 671/1; draft of an off-the-record briefing for the press, NAA, A5954/1 item 671/1.

38. Ray Denney, *The Long Way Home*, R. Denney Scottsdale, 1993, pp. 125–26.

39. War Cabinet Agendum 447/1943, 19 October 1943, NAA, 422/1942 item 672/1.

40. Eleanor Glencross to A. A. Calwell, 15 May 1945, NAA, SP 109/3 item 004/09.

41. Note for File, 'wireless message scheme for prisoners of war', 2 May 1944, NAA, A989/1 item 44/925/1/42 pt 2.

42. J. McEwen to PM, 4 August 1944, NAA, A989/1 item 1944/925/1/3 pt 2; Mrs Elsie Salter to Mrs Curtin, 18 September 1943, and Mrs Dawn Rickerby to Sir Earle Page, 28 September 1943, NAA, A989/1 item 1944/1/925/1 4243 pt 1.

43. Mrs Mary Bourke to PM, 2 September 1943, and Mrs E. M. Anderson to PM, 4 January 1944, NAA, A989/1 item 44/925/1/42 43 pt 1.

44. Memorandum for Director-General of Information from Short Wave Division, 12 May 1944, NAA, SP109/3/1 item 004/09; for numbers of letters NAA, A989/1 item 1944/925/1/42 pt 3; Sydney Smith to PM, 31 August 1944, NAA, A989/1 item 1944/925/1/42 pt 3.

45. Memo, Secretary External Affairs to Secretary Defence, 16 March 1945, NAA, A422/1942 item 672/1; Sydney Smith to Secretary External Affairs, 10 October 1944, NAA, A989 item 1944/925/1/42 pt 3.

46. File, D. W. Bruce, NAA, A705/15 item 166/6/796; *Age*, 7 September 1944.

3. 'That's the Eighth Division colour patch, isn't it?'

1. Mrs J. L. Thompson to PM, 17 September 1943, and reply 21 September 1943, NAA, A1608 item A20/1/1 pt 4.
2. A. J. Sweeting, 'Prisoners of the Japanese' in Lionel Wigmore, *The Japanese Thrust*, Canberra, 1957, pp. 614–15.
3. H. A. Graves to H. E. Stokes, Department of External Affairs, 25 January 1944; Graves to Stokes, 21 March 1944, NAA, A10322 item 13/1944.
4. Acting Secretary Department of Defence to Secretary External Affairs, 20 October 1944, NAA, A989 item 1944/925/1/153.
5. Sydney Smith to PM, 26 October 1944, NAA, A989 item 1944/925/1/153.
6. War Cabinet Agendum 552/1944, NAA, A5954/69 item 671/5.
7. Secretary Department of the Army to Secretary Department of Defence, 31 October 1944, NAA, A816 item 54/301/279; secretary Department of Defence to PM, 30 October 1944; *Sydney Morning Herald*, 20 November 1944.
8. War Cabinet Agendum 552/1944, NAA, A5954/69 item 671/5.
9. Secretary Department of Defence to secretary Department of the Army, enclosing undated letter from Mr Lindsay Pegler, 1 December 1944, and response 23 December 1944, NAA, A5954/69 item 671/5.
10. Frank Forde, acting prime minister to Sydney Smith, 22 December 1944, NAA, A989/1 item 1944/925/1/153; 'Extension of Disembarkation Leave for Aust PW Recovered from Japanese', 11 December 1944, NAA, MP742/1 item 255/15/565.
11. Gloria Muntz to 'Mr Harrison', 8 November 1944, NAA, B3856 item 144/1/128.
12. Secretary, Department of Air to M. Bruce, 2 November 1944; M. Bruce to Secretary, Department of Air, 7 November 1944; Secretary, Department of Air to M. Bruce, 20 November 1944, NAA, A705/15 item 166/6/796.
13. *Argus*, 6 December 1944.
14. *Daily Telegraph*, 25 January 1945; *Sydney Morning Herald*, 25 January 1945.

4. 'Twilight liberation'

1. A. J. Sweeting, 'Prisoners of the Japanese', in Lionel Wigmore, *The Japanese Thrust*, Australian War Memorial, Canberra, 1957, p. 633.
2. Hugh Clarke, *Twilight Liberation*, Allen & Unwin, Sydney, 1985, p. 10.
3. A. J. Sweeting, 'Prisoners of the Japanese', pp. 593–604.
4. I. C. B. Dear, *The Oxford Companion to the Second World War*, Oxford, 1995, p. 1106.
5. Hugh Clarke, *Twilight Liberation*, p. 59.
6. Ray Denney, *The Long Way Home*, R. Denney, Scottsdale, 1993, p. 140; Hugh Clarke, *Twilight Liberation*, pp. 5, 117.

7. Douglas McLaggan, *The Will to Survive*, Kangaroo Press, Sydney, 1995, pp. 175–79.

8. Tom Henling Wade, *Prisoner of the Japanese*, Allen & Unwin, Sydney, 1994, p. 169; Hugh Clarke, *Twilight Liberation*, pp. 91, 65.

9. Ray Denney, *The Long Way Home*, p. 140; Hugh Clarke, *Twilight Liberation*, pp. 107, 108.

10. Hugh Clarke, *Twilight Liberation*, pp. 64, 80; Douglas McLaggan, *The Will to Survive*, p. 175.

11. Hugh Clarke, *Twilight Liberation*, p. 109; Tom Henling Wade, *Prisoner of the Japanese*, p. 170.

12. Mrs Judith Shaw to author, Canberra, 29 June 2000.

13. Hugh Clarke, *Twilight Liberation*, pp. 130, 155; Douglas McLaggan, *The Will to Survive*, p. 186.

14. Linda Goetz Holmes, *Four Thousand Bowls of Rice*, Sydney, 1993, p. 36.

15. Jessie Simons, *In Japanese Hands*, Heinemann, Melbourne, 1954, pp. 106, 107.

16. Harry Windsor, *The Heart of a Surgeon*, New South Wales University Press, Sydney, nd [1988], p. 49; Jessie Simons, *In Japanese Hands*, p. 119.

17. Jessie Simons, *In Japanese Hands*, p. 124.

18. Report of Dr Harry M. Windsor, Major, 2/14 Aust Gen Hosp, 19 September 1945, NAA MP742/1 item 336/1/1289.

19. *Sydney Morning Herald*, 12 October 1945.

20. Linda Goetz Holmes, *Four Thousand Bowls of Rice*, p. 49.

21. Douglas McLaggan, *The Will to Survive*, p. 194.

22. Douglas McLaggan, *The Will to Survive*, p. 195.

23. R. H. Whitecross, *Slaves of the Sons of Heaven*, Dymock's, Sydney, 1951, p. 241.

24. Norman Carter, *G-String Jesters*, Currawong, Sydney, 1966, p. 195.

25. *Argus*, 7 September 1945.

26. *Argus*, 21 September 1945.

27. *Argus*, 8 October 1945; *Age*, 3 October 1945 (Callaghan).

28. *While You Were Away: a digest of happenings in Australia 1940–1945*, compiled, printed and published for you by the *Argus* Melbourne.

29. Russell Braddon, *The Naked Island*, Werner Laurie, London, 1952, p. 263; Hugh Clarke, *Twilight Liberation*, p. 71.

30. M. L. McGee to author, 9 February 1996.

31. Roy Bulcock, *Of Death But Once*, F. W. Cheshire, Melbourne, 1947, p. 207.

32. Sue Ebury, *Weary: The Life of Sir Edward Dunlop*, Viking, Melbourne, 1994, pp. 528, 529.

33. Hugh Clarke, *Twilight Liberation*, p. 113.

5. 'I will turn up like the proverbial penny'

1. F/Lt C. Greenwood to Mrs H. Greenwood, 14 September 1945, NAA, A705 item 32/6/67 pt 1.

2. Cable 19 August 1945, NAA, MP742/1 item 255/15/1455A pt 1.

3. 'The Prisoner of War Comes Home', History of Medicine Library, Royal Australasian College of Physicians, Sydney; Brig S. N. Burton, 21 March 1944, NAA, MP742/1 item 255/15/917, and note to DGMS, 23 March 1944.

4. Appendix A, undated, NAA, MP742/1 item 255/15/876, and RAN instruction 14 October 1944, NAA, MP1049/5 item 1951/2/82.

5. Report prepared for the Imperial Prisoner of War Committee and sent to Australia 11 May 1944, NAA, A1608 item AS20/1/1.

6. Director of Personnel Services (Navy) to 2nd Naval Member, 8 August 1944, NAA, MP1049/5 item 1951/2/82.

7. Lt Cmdr W. Seymour to Naval Board, 31 August 1944, NAA, MP1049/5 item 1951/2/82.

8. Scheme submitted by the Director of Education and Vocational Training, 24 October 1944, NAA, MP1049/5 item 1951/2/82.

9. Secretary of the Army to Secretary of Defence, 5 February 1945, NAA, A5954 item 673/1.

10. Lt Col AG 2 to Director of Operations, 6 June 1945, NAA, MP742/1 item 255/15/1375; Secretary Department of Air to Secretary Department of Defence, 3 January 1945, NAA, A5954/69 item 763/1.

11. Curtin to Australian Government Representative, London, 18 April 1945, NAA, A816 item 54/301/294.

12. Army order issued 14 June 1945, NAA, MP742/1 item 255/15/1455A pt 1; F. R. Sinclair to Secretary Department of Defence, 5 June 1945, NAA, A816 item 54/301/294.

13. Minute, 'Prisoners of war in Japanese Hands: Plans for Liberation', NAA, A705 item 32/6/114; report PWLO (Navy), 11 August 1945, NAA, MP1049/5 item 1951/2/82.

14. Draft letter, circa 2 July 1945, NAA, A705/1 item 32/6/51 pt 2.

15. 'Suggested Administrative Arrangements Regarding the Processing and Repatriation …', NAA, A7112/1 item 4; Secretary of Army to Secretary Prime Minister's Department, 25 August 1945, NAA, MP742/1 item 255/15/1081.

16. Cable to Landops from Forland [undated], NAA, A705 item 32/6/64 pt 2.

17. Acting Prime Minister to Acting Minister for the Army, 3 January 1945, NAA, MP742/1 item 255/15/876.

18. Draft letter, not sent, submitted 20 January 1945, NAA, MP742/1 item 255/15/876.

19. John Ritchie (general editor), *The Australian Dictionary of Biography*, vol. 15, Melbourne 2000, p. 103–4; David Horner, *Blamey: The Commander-in-Chief*, Allen & Unwin, Sydney 1998, p. 466.

20. Adjutant General to Minister for the Army, 16 July 1945, NAA, MP742/1 item 255/15/1375.

21. Army instruction quoted by A. L. Blythe, Chairman of the NSW Division of

the Red Cross in a letter to F. R. Sinclair, Secretary of the Department of the Army, 25 January 1945, NAA, MP742/1 item 255/15/876.

22. *Age*, 14 August 1945.

23. Director of Prisoners of War to Deputy Adjutant General 2, cable, 17 September 1945, NAA, B3856 item 500/2/45; Defence Committee directive, 4 September 1945, NAA, A1308 item 712/1/31. The issue recalls the concerns expressed about the return to Australia of men who served in Vietnam. By using aircraft to bring these men home, a soldier might be in a combat situation one day and on the streets of Sydney the next. A much longer interval between combat and civilian life seems to have been called for.

24. W. P. MacCallum, DDGMS to DGMS LHQ, 11 September 1945, NAA, MP742/1 item 255/17/168.

25. A. J. Sweeting, 'Prisoners of the Japanese', in Lionel Wigmore, *The Japanese Thrust*, Australian War Memorial, Canberra, 1957, p. 633.

26. A. J. Sweeting, 'Prisoners of the Japanese', p. 642.

27. Joan Beaumont, *Gull Force Survival and Leadership in Captivity 1941–1945*, Allen & Unwin, Sydney, 1988, p. 206.

28. Hansard (House of Representatives), 25 September 1945.

29. *Daily Telegraph*, 22 August and 28 August 1945; Hansard (House of Representatives), 12 September 1945; *Age*, 12 September 1945.

30. Cable from Milbase Sydney to Landforces, Melbourne, 30 September 1945, NAA, MP742/1 item 255/15/1455A pt 1; *Daily Telegraph*, 10 October 1945.

31. Summary of situation, 27 September 1945, NAA, A816 item 54/301/294; *Age*, 15 November 1945.

32. *Bulletin*, 5 December 1945; Col O2E to Director of Operations, 3 September 1945, NAA, MP742/1 item 255/15/1193.

33. Telegrams, 2 October 1945 and 8 October 1945, NAA, A705 item 32/6/67 pt 2.

34. Telegram Air Force to Mr M. Bruce, 2 October 1945, NAA, A705/15 item 166/6/796.

35. Telegram Air Force to Mr M Bruce, 9 October 1945, NAA, A705/15 item 166/6/796.

36. Mrs Enid Johnson to author, 14 February 1996.

37. Signal from Landforces to SACSEA, NAA, A816 item 54/301/294.

38. Report of Commissioned Gunner E. Blatchford RAN, 19 September 1945, NAA, MP150/1 item 567/201/98.

39. Cable Firstaf to 11 Gp RAAF Hq, 10 September 1945, NAA, A705 item 32/6/64 pt 2; 'Information for Use of RAAF Liaison Officer with 2nd Aust PW Reception Group' compiled 27 August 1945, NAA, A705 item 32/6/64 pt 2; Lt W. R. Smith to Lt Cmdr W. J. Seymour, 21 September 1945, 'Reports from POW Contact Officer Pt 1', NAA, A7112/1.

40. W. Roy Smith to Director of Naval Intelligence, Changi Camp, Singapore, 14 October 1945, 'Reports from POW Contact Officer Pt 1', NAA, A7112/1.

41. Minute from Lt Col DAG 2 to Director of Operations, 6 June 1945, NAA, MP742/1 item 255/15/1375.

42. Lt A. G. Steele RANVR to Cmdr R. B. M. Long, Director Naval Intelligence, 12 October 1945, 'Reports from POW Contact Officer Pt 1, NAA, A7112/1; Report on Activities of Personnel of 1 Aust PW Contact … attached to US Army's Forces Occupying Japan, NAA, MP742/1 item 255/15/1265.

43. Appendix 'B' to Major Thomas's report above; 'Report to 1 Aust PW Contact and Enquiry Unit by Lt Winter-Irving, Recovery Team 45, 9 October 1945, NAA, MP742/1 item 255/15/1280.

44. W. Roy Smith to Director of Naval Intelligence, Changi Camp, Singapore, 14 October 1945, 'Reports from POW Contact Officer Pt 1', NAA, A7112/1.

45. 'Directive: The Treatment and Evacuation of Recovered Allied Prisoners of War', HQ ALFSEA, 13 August 1945, NAA, MP742/1 item 255/2/867.

46. GOC Qld L of C Area to Landforces, 12 September 1945, and comment on this by Director General Medical Services, 28 September 1945, NAA, MP742/1 item 255/15/1375.

6. 'It wasn't as I had expected'

1. Interview with Lloyd and Muriel Ellerman, Canberra, 15 June 2000.

2. Secretary of State for Dominion Affairs to John Curtin, 5 July 1944, NAA, A5954/1 item 671/1.

3. Hansard, House of Representatives, 9 February 1944.

4. Colonel Wilson to Secretary, Department of Defence, 14 November 1944, NAA, A5954, item 671/5.

5. Paul Hasluck, *The Government and the People 1942–1945*, Australian War Memorial, Canberra, 1970, p. 499; meeting of the Advisory War Council, 23 May 1944, NAA, A5954/1 item 671/1.

6. Press release from the Attorney-General, 7 September 1945, NAA, A5954/1 item 671/1.

7. Lionel Wigmore, *The Japanese Thrust*, Australian War Memorial, Canberra, 1968, pp. 386–87.

8. *Age*, 18 September 1945.

9. Rohan Rivett, *Behind Bamboo*, Angus & Robertson, Sydney 1946, p. 379.

10. *Daily Telegraph*, 7 September 1945; Gavin Souter, *Company of Heralds*, Melbourne University Press, Melbourne, 1981, p. 207; *Sydney Morning Herald*, 2 October 1945.

11. *Argus*, 11 September 1945.

12. *Argus*, 1 September 1945; 17 September 1945.

13. *Daily Telegraph*, 10 September 1945; *Age*, 17 September 1945.

14. *Argus*, 17 September 1945; 4 September 1945.

15. *Daily Telegraph*, 11 September 1945; 13 September 1945.

16. Charles Bean, 'Do Atrocities Mean Japanese are Beyond redemption?', *Sydney Morning Herald*, 3 October 1945.
17. *Age*, 10 September 1945; Hansard, House of Representatives, 18 September 1945; *Bulletin*, 5 September 1945.
18. *Daily Telegraph*, 15 September 1945.
19. *Bulletin*, 19 September 1945.
20. *Daily Telegraph*, 15 September 1945.
21. *Argus*, 20 September 1945.
22. Linda Goetz Holmes, *Four Thousand Bowls of Rice*, Allen & Unwin, Sydney, 1993, p. 145.
23. F. R. Sinclair, Secretary Department of the Army to Secretary Prime Minister's Department, 30 April 1945, NAA, A1608/1 item A20/1/1 pt 4.
24. *Age*, 1 October 1945.
25. *Argus*, 1 October 1945.
26. *Argus*, 13 October 1945; Acting Minister for the Army, Senator Fraser, to Victorian Branch APOWRA, 3 July 1945, NAA, MP742/1 item 255/15/1375.
27. *Australian*, 8 December 1999.
28. Kenneth Harrison, *The Brave Japanese*, Rigby, Adelaide, 1966, p. 274.
29. *Argus*, 13 October 1945; Richard Cashman et al. (eds), *The Oxford Companion to Australian Cricket*, Oxford University Press, Melbourne, 1996, p. 49.
30. Linda Goetz Holmes, *Four Thousand Bowls of Rice*, p. 143.
31. H. L. C. Read to author, 17 February 1996.
32. Mrs Rosemary Reynolds to author, undated [March 1996].
33. K. A. McN. Thompson to author, 19 February 1996.
34. Recollection of Mrs Phyll Collins, Canberra, 21 June 2000; Mrs R. Reynolds to author.
35. *Sydney Morning Herald*, 12 October 1945.
36. *Daily Telegraph*, 15 September 1945; *Argus*, 24 September 1945; *Age*, 8 September 1945.
37. *Daily Telegraph*, 7 September 1945.
38. Information supplied by Mrs Nola Ashcroft, Sydney, 14 December 1999.

7. 'You are not going home as prisoners'

1. John Ritchie (ed.), *Australian Dictionary of Biography*, vol. 14, Melbourne, 1996, pp. 243–44 (the article is by David Griffin).
2. Bede Nairn and Geoffrey Serle (eds), *Australian Dictionary of Biography*, vol. 7, Melbourne, 1979, pp. 307–8.
3. *Herald*, 21 September 1945.
4. Air Board Agendum 6060, 1944, 'Courts of Enquiry — Recovered Prisoners of War', NAA, A705/1 item 32/6/105.
5. *Bulletin*, 12 September 1945; Hugh Clarke, *Twilight Liberation*, Allen & Unwin,

Sydney, 1985, p. 157; Tom Uren, *Straight Left*, Random House, Sydney, 1994, p. 57.

6. Lavinia Warner and John Sandilands, *Women Beyond the Wire*, Michael Joseph, London, 1982, p. 265.

7. Lloyd Ellerman to author, 15 June 2000; Sister Greer in Warner and Sandilands, *Women Beyond the Wire*, p. 267; Joan Beaumont, *Gull Force: Survival and Leadership in Captivity 1941–1945*, Allen & Unwin, Sydney, 1988, p. 203; Hank Nelson, *POW: Australians Under Nippon*, ABC Books, Sydney, 1985, p. 211.

8. Douglas McLaggan, *The Will to Survive*, Kangaroo Press, Sydney, 1995.

9. Beverley Mutch, Canberra, interview with author, 28 March 2000.

10. Betty Taylor, *To Hell and Back*, B. Taylor Bega, 1996, p. 66.

11. A. S. Blackburn to Eric Millhouse, 21 November 1945, RSL Papers, NLA, MS6609, File 2007C.

12. *Smith's Weekly*, 5 January 1946; 'Reception, Treatment and Disposal of AMF Ex Prisoners of War on Arrival in Australia', NAA, A5954/69 item 673/1.

13. *Smith's Weekly*, 8 March 1947.

14. *Age*, 10 September 1945; see many letters in NAA, A1608/1 item AH 20/1/1.

15. Hon Sec Australian Legion of Ex-Servicemen and Women 8th Division Sub-Branch to PM, 9 November 1946, NAA, A1607, item IC46/50/5.

16. P. M. Tully to PM, 1 May 1947, and Note for File, 10 December 1947, NAA, A1607 item IC46/50/5.

17. *Smith's Weekly*, 18 January 1947.

18. *Smith's Weekly*, 25 January 1947; Sue Ebury, *Weary: The Life of Sir Edward Dunlop*, Viking, Melbourne, 1994, p. 534.

19. *Smith's Weekly*, 15 February 1947; Brian Noonan to Frank Brennan MHR, 28 January 1947, NAA, A1607 item IC46/50/5.

20. General Secretary Sailors' Soldiers' and Airmen's Fathers Association to PM, 20 August 1945, and reply Secretary of the Army to Secretary of the PM's department, 19 September 1945; and PM to General Secretary RSS&AILA, 30 October 1946, NAA, A461 item G337/1/1.

21. *Smith's Weekly*, 14 June 1947.

22. Interview with John Ringwood, Canberra, 18 July 2000.

23. *Sydney Morning Herald*, 9 January 1946; 8 January 1946.

24. *Reveille*, 1 February 1947.

25. Robert Menzies to J. C. Neagle, 15 November 1950, and Senator Denham Henty to A. W. Fadden, NAA, A462/8 item 446/1/5; E. E. Dunlop, *The War Diaries of Weary Dunlop*, Penguin Books, Melbourne, 1986, p. xxi.

26. Charles Huxtable, *From the Somme to Singapore*, Kangaroo Press, Sydney, 1995, pp. 7–8.

27. *Sydney Morning Herald*, 31 May 1948; 8 June 1948; 16 June 1948; 9 June 1948 (Griffin).

28. *Sydney Morning Herald*, 31 May 1948.

8. 'Stirring up trouble by segregating POWs from their fellow servicemen'

1. George Wootten to Secretary Public Service Board, 2 October 1947, NAA, A2421/1 item G1846; Peter Dennis et al. (eds), *Oxford Companion to Australian Military History*, p. 680; Clem Lloyd and Jacqui Rees, *The Last Shilling: A History of Repatriation in Australia*, Melbourne University Press, Melbourne, 1994, pp. 307–8.

2. Sue Ebury, *Weary: The Life of Sir Edward Dunlop*, Viking, Melbourne, 1944, pp. 548–51.

3. Chairman Repatriation Commission to Director of Re-Establishment, 9 May 1949, NAA, A2421/1 item G1846 pt 2; Wootten to Minister, 15 May 1947, NAA, A2421/1 item G1846.

4. 'Survey of Selected Groups of those who served in the 1939–45 War, General Instructions', NAA, A2421/1 item G1846.

5. 'Fisher, Walter Edward', in *Roll of the Royal Australasian College of Physicians*, vol. 1, Sydney, 1988, pp. 91–92; *Medical Journal of Australia*, 6 August 1966, pp. 284–86.

6. 'Hunt, Bruce Atlee', in *Roll Call of the Royal Australasian College of Physicians*, pp. 140–41; copy of a letter from Hunt to Fisher, 30 June 1947, NAA, A2421/1 item G1846.

7. Acting Deputy Commissioner (NSW) to Secretary Repatriation Commission, 6 April 1948, NAA, A2421/1 item G1846 (admissions to Concord); 'Indications as to the Health of Ex-Ps.O.W.–J' by W. E. Fisher (Fisher Report), NAA, A2421/1 item G1846 pt 4.

8. Clerk-in-Charge, Metropolitan Treatment Section to Officer-in-Charge, M&G Section, 23 August 1948, NAA, A2421/1, item G1846 pt 2.

9. Deputy Commissioner (New South Wales) to Secretary Repatriation Commission, 15 September 1948, NAA, A2421/1 item G1846 pt 2.

10. Senior Medical Officer to Deputy Commissioner (Victoria), 17 February 1948, NAA, A2421/1 item G1846.

11. Chairman Repatriation Commission to Minister, 14 June 1949, NAA, A2421/1 item G1846 pt 2.

12. *Smith's Weekly*, 27 August 1948.

13. Sue Ebury, *Weary*, p. 553.

14. 'AS' to Deputy Chairman, Repatriation Commission, 16 August 1950, NAA, A2421/1 item G1846 pt 3.

15. *Australian*, 19 September 1964.

16. Kim E. Beazley to H. V. Evatt, 31 July 1947, NAA, A1067/1 item 1C 46/50/5.

17. John Ritchie (ed.), *Australian Dictionary of Biography*, vol. 15, Melbourne 2000, pp. 551–52; Peter Dennis et al. (eds) *Oxford Companion to Australian Military History*, pp. 528–30.

18. Cabinet Committee on Prisoners-of-War Subsistence Allowance, minutes of

    meeting 10 October 1950, and press release, 12 October 1950, NAA, A463/34
    item 68/2922 pt 1.

19. Arthur S. Blackburn to Secretary Prime Minister's Department, 26 April 1951,
    and Assistant Secretary Department of the Treasury to Secretary Prime
    Minister's Department, 25 June 1951, NAA, A463/34 item 68/2922 pt 1.

20. J. W. Rymill, President 2/3rd M.G. Battalion Club, to Chairman of Trustees,
    Prisoners of War Trust Fund, 3 May 1952, NAA, A463/34 item 68/2922 pt 1;
    Clem Lloyd and Jacqui Rees, *The Last Shilling*, pp. 303–4.

21. Prisoners of War Trust Fund, 'Report of Activities of the Fund up to 31 January
    1960', NAA, A463/34 item 68/2922 pt 1.

22. Prisoners of War Trust Fund, 'Report of Activities of the Fund up to 31 January
    1960', NAA, A463/34 item 68/2922 pt 1; R. G. Menzies to Acting Secretary
    Ex-Servicemen's POW Claims Committee, 10 October 1952, NAA, A463/34
    item 68/2922 pt 1.

23. POW Liaison Officer quoted in Colin Simpson, Trip Diary, 1946, Mitchell
    Library (ML) MS 3343 Box 00722.

24. K. S. Inglis, *This Is the ABC*, Melbourne University Press, Melbourne, 1983, p.
    164; William H. Wilde et al. (eds), *The Oxford Companion to Australian Literature*,
    Oxford University Press, Melbourne, 1985, p. 631; Colin Simpson to Owen
    Campbell, 22 February 1947, ML, MS 3343, MLK 718.

25. Colin Simpson to his wife, 30 December 1946, ML, MS 3343, MLK 718.

26. Colin Simpson to 'Mr Botterill', 13 February 1947, and Colin Simpson to
    Owen Campbell, 22 February 1947, ML, MS 3343, MLK 718.

27. Joyce Braithwaite to author, Sandakan, 11 July 1995.

28. Script, 'Six from Borneo' by Colin Simpson, ML, MS 3343, MLK 718; Colin
    Simpson to Dick Braithwaite, 14 June 1947, ML, MS 3343, MLK 718.

29. Colin Simpson, Trip Diary, ML, MS 3343, MLK 00722.